THE UNCERTAINTY SOLUTION

"In *The Uncertainty Solution*, Jennings provides exactly what you need to know about investing, even though it's really about how the mind works. Through his clever storytelling and examples, he delivers terrific insights into what can be a complicated topic but in a very accessible and entertaining way. If you want to learn how investing really works and cut through all the hype, start with this brilliant book."

—**Patrick Geddes,** Cofounder of Aperio Group and author of *Transparent Investing*

"Jennings shows why successful investing requires accepting that the investment world is full of uncertainty and randomness and that the future is unpredictable. However, he also shows that investors aren't powerless in the face of uncertainty. In fact the key to success is to shut out the noise of the markets and the media, ignore the forecasts of market gurus, avoid making decisions based on fear or greed, and avoid the mistakes of loss aversion, overconfidence, and hindsight bias. Success requires embracing uncertainty and preparing for it through the development of an investment plan that is well diversified and lays out simple algorithmic rules of engagement, such as when to rebalance."

—**Larry Swedroe,** Chief Research Officer of Buckingham Wealth Partners and the co-author of *Your Essential Guide to Sustainable Investing*

"The habits that serve us well in most of life serve us badly in investment management. In most things, for example, the past is a perfectly useful guide to the future—but not when it comes to investing money, where uncertainty and luck play a far larger role than most people realize. *The Uncertainty Solution* identifies the worst of our bad behaviors and helps us navigate the randomness of the stock market. Any investor would benefit from John Jennings' insights and advice."

—**Craig Lazzara,** Managing Director of S&P Dow Jones Indices

THE
UNCERTAINTY
SOLUTION

THE
UNCERTAINTY
SOLUTION

HOW TO INVEST WITH CONFIDENCE
IN THE FACE OF THE UNKNOWN

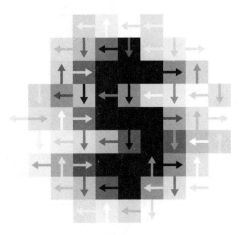

JOHN M. JENNINGS

GREENLEAF
BOOK GROUP PRESS

Published by Greenleaf Book Group Press

Austin, Texas
www.gbgpress.com

Distributed by Greenleaf Book Group

For ordering information or special discounts for bulk purchases, please contact Greenleaf Book Group at PO Box 91869, Austin, TX 78709, 512.891.6100.

Design and composition by Greenleaf Book Group and Brian Phillips
Cover design by Greenleaf Book Group and Brian Phillips
Cover image © Andrius Repsys. Used under license from Shutterstock.com

For permission to reproduce copyrighted material, grateful acknowledgment is made to the following sources:

The Vanguard Group: Figure 3.5, "Most popular metrics have had little or no correlation with future stock returns," from "Forecasting stock returns: What signals matter, and what do they say now?" October 2012. Copyright © 2012 The Vanguard Group, Inc. Used with permission.

The New York Times: Excerpt from "How Did Economists Get It So Wrong" by Paul Krugman from the *New York Times*, September 2009. Copyright © 2009 by the New York Times Company. All rights reserved. Used under license.

Elsevier: Figure 5.3 from "Effects of Amount of Information on Judgment Accuracy and Confidence," 4, by Claire I. Tsai, Joshua Klayman, and Reid Hastie from *Organizational Behavior and Human Decision Processes* 107, no. 2. Copyright © 2008. Reproduced with permission.

Andrew Clare: Figure 6.6, "Proportion of Monkeys Beating Market-Cap on Three-Year Rolling Basis" by Andrew Clare, Nick Motson, and Stephen Thomas. Copyright © 2013 by the authors. Reproduced by permission.

Eastman Kodak Company: Figure 7.1, image of the first digital Kodak camera. Copyright © by Eastman Kodak Company. Reproduced by permission.

ARK Investment Management LLC: Figure 7.10, "Motor Vehicle Registration and Number of Horses and Mules in the US." Printed with permission.

Basic Books: Figure 8.11 from *The (Mis)behavior of Markets* by Benoit Mandelbrot. Copyright © 2004. Reprinted by permission of Basic Books, an imprint of Hachette Book Group, Inc.

Publisher's Cataloging-in-Publication data is available.

Print ISBN: 979-8-88645-032-3

eBook ISBN: 979-8-88645-033-0

To offset the number of trees consumed in the printing of our books, Greenleaf donates a portion of the proceeds from each printing to the Arbor Day Foundation. Greenleaf Book Group has replaced over 50,000 trees since 2007.

Printed in the United States of America on acid-free paper

23 24 25 26 27 28   10 9 8 7 6 5 4 3 2 1

First Edition

For Tammy and Dylan,
my supportive companions during
my writing journey.

There are two kinds of forecasters:
those who don't know, and
those who don't know they don't know.

—JOHN KENNETH GALBRAITH

CONTENTS

Preface xv

Introduction 1

1   The Quest for Certainty 9

2   Looking for Causes in All the Wrong Places 25

3   The Stock Market Is Not the Economy
    (or What Toilet Paper Can Teach Us About Investing) 51

4   Market Cycles and the Two Axioms of Investing 69

5   Beware Experts Bearing Predictions 87

6   Skill and Luck in Investing 109

7   The Trend Is Not Your Friend 137

8   The Trivial Many Versus the Vital Few 169

9   Navigating Our Behavioral Biases 193

10   Behavior—The Most Important Ingredient 219

Conclusion: There's Grandeur in this View of Investing 243

Acknowledgments 247

Appendix: The Mental Models 249

Notes 257

About the Author 271

AUTHOR'S NOTE

The stories and examples in this book are based on real events, but the facts have been materially altered and names changed to protect the privacy of those involved.

PREFACE

You can think of your life in two parts. Or, more accurately, as a continual "before" and "after." You're moving through your life, then something happens, and you step through a door into another reality—physically, emotionally, mentally, or spiritually. After that, everything changes. We tend to think of ourselves as the same person, but when we move into the *after*, who we are fundamentally shifts. A new normal, if you will.

Having a baby creates such a door, and after the baby, everything changes. Before, you weren't a parent; after, you are. The immense responsibility of caring for and raising another human is suddenly, irrevocably yours. Entering the workforce is another before-and-after moment. You spend two-plus decades going to school and preparing to do something. Then, you do it. You enter the working world, and there's no going back (no more naps!).

Then there's the Financial Crisis of 2008—a watershed event that sliced my life into two parts and changed who I am professionally and intellectually. It exposed massive cracks in my understanding of how the financial world works and forced me to face the uncertainty inherent in investing and stop searching in vain for certainty where it doesn't exist.

I was inspired to write this book after my view shifted on how to help my clients after the Financial Crisis. Instead of delivering the false certainty of expert predictions and bell curve–based projections or drowning them in torrents of financial statistics and data, I've learned that it's best to tell clients the truth. That means conveying the investment world as it really is—full of uncertainty and wild randomness, where luck plays a sizable role, rendering the future inherently unpredictable. This truth is hard to accept (cue Jack Nicholson screaming, "you can't handle the truth" in the movie *A Few Good Men*), but ignorance of reality won't make you a better investor.

Yet, investors aren't powerless in the face of uncertainty. There are things we *can know* and things over which *we do have control*. We're better investors when we shut out the noise of the unknowable and uncontrollable swirling around us and instead focus on what matters. I wrote this book to help you do this. Give me five hours of reading time, and I'll show you how to improve your thinking about investing, practice better investment behavior, and ultimately, have more money.

INTRODUCTION

DRINKING FROM THE INFORMATION FIRE HOSE

Before the financial crisis, I thought that to be an effective advisor I had to know as much as possible about everything happening in the financial markets. I drank from the fire hose of information. I read the *Wall Street Journal, Investor's Business Daily*, the *Financial Times, BusinessWeek, Barron's*, and *The Economist*. I subscribed to numerous investment research services and devoured their reports. I consumed quarterly commentaries from our multitude of investment managers and research consultants. And I attended conferences and webinars where I learned about the hot investment trends of the moment.

I always knew the price-to-earnings ratios of the major stock markets, how value stocks were faring relative to growth stocks, what the shape of the yield curve was (and was predicted to be), how global shipping costs were trending (via the *Baltic Dry Index*), the level of Volatility Index (the "VIX"), and on and on. In short, I was a walking, talking encyclopedia of economic indicators and investment news.

It was exhausting, exhilarating, stressful, and hectic. I loved it, and sometimes I hated it. But my vast store of knowledge always made me feel like I had a good handle on the economy and the stock market. I thought I generally knew what was coming in the financial markets.

But it turns out I was kidding myself.

The global economy and markets were rocked by the Financial Crisis that began in late 2007. The S&P 500 fell 57 percent from its peak to its trough, and the world's financial system teetered on the brink. And I hadn't seen it coming. All the information I'd consumed hadn't helped me foresee or prepare for the meltdown. I had no idea what to do. I became frantic. So, I ratcheted up my reading about the economy and markets, met with economists and investment consultants, and attended conference calls hosted by investment managers. Everyone I spoke to in the investment world was in a lather, just like me. I couldn't see how things could end well—there was just too much bad news. I was paralyzed with fear and didn't know how we should be advising our clients.

During one of the darkest periods of the crisis—February 2009—I attended a client meeting with Liz, one of my colleagues and a fellow founding member of my firm. While I spent hours reading and keeping up with what was happening in the markets daily, Liz took a different tact. She had more of a big picture approach and merely kept lightly abreast of the happenings in the financial markets. At the meeting, I was struck by Liz's calm demeanor as she counseled our client to take a long-term perspective. She said the market would be back up; we just couldn't say when. Liz reminded our client that, in her portfolio, she had plenty of cash and bonds and was well-positioned to ride out further market declines. She told the client not to look at her portfolio because it would cause her needless anxiety. Liz said *we* were worrying about her investments, so *she* didn't have to. It was great advice, and our client followed it. And when the market began its historic rebound a month later, the client enjoyed strong returns.

After that meeting, I thought about how, while I was more knowledgeable than Liz about the economy and financial markets, she was more focused on what mattered. While I was cataloging trees, Liz was looking at the forest. For me, this was an epiphany. I realized I needed to change my focus and that I'd been wasting my time by concentrating on irrelevant noise.

So, I changed. I stopped spending hours every day reading investment news and analysis and stepped through the door to the *after* of my wealth management career. I embarked on a quest for investment wisdom.

THE WISDOM HIERARCHY

So, what is wisdom? I think it's best captured by a concept known as the "Wisdom Hierarchy," first developed by organizational theorist Russell Ackoff in 1989. In this model, Ackoff divides the types of things we hear and learn every day into four categories: data, information, knowledge, and wisdom. Then he ranks them in order of usefulness and availability: wisdom is rare and most useful, while data is plentiful and not terribly helpful.

THE WISDOM HIERARCHY PYRAMID

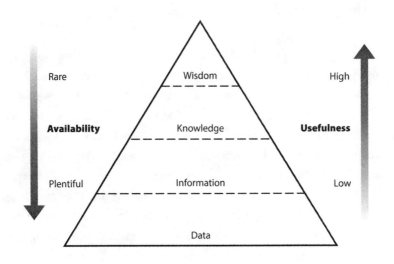

A key to making sound investment decisions is to base more of your choices on wisdom rather than on knowledge, information, or data. But to do that, you must first understand the differences between them:

- *Data* is raw facts, events, experiences, and observations; stuff like housing starts, stock prices, weekly unemployment claims, and interest rates.

- *Information* is data with context. For example, housing data becomes information when organized by region and price because it indicates which market segments are doing better than others.

- *Knowledge* is data or information coupled with experience, understanding, and expertise. For example, an economist armed with housing starts, unemployment, and GDP data can tease out insights about the overall state of the economy.

- *Wisdom* is knowledge applied with judgment earned through experience. For example, suppose experts—using data, information, and knowledge—conclude that the stock market is becoming overheated. In that case, wise investors will understand that the market tops are nearly impossible to time and, consequently, they will take a long-term view.

Wisdom is a rarer commodity that often sounds simple but isn't easy to implement because it runs counter to our instincts and emotional reactions. When you view the investment industry through the lens of the wisdom hierarchy, it becomes apparent that most of the expert opinions we read in the news or hear on TV aren't wisdom but mere knowledge or information. Before the Financial Crisis, I spent way too much time and effort in the data, information, and knowledge realms.

My pursuit of investment wisdom meant scaling the Wisdom Hierarchy Pyramid. I began by limiting my financial information and news consumption to just fifteen minutes a day. It felt great to turn off all that noise—like coming up for air after being underwater. Instead of my previously frenetic information intake, I read books—stacks and stacks of them—about investing and other relevant areas like mathematics, statistics, physics, economics, complex adaptive systems, and psychology. I supplemented the books with academic research on investing, uncertainty, brain physiology, behavioral biases, and evolutionary psychology. The common thread was to step back and try to understand how humans interact with each other in financial markets.

A few years into my investment wisdom journey, I discovered the concept of "mental models," which make nuggets of investment wisdom and knowledge useful to investors of all experience levels and sophistication.

THE WISDOM OF INVESTMENT MENTAL MODELS

How often have you sent an email and not gotten a response? All the time, right? It's off-putting, and it's common to think, "Do they think I'm not important?" or "Are they blowing me off or sending me a message?" All seemingly reasonable thoughts, which can lead to anger or hurt feelings.

But there's a more productive way to think about not getting a response to an email. It's called Hanlon's razor. In philosophical terms, a razor is a guiding principle or mental model that allows us to shed unlikely explanations. The most famous razor is Occam's, which posits that simpler explanations are more likely to be correct than complex ones. Hanlon's razor is similarly straightforward. It states:

> Never attribute malice to that which can be adequately explained by stupidity (or carelessness, disorganization, forgetfulness, etc.).

So, when someone doesn't return an email or text, it's best to assume they just messed up and didn't mean to slight you. When your friend keeps you waiting at a restaurant, chalk it up to her disorganization. When someone cuts you off in traffic, he probably hasn't targeted you; he's just a crummy driver. Your brother forgot your birthday? Maybe something is going on in his life you don't know about. Hanlon's razor is an important concept that can save us a lot of wasted negative emotion. It's an excellent example of what is known as a *mental model*.

Mental models are *conceptual* structures that help us understand how the world works. They are bits of knowledge or wisdom we file away in our heads to help us make decisions. Warren Buffett's business partner Charlie Munger is the pioneer of the concept. Here's how he described mental models in a 1994 speech at USC's business school:

> What is elementary, worldly wisdom? Well, the first rule is that you can't really know anything if you just remember isolated facts and try to bang 'em back. If the facts don't hang together on a latticework of theory, you don't have them in a usable form. You've got to have models in your head . . . You've got to have multiple models—because if you just have one or two that you're using, the nature of human psychology is such that you'll torture reality so that it fits your models, or at least you'll think it does . . . 80 or 90 important models will carry about 90 percent of the freight in making you a world-wise person.[1]

In his talk, Munger was referring to mental models that help us make business and personal decisions, but the concept of mental models is equally applicable to investing. In my decade-plus-long quest for investment wisdom, I discovered that great investors create a latticework of mental models.

An example of an investment mental model is Warren Buffett's simple and straightforward advice that successful investing requires being "fearful when others are greedy, and greedy when others are fearful."[2] This is a model to apply when you feel investment FOMO (fear of missing out) when the stock market is soaring and investors are euphoric. It also reminds you that the best time to invest is when the market is down, and everyone is panicking.

Investment mental models serve as guideposts to help you make the best possible decisions in the face of uncertainty. Here's an example: in March 2020, as the dimensions of the COVID-19 pandemic were becoming clear, the stock market was in free-fall, dropping nearly 35 percent in a month. The outlook was dire; the United States and the rest of the world were entering a recession, and sickness and death inevitably would sweep the globe.

During the Financial Crisis, I didn't know how to advise our clients. But I knew what to tell them as the COVID-19 crisis unfolded. I used the mental model that *the stock market is not the economy*. We'll look at this in-depth in Chapter 3, but for now, I'll summarize it: You cannot use what is happening in the economy to predict what will happen in the stock market. Using *the stock market is not the economy* model (and others) as a guide, we advised our clients not to panic and, if it helped them maintain their asset allocation strategy, to sell bonds (which had held their value) and buy stocks (which were down). Our clients navigated the brief bear market with flying colors and enjoyed the strong stock market recovery.

HOW TO THINK BETTER ABOUT INVESTING

The purpose of this book is to provide individual investors with mental models that will help them make better investment decisions, practice better investment behavior, and be better consumers of investment advice—to build a latticework of wisdom. This book is not about *how* to invest but rather *how to think* about investing. It is the culmination of my thirteen-year quest for investment wisdom. In the following chapters, I share the essential wisdom for creating a latticework of mental models for investing; they are vital tools for investors to make better decisions when faced with uncertainty and the unknown.

This book is not about how to invest because there isn't a single right way to do it. For some investors, public securities are best; for others, private assets like private equity and venture capital are the way to go. For most investors, being in index funds is the surest road to success. For others, active management is better. Additionally, this investment book is "G-rated"—suitable for all levels of experience and sophistication.

Two years ago, as I was working with my editor outlining this book, she noted that learning about investment mental models laid out in this book is like finding out there's no Santa Claus. I get it. The mental models in this book describe the investment world as full of uncertainty, wild randomness, unpredictability, and pitfalls. There's no easy path. But mental models that embrace reality—that take the world as it is, not how we think it is or want it to be—will make you a better investor and a better consumer of investment advice.

Now let's dig in.

CHAPTER 1

THE QUEST FOR CERTAINTY

What men really want is not knowledge but certainty.
—BERTRAND RUSSELL

Would you rather *know for sure* that you'll receive a painful electric shock or have *the possibility* that you might? A study performed at University College London answered this question by having volunteers play a strange, painful video game while their stress levels were measured.[1]

The game required the volunteers to turn over rocks that, at times, had snakes underneath them. If they turned over a rock with a snake, they received a painful shock on their wrist. At first, there was a pattern and the players quickly learned which rocks harbored snakes, and they could avoid shocks. Then the snakes were distributed randomly, and the players received shocks about half the time.

Then the game changed again. Now there were snakes under *all* the rocks, and the players were shocked every time. In other words, the game progressed. In the first version, the participants had a zero percent chance of being shocked. Then they had about a 50 percent chance. Finally, they were shocked every time, a 100 percent certainty.

What were the players' stress levels in each scenario? Predictably, the stress was low after they learned how to avoid shocks. When they were faced with randomly distributed snakes and uncertain shocks, their stress skyrocketed. But what happened when the shocks were 100 percent certain was surprising. Their stress level was about the same as when they had a zero percent chance of being shocked. Knowing that they were going to be shocked was less stressful than being randomly shocked; the participants preferred inevitable pain to an uncertain chance of pain. If you stop and think about how you'd feel if you played the game, you can probably imagine how anxious you'd be to turn over a rock, not knowing if you'd be shocked. And you'd feel less stress if you knew a shock was coming, and you could steel yourself against it.

This conclusion—that we prefer certainty to uncertainty, even if the certainty is bad—is consistent with numerous other studies, including the following:

- We'd rather have a boss who is always unfair compared to one who is sporadically unfair; variability results in more significant psychological stress than both consistently fair and consistently unfair treatment.[2]

- When given a countdown to a possible electric shock, a group informed that their chance of a shock was 5 percent experienced greater anxiety than a group told that their chance was 95 percent.[3]

- Even our immune systems don't like uncertainty. A 1995 study found that the immune systems of a group of volunteers who were subjected to unpredictable exposure to cold experienced more stress than when the exposure was predictable. The researchers found that "predictability buffered the effect of the [cold] stressor on immune function."[4]

Bottom line? Humans hate uncertainty. We prefer certainty, even if it comes with pain.

OUR PATTERN-SEEKING BRAINS

Our brains are pattern-recognizing machines. For eamxlpe, it deson't mttaer in waht oredr the ltteers in a wrod aepapr, the olny iprmoatnt tihng is taht the frist and lsat ltteer are in the rghit pcale. The rset can be a toatl mses and you can sitll read it wouthit pobelrm. S1M1L4RLY, Y0UR M1ND 15 R34D1NG 7H15 4U70M471C4LLY W17H0U7 3V3N 7H1NK1NG 4B0U7 17.

Our mind's ability to recognize patterns is an inherited trait, a survival advantage. Imagine you lived in a small tribe of hunter-gatherers 100,000 years ago. Your ability to survive as a hairless, relatively weak, and slow mammal depended on your ability to recognize patterns that signaled threats. Was that rustling in the bushes a predator? Did those clouds predict a storm that would require you to find shelter? Were those red berries nourishing or poisonous? This was all critical to your survival. And if you were good at it, your chances of living long enough to breed and pass on your pattern-recognition ability to your children increased. As a result, our minds are superbly attuned to finding patterns. And when we can't detect a pattern, we get antsy.

The physiology is fascinating. When you feel uncertain or threatened, your brain enters a vigilant state as it seeks information and searches for patterns to resolve the uncertainty. Your brain triggers the sympathetic nervous system, which unleashes the fight-or-flight response, and you become hyper-alert. Your respiration and heart rate quicken, and glucose is released into the bloodstream for a quick shot of energy. You're primed for action. You're ready for anything. This all happens in a flash, and you usually don't even realize it. You just know you feel keyed up and stressed.

When we resolve uncertainty, the opposite happens. The parasympathetic nervous system kicks in and calms us

> OUR MINDS ARE SUPERBLY ATTUNED TO FINDING PATTERNS. AND WHEN WE CAN'T DETECT A PATTERN, WE GET ANTSY.

down; our brain releases dopamine, creating a sense of pleasure, and our stress and anxiety melt away. Nice.

These opposing sensations of feeling anxious during uncertainty and pleasure when we resolve it create a complex relationship with uncertainty. We like a bit of it—especially when it's nonthreatening—because we enjoy the dopamine that comes with its resolution. That's why we like suspense novels and horror movies and why some people like to gamble. But too much uncertainty creates anxiety, and our brains seek ways to resolve it.

HOW WE REACT TO UNCERTAINTY

The combination of feeling stress when we experience uncertainty and pleasure when it's resolved makes our need for certainty a primary human motive that drives large swaths of our behavior.[5] Most of the time, we're unaware of it. We don't realize that our drive to seek certainty is underpinning our behavior. It all happens subconsciously, which has the advantage of speeding up the process.

You didn't *think* when the bush rustled; you *ran*, giving you a head start on that fast predator. That made a lot of sense. But in our modern world, many of those subconscious reactions are neither rational nor helpful. Today, there are rarely tigers hiding in our hedges, but we still react as if there are because our brains don't distinguish between real tigers and imaginary ones. Consequently, today our fight-or-flight response is triggered by work deadlines, our daily commute, political discussions, perceived social snubs, or the stock market's ups and downs. When the stock market becomes volatile, we can feel the same way we would if a saber-toothed tiger were chasing us, even though we're in no physical danger. That's because the world has changed a lot faster than our brains.

The actions we take in such situations may give us a feeling of certainty, but more often than not, they make things worse. As this mostly happens subconsciously, we don't always realize what we're doing. It's essential to understand how we typically react to feeling uncertain, so we can make better decisions. In general, there are four primary things we do when faced with uncertainty:

1. WE SEEK COGNITIVE CLOSURE

Our aversion to uncertainty creates a need for immediate answers. We achieve resolution by grabbing the first possible explanation that fits our worldview, and we stick to it even if contrary information surfaces because we don't want to revisit the uncertainty. First proposed by psychologists Arie Kruglanski and Donna Webster, these responses are known as "seizing and freezing." As Dr. Kruglanski wrote recently about our reactions to the COVID-19 pandemic, "Under conditions of diffuse uncertainty, people are drawn, as if by a magnet, to simplistic solutions and black-and-white reasoning. Some gravitate to the pole of denial that nothing is wrong, others to that of utter panic, the belief that the worst is sure to come."[6] In other words, when faced with the uncertainty that COVID-19 brought us, people grasped for explanations that fit their worldview and then clung to their conclusions even if contrary to fact.

Investors do this all the time by presuming overly simplistic rationales for complex events. When faced with uncertainty, investors grasp any plausible explanation and cling to it even when facts and events contradict it. For example, it's common for investors to have an opinion about what causes inflation and what should be done about it. Yet, economists don't wholly understand inflation, and their theories about what causes inflation and even how to best measure it are the subject of debate. But acknowledging that the causes of inflation aren't wholly understood and that future inflation is unpredictable is hard to stomach. Instead, investors typically pick an explanation like "the Fed's monetary policy has been too accommodative" or "the government has been spending too much" and then cling to it.

We also see our need for explanations play out in headlines that attribute stock market movements to a single piece of news. Headlines such as "The S&P 500 Drops 2 Percent as Disappointing Retailer Earnings Stoke Global Recession Fears" are commonplace. But there's usually no simple answer (like retailers reporting disappointing earnings) to why the stock market is up or down. Hour-to-hour, day-to-day, and week-to-week stock market gyrations are caused by tens of millions of investors buying and selling shares of thousands of stocks. There is vast complexity and myriad reasons behind each buy and sell, which causes the market to rise and fall. A single piece of news is rarely "the cause" of what the stock market does.

Investors gobble up these single cause explanations from the financial media and market pundits because of the need for closure. Explanations like this give us a sense of certainty. We need the stock market to make sense. But, as discussed in Chapter 3, the stock market is a complex adaptive system and thus generally defies simple explanation.

2. WE TURN INTO INFORMATION JUNKIES

During the spring of 2020, as COVID-19 swept across the United States, I reacted to the uncertainty of the pandemic by furiously seeking information. Every day, I spent hours reading about COVID-19 in news reports and medical journals. I logged into webinars where epidemiologists and infectious disease experts shared their knowledge and thoughts about how the pandemic might progress. I acted similarly during the Financial Crisis of 2008.

Uncertainty can make us feel like we must be missing something, and we respond by seeking more information. We get a hit of dopamine when we take in information, which makes our brains crave more. Sometimes this search can be helpful and lead to better-informed decisions. But many things in life are unknowable, and no amount of information will change that. Harvard economist Richard Zeckhauser thinks of knowledge as falling in three categories: the known, unknown, and unknowable.[7] Thinking in terms of these three categories (see Figure 1.1) helps us determine when information will be helpful and when it won't.

THE KNOWLEDGE CONTINUUM

FIGURE 1.1

At one end of the spectrum is *the known*: George Washington was the first US President; the S&P 500 dropped 38 percent in 2008; dogs drool. This category also includes future events where the outcomes have known probabilities. For instance, the chance of heads coming up sixty times in one hundred flips is known, as is the likelihood that a roulette ball will land on red.

In the middle of the continuum is *the unknown*. The first type of unknowns are future events with discrete outcomes where we aren't sure of the probabilities. For instance, doctors usually can provide guidance about the course of a disease within a specific range but can't provide certainty; each patient's specific outcome falls within a realm of uncertainty. The unknown also includes things you don't know but could know. For example, I don't know the Norwegian word for "gray," how many kilowatt-hours of energy my household uses in a year, or the name of the heaviest element in the periodic table. But I could find out and move those things from the unknown category to the known.

At the far end of the spectrum is *the unknowable*. These are things that we can't currently know, no matter how hard we try, such as whether a giant asteroid will impact the earth in the next thousand years, who will win the presidency in 2032, what the next pandemic will be like, or whether we'll ever meet aliens from outer space. No matter how hard you try and how much information you acquire, you can't move the unknowable to the unknown, much less the known. The unknowable is unresolvable; no matter how much information we gather, we get no closer to knowing (unless the passage of time reveals it).

Dividing knowledge into these three categories is helpful because it lets you know whether seeking information will be productive. Looking for information about the unknown but potentially knowable is useful. But when you're dealing with the unknowable, more information isn't worthwhile and may generate a false sense of certainty. The key is to recognize what's unknowable versus what's merely unknown.

Investment knowledge also falls into these three categories. We know what's happened in the past and such knowledge can reveal patterns that we can project into the future, within a range. For instance, the US stock market tends to go up (see Figure 1.2) about two out of every three years, no matter what has happened in the prior year: market ups and downs, Republican or Democratic presidents, or a leap year.

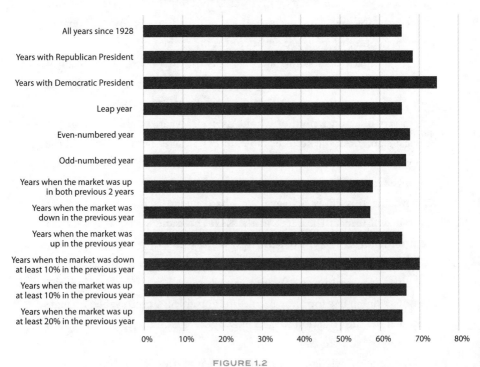

THE PROBABILITY OF THE S&P 500 RISING IN ANY CALENDAR YEAR

FIGURE 1.2

Of course, this pattern could change; Japan's stock market still hasn't regained its 1989 high watermark, and a similar scenario could play out in the US market.

Unfortunately, much of what we'd like to know to help us invest falls in the realms of the unknown or unknowable and thus generates a ton of uncertainty and anxiety. We can't know what the stock market will return tomorrow, next month, or next year. We can't know when the next bear market will start, or the next bull market will begin. The path of interest rates, future inflation, and economic growth are all unknowable. That stinks, doesn't it?

But viewing investing through the known, unknown, and unknowable lens is a good habit. When you feel the stress of uncertainty and begin looking for answers and explanations, feeling like a rat caught in a scary maze, ask yourself which category of uncertainty you are dealing with and whether additional information will help.

3. WE SEEK PREDICTIONS FROM EXPERTS

When wrestling with uncertainty, we seek out experts, hoping they'll have the crystal ball we lack. Expert predictions can be comforting because they make us feel we've gained some sense of certainty. When a confident expert predicts what the future holds for market returns, inflation, or economic growth, our uncertainty ebbs. We feel a greater sense of control.

The problem is that expert predictions of the future are pretty much useless in investing. In Chapter 5, "Beware Experts Bearing Predictions," you'll see the experts' dismal track record in predicting just about everything. For now, suffice to say, don't click on investment predictions. The biggest investment misconception, which we dig into in later chapters, is that to invest well, you must know the future. In fact, the opposite is true. If you think you know the future, you won't invest as well as when you admit your ignorance. Knowing what you don't know and what you can't and won't know is necessary for successful investing.

4. WE ASSOCIATE WITH GROUPS WHO THINK LIKE WE DO

Do you ever wonder how other people can hold such profoundly different views than you do? Take COVID-19 and our country's response to it. Suppose you favored wearing masks and getting vaccinated. In that case, it probably seemed that those who thought COVID-19 was no big deal and that wearing masks and getting vaccinated were unnecessary (or even inadvisable) were from a different planet. And vice versa. How could we have such differing views based on the same set of facts?

One feature of groups is that *what we view as being true* is largely defined by our social group. Here's what sociologist and expert on groups Arie Kruglanski has to say about groups and truth:

> An opinion, a belief, an attitude is perceived as "correct," "valid," and "proper" to the extent that it is anchored in a group of people with similar beliefs, opinions, and attitudes. Individuals' understandings of the world are held as true to the extent that they can be affirmed by some social group.[8]

Thus, the "truth" is whatever our social group believes it to be.

When we feel uncertain, we find comfort and support in groups whose members share our values, views, and beliefs—our "truths." The desire to associate with groups is known as the uncertainty identity theory, pioneered by Michael Hogg of Claremont Graduate University. According to Dr. Hogg, we attempt to reduce uncertainty and protect ourselves from its discomfort by associating with others who agree with and validate our attitudes and values.

Groups vary in how homogeneous they are in their beliefs and norms. Some groups have minimal variation in beliefs, while others tolerate a wider range of opinions. A way to think about this is that some groups are more group-y than others. The technical term for this is entitativity. For example, "Christians" have certain shared beliefs and worldviews. Still, as a group, it's more heterogeneous and has less entitativity than subgroups of Christians such as Pentecostals or Presbyterians, who have a narrower set of beliefs than Christianity as a whole.

The more uncertain we feel, the more we want to associate with high-entitativity groups. While this reduces our feelings of uncertainty, homogeneous thinking has its drawbacks. Being with others who share the same views can be like living in an echo chamber that amplifies fringe and extremist views. We see this concept playing out in social media, where everyone can pick their news source based on their affinity groups. Extremist and fringe views like the QAnon conspiracy or the idea that 5G towers cause COVID-19 can take hold as our society stratifies into smaller groups with homogeneous views.

Why is this happening? "Studies suggest that conspiracy theories flourish when people feel anxiety, alienation, paranoia, or loss of control," political scientists Joseph Uscinski and Joseph Parent wrote in their seminal book *American Conspiracy Theories.*[9] That is, when people feel uncertainty-induced anxiety. But rather than seeking that kind of spurious comfort, you'd be better served by being open to thoughts beyond your current groups.

LETTING IT BE

Our hardwired aversion to uncertainty is a theme that runs throughout this book. Uncertainty causes discomfort, and discomfort can lead us to make bad decisions—both in the investment realm and in other areas of our lives. Now that you know this mental model, pay attention to those times you feel uncertain and notice how you react. Are you stressed and anxious? Is your fight-or-flight response kicking in? When you recognize that uncertainty is causing you discomfort, instead of hunkering down in your group or listening to expert predications of the future, try these strategies instead.

1. SIT IN YOUR DISCOMFORT

Therapists suggest that when people experience uncomfortable feelings—anxiety, worry, frustration, or anger—they should do . . . nothing. By learning to sit in the discomfort of your emotions, over time you gain peace and equanimity and the skills to tolerate them.

Sitting in discomfort is a good strategy for painful emotions; it's also an essential behavior to practice in the face of uncertainty. When you take action to relieve uncertainty, it's like a sugar rush. Yes, you're doing something, but the action likely is counterproductive. Own the feeling; observe your discomfort. Breathe. It will pass.

I've sat in the discomfort of uncertainty when faced with volatile investment markets, business concerns, health scares, and worries about my children. It works, it's simple, but it's not easy. For example, in October 2021, I developed pain in my calf. I work out a lot, so I thought I had pulled a muscle. A week later, when my entire leg swelled up, I knew it wasn't just a pulled muscle. It turns out I had two blood clots in my calf and two more in my lungs. I was put on blood thinners and scheduled for a CT scan a week later to see if my clots were caused by cancer.

Waiting for the results of a medical test to tell me if I had cancer was the very definition of uncertainty-fueled anxiety. Yet, I'm proud to say that I remained calm because I acknowledged the uncertainty and viewed it as a challenge to overcome and an opportunity to apply all that I've learned over years in therapy and my research into uncertainty. Probably the thing that helped the most was a mantra developed by Dr. Claire Weekes in the 1960s. It goes like this: *Face, Accept, Float, Let Time Pass.*

- **Face** that you are experiencing uncertainty that's causing stress and anxiety. Acknowledge the discomfort and don't run from it.

- **Accept** the situation and that the uncertainty can't be immediately resolved.

- Let your feelings of stress, anxiety, and fear **float** by—observe your emotions but stay above them.

- **Let Time Pass** without impatience, fear, or anger. Let things play out.

This four-step process helps you sit in your discomfort. I've found it works equally well for health scares, stressful work situations, and dealing with the uncertainties of the stock market. Oh, my CT scan was fine. I didn't have cancer. And the clots are gone. It turns out I had a congenital defect related to how an artery and vein are arranged in my abdomen called May-Thurner syndrome that caused the clots, which has been fixed via surgery. I guess being vegan for twenty years and getting regular exercise don't make you bulletproof!

Not only is learning to sit in discomfort helpful in our daily lives, it's also essential to good investment behavior. From an investment perspective, we should all adopt the mantra "when in doubt, do nothing." Warren Buffett agrees with this notion, having said, "Much success can be attributed to inactivity. Most investors cannot resist the temptation to constantly buy and sell."

When markets are volatile, the best course is almost always to ignore both the markets and our investments. Follow the advice of Vanguard founder John Bogle, who when interviewed by CNBC advised that when faced with investment uncertainty, "the best rule you can possibly follow is not 'Don't stand there, do something,' but 'Don't do something, stand there!'" When you feel compelled to act on your portfolio, go for a walk. Read a good book. Start a home project. Try not to look at your portfolio. I know that the more I look at my portfolio, the more I'm apt to tinker. Tinkering seldom works out well. We revisit tinkering and what good investment behavior looks like in Chapter 10.

2. FOCUS ON WHAT YOU CAN CONTROL

Flying in a plane is much safer than riding in a car. Car deaths per mile are fifty times greater than airplane deaths. Yet the fear of flying is common; an estimated one in six people—or forty million Americans—suffer from fear of flying.[10] When you leave for a flight, it's common for friends to say, "travel safe," but you rarely hear that when you jump in your car for your evening commute.

Why is the fear of flying common while the fear of driving isn't? Multiple factors are at play, but primarily people are afraid to fly because they are giving up control to someone else—the pilot. When we don't have control, we feel uncertain. And we really hate that.

When you feel the stress of uncertainty, ask yourself if it's because you aren't in control. It's freeing to know the difference between what you can and can't control. And when you focus only on what you can control and don't fixate on what you can't, you spare yourself a lot of stress.

When the stock market drops and your investment portfolios decline, you may feel powerless. And you are. That's never any fun. Figure 1.3 is a diagram we use with our clients that lays out a helpful model of what we can control and what we can't.

FOCUS ON THOSE THINGS WITHIN YOUR CONTROL

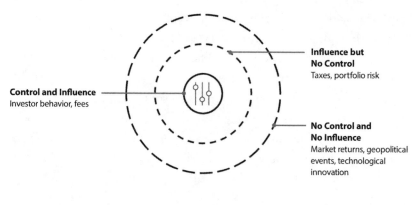

FIGURE 1.3

The key is to focus on the bullseye, pay some attention to the second ring, and ignore those things over which you have neither control nor influence.

THE UNCERTAINTY MENTAL MODEL

Making peace with uncertainty is unbelievably difficult, yet it's essential to successful investing. Train yourself to notice when you are faced with uncertainty and it's causing you discomfort. When you can recognize that uncertainty is causing discomfort and you don't react to it, you'll make better decisions and practice better behavior.

In addition to sitting in your discomfort and focusing on what you can control, it is also essential to develop a latticework of investment mental models to use when making decisions in the face of uncertainty. Without a foundation of investment wisdom to guide you, practicing good investment behavior is nearly impossible.

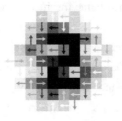

CHAPTER 2

LOOKING FOR CAUSES IN ALL THE WRONG PLACES

One of the first things taught in introductory statistics textbooks is that correlation is not causation. It is also one of the first things forgotten.

—THOMAS SOWELL, *THE VISION OF THE ANOINTED*

Not long after 9/11, a friend forwarded me an email asserting that the US government had engineered the attacks. The gist of the message was that a cabal of powerful officials were behind it, so they could better surveil and control American citizens. The email suggested that it made more sense that powerful people inside our government orchestrated the attacks than to believe that a ragtag group of rogue terrorists could inflict such damage on our country.

I thought the email was ludicrous. But it was also oddly compelling, especially in the wake of 9/11 as our collective fear helped pave the way for legislation like the Patriot Act, which gave the government powers that would have been unthinkable before 9/11.

I didn't get sucked into believing in this conspiracy, but a survey by University of Chicago political scientists Eric Oliver and Thomas Wood found that nearly 20 percent of Americans believed that "certain U.S. government officials planned the attacks of September 11."[1]

Belief in conspiracy theories is common in the United States. That same study found that 50 percent of Americans believe in at least one conspiracy theory. The authors define a conspiracy theory as "narratives about hidden, malevolent groups secretly perpetuating political plots and social calamities to further their own nefarious goals," contradicting commonly accepted explanations for . . . just about anything.[2] Belief in conspiracy theories is especially common for those with extremist political views—both on the right and the left.[3]

Some widely believed conspiracy theories include:

- Vapor trails left by aircraft are chemicals deliberately sprayed by a clandestine government program.

- Billionaire George Soros is behind a secret plot to destabilize the American government, take control of the media, and thereby rule the world.

- The US government is mandating the switch to compact fluorescent light bulbs because they make people more obedient and easier to control.

- The moon landings were fake.

- The Holocaust didn't happen.

- The rollout of 5G mobile phone technology is responsible for the spread of COVID-19.

- COVID-19 vaccines contain microchips, so Bill Gates can track you.

Why do people believe in conspiracy theories? Our dislike of uncertainty is a primary reason. As noted in Chapter 1, humans crave certainty, yet the world is rife with randomness and unpredictability. And sometimes it's easier to imagine that there's a group of secret, powerful people in charge of world events rather than accept the idea that many things happen for no good or fathomable reason. Attributing a cause or explanation to events gives us a sense of control and makes the world, and our lives, seem less uncertain.

Conspiracy theories are particularly compelling when they support our existing beliefs and worldviews. But complex, far-flung conspiracies that must involve many actors are, as G. Gordon Liddy, former advisor to President Nixon and mastermind (and bungler) of the Watergate break-in explained, "difficult to pull off, and so many people want their quarter-hour of fame that even the Men in Black couldn't squelch the squealers from spilling the beans. So, there's a good chance that the more elaborate a conspiracy theory is, and the more people that would need to be involved, the less likely it is true."[4]

But our yearning for explanations and causation isn't only expressed as a belief in conspiracy theories. Our brains have evolved to look for causes and explanations everywhere, even where they don't exist or can only be explained through mathematics and probability, rather than anecdote.

Becoming wary of attributing causation to circumstance is a mental model essential to making good decisions, both in the investment realm and the real world. Decisions based on faulty explanation or imaginary causation are like coin flips (or worse). Consequently, knowing how to sniff out when causation exists and when it doesn't is critical . . . unless flipping a coin is your go-to decision-making model.

> BECOMING WARY OF ATTRIBUTING CAUSATION TO CIRCUMSTANCE IS A MENTAL MODEL ESSENTIAL TO MAKING GOOD DECISIONS, BOTH IN THE INVESTMENT REALM AND THE REAL WORLD.

THE CHICKEN AND THE EGG: THE DIFFICULTY IN DETERMINING CAUSATION

What does it mean for something to cause something else? That's been debated since Socrates, and probably before. There's no single accepted definition of causation and determining that one thing causes another is often extremely difficult. According to Stephen Mumford and Rani Lill Anjum in their book *Causation*, "To a large extent, it is a vast scientific endeavor to figure out what causes what, and even when we think causation has been established, there is no guarantee that we are right."[5]

Let's focus on some of the common issues that make determining causation challenging.

CONFUSING SYMPTOMS WITH CAUSES

Years ago, during the cocktail hour at an investment conference, I met the CEO of a successful investment firm. As we sipped our nondescript conference wine and exchanged niceties, I asked her about her firm's investment strategy. She replied that it was simple: the firm invested in companies that had female leaders because female-led companies outperform male-led ones. By using this simple strategy, their fund had beaten the market over the previous three years—and handily. I loved this. It was so simple, so compelling. My mind jumped to how female-led firms' culture might be different and could lead to better performance.

Back at my office, I dug into the research that confirmed that firms with female leadership had tended to outperform male-led ones. For instance, a 2013 Credit Suisse study of over 3,000 businesses found that "companies with more than one woman on the board have returned 3.7 percent compound a year over those that have none since 2005."[6] Similarly, Quantopian, a quantitative research firm, found that firms in the Fortune 1000 with female CEOs (eighty of them on average) outperformed the S&P 500 by 226 percent between 2002 and 2014.[7]

Why might female leadership be linked to better company performance? My research uncovered that:

- Females generally have a higher risk tolerance than males, which leads them to make fewer mistakes.

- They are more in-tune with female consumers, and women make over 70 percent of all purchase decisions.

- Women tend to focus more on long-term priorities than men.

- Diverse teams are more innovative and tend to outperform more homogeneous ones.[8] Including females in leadership positions increases diversity and strengthens corporate leadership teams.

- Finally, females are more likely to be rock stars than their male peers because they've had more obstacles to overcome on their journey to the corner office (aka the "glass ceiling"), and those who make it to the top are, indeed, the cream of the crop.

These are compelling explanations for why female-led firms perform so well, and they inspired me to introduce this to our Investment Committee as a strategy we could adopt.

Shortly after that, I met with a long-standing client, a retired CEO of a large publicly traded company and one of the smartest people I know. When he asked if I'd learned anything worthwhile at the aforementioned conference, I told him about the female-led firm idea. He asked, "Does female leadership cause those firms to outperform others, or is female leadership and performance merely correlated but not causally related? Maybe female leadership is a symptom and not a cause?"

I was embarrassed. In my excitement about uncovering a potentially profitable investment strategy, I'd jumped straight to the conclusion (buoyed by compelling but not dispositive evidence) that female leadership was causal. Of course, I wasn't alone in my conclusion as the authors of the research papers I read also assumed that female leadership caused the strong corporate performance.

My client's question was precisely the right one to ask because there's an alternate explanation of the female leader phenomenon: firms that already are performing well may be more likely to hire female board members and executives.

Alice Eagly of Northwestern University has studied the issue, and she thinks this alternate explanation has a great deal of validity. Even though "considerable social science evidence shows women tend to have leadership styles that researchers have established are advantageous," she has found no evidence of a causal correlation between women in high positions and firm performance or that "women's participation makes groups more creative and productive or corporations more profitable."[9]

Psychologist James Thompson takes this a step further. He posits that "successful companies are able to spend money on public relations, of which appointing a few women to top posts would be part, a cynical measure like giving to selected charities or implementing policies to encourage the recycling of company reports."[10]

So, which is it? Do female leaders drive corporate performance or do strong performing companies tend to hire more women? The jury's out. Experts in the field suggest more research is needed, particularly longitudinal studies that compare companies to each other over long periods of time.

As a postscript, and with years more data, the conclusion that female-led firms outperform male-led ones isn't as solid as it once seemed. In recent years, investment funds that focus on female-led firms have underperformed. For example, as of the end of 2020, the Pax Ellevate Global Women's Leadership Index Fund has trailed the world stock index over the past one, three, five, and ten years.

We need to be careful not to ascribe causation when we think we see a pattern. Just because two variables are correlated (in this case, female leaders and company performance) doesn't mean that one variable caused the other. Acting as if it does can lead to bad decisions and nasty surprises. And it's possible that what you thought was a cause (female leaders driving firm performance) might instead be a symptom (maybe female leaders are more likely to be hired by already high-performing firms).

My embarrassment about jumping to causation as an explanation and having my client question my conclusion left its mark. Now, when I see two linked variables, I stop, and then try to hammer down whether there's a causal link. This may sound simple. It's not.

CAUSE OR COINCIDENCE?

Here's an example of how hard it is to establish causation: Imagine you live in a city in which an illness has been sweeping through the population for a few weeks. (These days, that shouldn't be hard to picture.) When the infection first appeared, the city experienced an unprecedented infestation of rats. Did the rats cause the disease? Given that the appearance of the rats and the disease coincided, it would seem so to our pattern-seeking brains.[11]

But perhaps the incidence of illness and the appearance of rats was a mere coincidence. Maybe mosquitoes transmitted the disease. Maybe a person returning from an overseas trip brought it back. It would take a lot of work to trace the disease's actual cause and determine if the rats (or bats) were the source.

Always ask whether two simultaneously occurring events could be coincidental. If coincidence could explain the events, further digging is warranted to develop a causal link.

THE HAWTHORNE EFFECT:
OBSERVATION CHANGES BEHAVIOR

In the 1920s and 1930s, Harvard professor Elton Mayo performed a series of experiments at Hawthorne Works, a factory outside of Chicago. The purpose of the experiments was to determine whether various changes to working conditions would boost worker productivity.

The first experiment increased the brightness of the work floor lights for one set of workers. And productivity increased for the group working under brighter lights. Other experiments included lengthening work breaks, making work breaks shorter but more frequent, changing the humidity in the factory, and tidying up workstations. With each change, productivity rose. Finally, the experimenters reestablished the initial conditions—dimmer lights, original break structures, etc.—and productivity hit an all-time high. Regardless of the variable manipulated, worker productivity improved!

The phenomenon observed in these experiments, now dubbed the Hawthorne effect, is that subjects in behavioral studies often change their performance in response to being observed. While there are numerous lessons to be learned from the Hawthorne experiments, a key one is that we should beware of concluding that Occurrence A produced Effect B. If the Hawthorne researchers had merely boosted the lighting and stopped there, they would have concluded that brighter lights boost productivity and handed out sunglasses to the workers. Only when they dimmed the lights and saw that productivity increased again did they understand that something else was going on.

MULTIPLE CAUSES

Another problem with trying to pinpoint causation is that the world is complex, and any event tends to have multiple causes. For example, Greg attends a party at his friend Gretchen's apartment. At the party, egged on by Gretchen, he engages in a drinking game and becomes highly intoxicated. Even though Gretchen knows that Greg is drunk, she doesn't say or do anything when he grabs his keys to drive home. On the way, Greg runs a red light and smashes into another vehicle, injuring its driver who wasn't wearing his seatbelt. The driver's injuries are severe but not life-threatening. However, while in the hospital recovering, a nurse misreads a prescription and administers a fatal overdose.

So, who caused the driver's death? Was it Gretchen for pushing Greg to drink and not stopping him from driving? Was Greg the cause because he drove drunk and ran a red light? Maybe it was the injured driver's fault; if he'd been wearing his seatbelt, he might not have been injured seriously enough to require hospitalization. Was the nurse who administered the wrong medication the cause? Was some nameless hospital administrator at fault for not instituting better procedures that would have ensured that patients wouldn't receive incorrect medications? The answer, of course, is—to some extent—yes to everything. Each of the events conspired to cause the death. The absence of any of these people and their actions would have broken the chain of causation and prevented the result.

The lesson of multiple causes is that you can't simply say that taking shots of whiskey leads to death or that drinking and driving always results in wrecks. Doubtless, these were contributing factors (and none of them a best practice), but it took many events to link up in just the right combination to produce the driver's demise. And that's not including the inventor of drinking games, the haphazard enforcement of seatbelt laws, the design of automobiles, etc., ad infinitum. Consequently, we should be wary of causally linking two occurrences because without other causes, the link between them might be severed.

A good way to think about multiple causes is that a cause, like the driver not wearing his seatbelt, may be *necessary* for the result to occur, but may not be *sufficient* on its own to be *the* cause.

CORRELATION DOESN'T IMPLY CAUSATION

Correlation is the strength of the relationship between two variables and is expressed via the "correlation coefficient" as depicted in Figure 2.1. Correlation tells you how one variable acts with reference to its average compared to another variable and its average.

Variables that are positively correlated move together in the same direction compared to their means. For example, height and shoe size are positively correlated. Taller people tend to have bigger feet than shorter people.

Negatively correlated variables move in opposite directions compared to their means. For example, altitude and temperature are negatively correlated. As you move higher above sea level, temperatures tend to drop.

Uncorrelated variables have no linear relationship; one variable's movement doesn't tell us anything about another's. For example, there's no correlation between the amount of time a person spends watching TV each week and the size of their TV.

THE CORRELATION COEFFICIENT

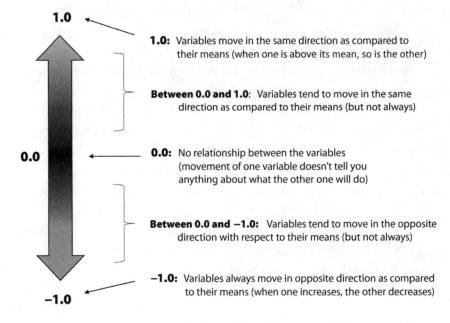

1.0: Variables move in the same direction as compared to their means (when one is above its mean, so is the other)

Between 0.0 and 1.0: Variables tend to move in the same direction as compared to their means (but not always)

0.0: No relationship between the variables (movement of one variable doesn't tell you anything about what the other one will do)

Between 0.0 and −1.0: Variables tend to move in the opposite direction with respect to their means (but not always)

−1.0: Variables always move in opposite direction as compared to their means (when one increases, the other decreases)

FIGURE 2.1

Strongly correlated variables confuse our ability to determine causation because if one variable always moves when another does, it can appear that there is a causal link. Consequently, because our brains demand and prefer explanations, we're quick to see causation when there is none.

CORRELATION DOESN'T NECESSARILY IMPLY CAUSATION.

That something is correlated doesn't mean it's an absolute relationship (unless the correlation coefficient is 1.0 or −1.0). For example, a short person can have big feet, and sometimes it's hotter at higher altitudes. Correlation generally references a tendency: if one variable moves, correlation describes how the other variable might.

SPURIOUS CORRELATIONS

To make the point that correlation doesn't imply causation, data scientists David Leinweber and David Krider compared S&P 500 returns from 1983–1993 to various other data streams. They found that S&P 500 returns and butter production in Bangladesh were highly correlated. When butter production was up, so was the stock market, and when butter production was down, the stock market was also.[12] What is the causal relationship between those factors? None. And that's the point. Completely unrelated factors can be highly correlated.

Other data scientists have followed Leinweber and Krider's footsteps and identified a bevy of spurious correlations, including:

- The change in the number of nine-year-olds in the US exactly predicts the stock market.[13]

- The divorce rate in Maine is nearly perfectly correlated with the per capita consumption of margarine.[14]

- Chief executives that said "please," "thank you," and "you're welcome" more often enjoyed a better subsequent share price performance.[15]

Whenever I see factors that are strongly correlated, I think about Bangladeshi butter production.

CORRELATED FACTORS MAY HAVE A COMMON CAUSE

A tricky situation occurs when two correlated variables share a common cause because it can erroneously seem like one variable causes the other. A good example is the relationship between books and educational attainment. A study titled "Family Scholarly Culture and Educational Success: Books and Schooling in 27 Nations" concluded that there's a strong positive correlation between a child's academic achievement and the number of books his or her parents own.[16] Key findings included:

- Children who grew up in a home with more than 500 books spent three years longer in school and were almost 20 percent more likely to finish college than children whose parents had only a few or no books.

- Having books in the home is twice as important as the parents' education level and more important than whether a child was reared in China or the United States.

- The number of books in the home was more important than the home country's GDP or political system.

Does this make you want to run out and buy books for your kids or grandkids, so they'll succeed academically? That's probably not a bad thing, but if you're betting that will get them into Harvard you may want to examine the findings more closely. The study merely found a *correlation* between the number of books in a home and the amount of education attained. It did not necessarily uncover a causal link.

In the bestseller *Freakonomics*, the authors acknowledged that having an abundance of books in the home positively correlated to higher test scores but, surprisingly, how often a parent read to their child in their early years did not. So, according to the data relating to what correlates to higher test scores, the authors noted:

Matters: The child has many books in his home.
Doesn't: The child's parents read to him every day.[17]

What's the explanation for this? The authors posited that the correlation of books in the home to educational achievement was due to a different common cause: Parents who buy a lot of books for their children tend to be smart and well-educated. And they pass on their smarts to their children through their genes. Or perhaps they care a great deal about education and about their children in general, which means they create an environment that encourages and rewards learning. Such parents may believe that every book they bring into the home is a talisman for their child's future success in school, but they're probably wrong. A book, in fact, is less a *cause* of intelligence than an *indicator*. And it's an indicator of the type of parents who buy a lot of books for their children. In other words, the bevy of books say more about the parents than they do about their kids' chances of getting into an Ivy League school.

Whenever we see two correlated variables, we should stop to ask whether they have a common cause rather than jumping to the conclusion that one variable caused the other.

DETERMINING CAUSATION IS DIFFICULT

As the previous examples illustrate, determining causation is tricky. The rooster crowing at dawn does not cause the sun to rise. Just because when one thing happens the other also happens doesn't mean there's a causal link. Unfortunately, our brains are wired to jump to those sorts of conclusions.

Data scientists and researchers use sophisticated statistics and design experiments to avoid the traps our brains lay for us and to tease out whether causation actually exists. The gold standard for determining causation is the randomized clinical trial, commonly used in drug studies. In these studies, subjects are randomly assigned to groups. A placebo is given to the control group while the experimental group receives the active drug. By comparing the two groups' outcomes, researchers can determine whether the drug produced (caused) an effect.

. . . WHEN WE SEE THAT WHEN ONE THING HAPPENS THE OTHER OCCURS AS WELL, OUR BRAINS SEARCH FOR A CAUSE.

It's tough to determine causation in the investment world because we can't run a randomized trial. And even if you could, it would be of limited value because, as discussed in Chapter 3, the stock market is a complex adaptive system and is continually changing. What might be a cause in one

INSTEAD, AS
INVESTORS, WE NEED
TO BUILD MENTAL
MODELS AROUND
CAUSATION THAT
RECOGNIZE THAT
OUR BRAINS WANT
EXPLANATIONS, AND
WE ARE PRONE TO SEE
CAUSATION WHERE IT
DOESN'T EXIST.

period may not be a cause in another due to market participants learning and adapting. Additionally, as discussed in Chapter 6, randomness and luck play a large role in investing, so determining causation is always difficult.

This is not to say that causation doesn't exist in investing or that all investment correlations are spurious. That's not the case. Instead, as investors, we need to build mental models around causation that recognize that our brains are prone to perceive causation where it doesn't exist. Accordingly, it's important to question presumed causal links and dig below the surface to test whether causation truly exists.

REGRESSION TO THE MEAN

Years ago, our firm employed a junior investment analyst who left us for pastures he supposed would be greener. In his exit interview, he told me he was leaving in part because he thought he was great at picking investment managers who outperformed the market, and he wanted more opportunities to pick them. So, we made a $100 bet. We'd each pick an actively managed mutual fund in three categories: domestic stocks, international stocks, and bonds. We would equal-weight their performance, and whoever had the highest value portfolio after three years would win a C-note.

The junior analyst spent days combing through the characteristics and statistics of funds to pick his three, which had all consistently outperformed the market in the past. I took a different approach: I randomly picked three funds on our investment consultant's watch list due to poor performance. That took me about three minutes.

How'd we do? After three years, I won. It wasn't even close. I didn't cash my former colleague's $100 check. I taped it to my wall to remind me of the importance of an often-misunderstood concept that I used to win the bet: *regression to the mean.*

A lot of people are aware of this concept, but they overlook it when making investment decisions. They select investments based on past performance, assuming there's a reason these portfolios are performing well and assuming they will continue to do so for that reason. However, luck and randomness are a significant aspect of markets and investing, whereas regression to the mean is predictable and happens all the time. Understanding what it is and how it applies to the markets is essential to maximizing your investments' performance.

WHAT IS REGRESSION TO THE MEAN?

Regression to the mean is a statistical phenomenon in which extreme events are followed by those closer to the average. It happens whenever the correlation between two factors is less than one. You can think of regression to the mean and correlation as the flip sides of the same coin: the weaker the correlation, the greater the regression.

For example, height is based on genetics and other factors such as childhood nutrition and disease incidence. Because of the complex combination of factors that determine height, the correlation between parental height and their children's is less than one (it's about 0.5[18]). Because the correlation is less than one, regression to the mean occurs. This suggests that although tall parents usually have tall children, their children will likely be shorter than they are and closer to average height.

Regression to the mean also explains why the "*Sports Illustrated* cover jinx" is imaginary. According to this urban legend, an athlete will begin to perform worse after they appear on the cover of *Sports Illustrated*. But athletes are typically featured on the cover during a period of extreme performance. Inevitably, their future performance will return toward the average. This is a matter of statistics—not some sort of voodoo.

WHY REGRESSION TO THE MEAN IS DIFFICULT TO APPLY

On its face, the idea that more moderate events typically follow extreme circumstances is not difficult to grasp. "What goes up must come down," right? Gravity. But until we fully understand regression to the mean, it's human nature to look beyond simple math for reasons why something happened.

In the height example, regression to the mean explains why tall parents tend to have children who are shorter than they are. But the reverse is also true: tall children are likely to have parents shorter than they are. When I first heard this inverted example, it made my head hurt because it was difficult to explain why. It is easy to think of reasons why a child might be shorter than her tall parents. Maybe she was a picky eater growing up, or perhaps she was sickly. It is more difficult to ascribe causes for how tall children would have shorter parents. And that's the point. Regression to the mean is a mathematical tendency that occurs whenever two variables aren't perfectly correlated. So, although we try to ascribe reasons for these fluctuations, "the truth is that regression to the mean has an explanation but does not have a cause," economics Nobel laureate Daniel Kahneman says.[19]

Kahneman uses the following example to drive home the point that we often ascribe causation inappropriately to regression-to-the-mean situations: "Why is it that highly intelligent women tend to marry men who are less intelligent than they are?" Our brains jump to causes and explanations such as the possibility that intelligent men don't want to compete with their equally smart spouses, or that females may have evolved to prefer physical stature over intelligence. But these causes aren't the answer. The answer is that spousal intelligence isn't perfectly correlated. According to Kahneman, "It is a mathematical inevitability that highly intelligent women will be married to husbands who are on average less intelligent than they are (and vice versa, of course). The observed regression to the mean cannot be more interesting or more explainable than the imperfect correlation."[20]

Note, however: regression to the mean does not imply that everyone will end up around the average over the long term because people, teams, and companies have varying levels of skill, which is correlated to performance. For example, Michael Jordan was extraordinarily skilled and thus consistently delivered much better than average performance. What regression to the mean *will tell you* is that Michael Jordan's sixty-nine points scored against the Cavaliers on March 28, 1990, was likely to be followed with a less astounding performance (and it was—that was his career best). The effect of skill on performance is addressed in more detail in Chapter 6.

HOW REGRESSION TO THE MEAN RELATES TO INVESTING

The failure to recognize the phenomenon (and the applicability) of regression to the mean in various situations is ubiquitous and occurs across fields. According to mathematician Jordan Ellenberg, "Biologists are eager to think regression stems from biology, management theorists . . . want it to come from competition, literary critics ascribe it to creative exhaustion—but it is none of these. It is mathematics."[21]

Misunderstanding regression to the mean is commonplace in investing, and that can be costly, leading people to read too much into both good and bad outcomes that have no explanation other than math. For example, more money flows into high-performing mutual funds, while cash flows out of low-performing funds. This is because investors assume that high-performing funds will continue to perform well and vice versa.

However, investors would often be better off doing the opposite because there's a weak-to-negative correlation between how a fund has performed in the past and how it will perform in the future, according to research from the Yale School of Management.[22] This is confirmed by a *Wall Street Journal* study that found that domestic equity funds ranked as five-star by research firm Morningstar were more likely than other funds to have one-star performance ratings three, five, and ten years later. "A five-star rating was no more an omen of success than it was one of failure," the researchers said.[23] Similarly, academic research has found that investors who chose funds with poor recent performance earned higher returns than those who

MISUNDERSTANDING REGRESSION TO THE MEAN IS COMMONPLACE IN INVESTING, AND THAT CAN BE COSTLY.

selected funds with superior recent performance, which is what I was banking on in my bet with our departing junior analyst.[24]

So, does this mean you should invest more money in funds that are doing poorly and less in those with high returns? Sometimes. But what it really means is that over time low-performing funds will do better and high-performing funds will do worse—regression to the mean. Again, it's just math.

WHAT INVESTORS SHOULD DO ABOUT REGRESSION TO THE MEAN

You can avoid making decisions based on reasons that simply aren't there by making regression to the mean a mental model that you turn to first, *before* casting about for causes. Doing this can also help you be more patient with investments—both in investment managers and asset classes—by understanding that poorer performers will likely do better in the future, and higher performers (both asset classes and managers) will probably do less well. And all this happens for no other reason than the mathematics of regression to the mean.

THE LAW OF LARGE NUMBERS

I've been a vegan for over twenty years. Early in my plant-based journey, I went to lunch with a business acquaintance who asked me about my "strange" food order. When I explained I was vegan primarily for reasons of health, he said I was being ridiculous. He told me his grandfather lived to age 102 on a daily diet largely consisting of bacon washed down with a glass of whole milk. Furthermore, a friend of his mother's, who was a vegetarian, recently died of cancer at sixty-six. So, he concluded, being a vegetarian or vegan wasn't healthy, and I should wise up.

Was my lunch partner correct? No. While I don't doubt his stories, he was drawing conclusions from a tiny sample size. Two, by my count. Studies that look at larger populations (tens of thousands of people) have found that a plant-based diet is associated with a lower body mass index, less heart disease, less cancer. and less diabetes. Plus, vegetarians live about eight years longer than the general population.[25] But don't let me interrupt your hamburger!

The importance of considering sample size results from the law of large numbers, which holds that as a sample size grows, the average (mean) of the sample gets closer to that of the whole population. The flip side of the law of large numbers is that small sample sizes often vary significantly from that mean. In other words, drawing conclusions from small sample sizes can be dangerous to your health.

THE MOST DANGEROUS EQUATION

In 2007, author and statistician Howard Wainer published an article in *American Scientist* called "The Most Dangerous Equation." The article proposes that two types of equations can be dangerous:

1. Those that are dangerous if you know them (like $e = mc^2$, which opened the door to the atom bomb), and

2. Those that are dangerous if you don't know them.[26]

According to Dr. Wainer, the *most* dangerous equation lives in the second category—de Moivre's equation (derived by the eighteenth-century French mathematician Abraham de Moivre)—which says that as the sample size decreases, the variability from the average increases exponentially. When you measure less than the whole population, the average of sub-populations will vary from the actual average, and that variation increases exponentially (i.e., quite a lot) as sample sizes get smaller. The inverse is also true: as the sample size gets closer to the population's actual size, the sample means cluster more and more around the whole population's mean. Why is this the most dangerous equation? Let's look.

RURAL COUNTIES AND KIDNEY CANCER

In his article, Wainer noted that if you plot the incidence of kidney cancer cases by US counties, you notice something interesting: counties in the highest decile for kidney cancer are rural. This fact, on its own, might cause you to infer (if you are relying on stereotypes) that rural living might lead to more cancers due to poor diets and too much alcohol and tobacco. However, it's equally noteworthy that the map also shows that those counties in the *lowest* decile for kidney cancer are also rural. This might suggest that these low cancer rates are due to a life spent outdoors, less pollution, and lower stress. But how can we explain that rural counties have both the highest and lowest incidence of kidney cancer?

The answer lies in de Moivre's formula. Counties with a small population have a substantial variation around the mean, while densely populated urban counties have a much lower variation because they more closely track the whole population's given their size. So, small population counties had the most significant variation in cases, putting them on both the best and worst outcomes list.

INSURANCE CLAIMS BY CAR BRAND IN THE NETHERLANDS

Another great example of this effect is found in an article about insurance claims in the Netherlands. The article observed that Mazda drivers had the highest incidence of insurance claims and Citroen drivers had the lowest.[27] Based on that data alone, we might speculate that as Mazda advertisements claim, their drivers enjoy their *Zoom Zoom*, which could lead to more insurance claims, while Citroen drivers must be more careful putt-putt drivers. That sounds plausible, but the real answer lies (surprise!) in the sample size. As the twentieth most popular car brand in the Netherlands, Mazdas make up a tiny sample, so you *should* expect Mazda to have a large variation in claims history. You *should* expect that Mazda drivers will likely have great claims history in some years and a terrible record in others, based on de Moivre's formula. A case in point is Skoda, a small-sample-size brand, the eighteenth most popular in Holland. As the article points out, it went from the best claim record to one of the worst in back-to-back years, illustrating both the power of de Moivre's formula, and how not knowing it could leave you the proud owner of a Skoda.

THE SMALL SCHOOLS MOVEMENT

Small sample sizes can even fool geniuses like Bill Gates. In the 1990s, data showed that the best performing schools were often small.[28] As a result, The Bill and Melinda Gates Foundation, the Annenberg Foundation, and the Pew Charitable Trusts provided billions in grants promoting small schools as a way to boost academic performance, in effect combining a bias (small schools feel better) with faulty data (because small schools have small student bodies their overall performance is highly variable compared with larger schools that are closer to the mean). Not surprisingly, the massive investment in small schools didn't pan out. Of course, Bill Gates dropped out of Harvard during his sophomore year, perhaps before he encountered de Moivre's formula.

THE TAKEAWAY

Small sample sizes skew results. Because variability increases exponentially as the sample size decreases, it's easy to be surprised and sometimes wrongly impressed by the results of small sample sizes. Asking "what's the sample size?" is the most critical question when evaluating data, and it's a vital mental model to have in your tool kit. When sample sizes are too small, mistaken conclusions are the norm.

THE HIGHLY IMPROBABLE HAPPENS ALL THE TIME

A few years ago, I experienced a fantastic coincidence. I was on vacation in a foreign city, and one night my wife and I went to dinner. We were directed to a table—right next to Dave, one of my fraternity brothers from college whom I hadn't seen in decades. Dave said, "Wow. How crazy is this? What are the chances that we'd find ourselves in the same restaurant at the same time thousands of miles from home?"

"Probably like one in a million or one in a *hundred* million!" I said, not really knowing what I was talking about.

Was our encounter really a one-in-a-million or hundred-million chance? It was surely surprising and even a bit strange. When I groped for the odds, I was trying to get a handle on what seemed like a miracle, or the Universe trying to tell me something. Would Dave be playing a key role in my life going forward?

Everyone does it. We all try to make sense of events that seem improbable. We all do it because under the pressure of surviving (hunting for food; trying not to become food), our brains evolved to perceive patterns and meanings. That's how we reassure ourselves that we are on top of things, especially when they get weird.

But coincidental events only seem extraordinary due to improper framing or a misunderstanding of the laws of probability. While it seems counterintuitive, the highly improbable happens all the time. As summed up by the British statistician R.A. Fisher: "The 'one chance in a million' will undoubtedly occur, with no less and no more than its appropriate frequency, however surprised we may be that it should occur to us."[29] Similarly, Aristotle observed that "it is probable that improbable things will happen. Granted this, one might argue that what is improbable is probable."[30]

Understanding that the highly improbable occurs rather commonly is an essential mental model. It may make the world seem less mystical and fantastic, but it will also help us to see things more clearly and make better decisions knowing that the unexpected is our constant companion.

LITTLEWOOD'S LAW OF MIRACLES

"Miracles" happen all the time. Mathematician John Littlewood calculated that the average person would experience a miracle about once a month, a miracle being a one-in-a-million occurrence. The math behind the concept is simple. Littlewood surmised that during our waking hours (assumed to average sixteen hours a day) we see new events at a rate of one per second. That translates into experiencing 30,000 events a day, or about one million a month. Thus, miracles happen, on average, about once a month. Even if the assumption that we have 30,000 experiences a day is too high an estimate, the point still stands that experiencing the improbable is not all that unusual.

COINCIDENTAL EVENTS ONLY SEEM EXTRAORDINARY DUE TO IMPROPER FRAMING OR MISUNDERSTANDING THE LAWS OF PROBABILITY.

The reason coincidences seem so rare is that we aren't paying attention to the other million boring, unremarkable experiences that occur the rest of the time. Only the noteworthy stands out. This notion is captured perfectly by physicist Richard Feynman:

> You know, the most amazing thing happened to me tonight. I was coming here, on the way to the lecture, and I came in through the parking lot. And you won't believe what happened. I saw a car with the license plate ARW 357. Can you imagine? Of all the millions of license plates in the state, what was the chance that I would see that particular one tonight? Amazing![31]

PROPER FRAMING IS ESSENTIAL

Let's look at the miraculous—and how to put it in the proper frame—with an example from University of Wisconsin math professor Jordan Ellenberg's book *How Not to Be Wrong: The Power of Mathematical Thinking*:

> Most coincidences lose their snap when viewed from the appropriate distance. On July 9, 2007, the North Carolina Cash 5 lottery numbers came up

4, 21, 23, 34, 39. Two days later, the same five numbers came up again. That seems highly unlikely, and it seems that way because it is. The chance of those two lottery draws matching by pure chance was tiny, less than two in a million. But that's not the relevant question if you're deciding how impressed to be. After all, the Cash 5 game had already been going on for almost a year, offering many opportunities for coincidence; it turns out the chance some three-day period would have seen two identical Cash 5 draws was a much less miraculous one in a thousand. And Cash 5 isn't the only game in town. There are hundreds of five-number lottery games running all over the country and have been for years; when you put them all together, it's not at all surprising that you get a coincidence like two identical draws in three days. That doesn't make each individual coincidence any less improbable. But here comes the chorus again: improbable things happen a lot.[32]

Returning to me and Dave at the restaurant, how should I frame it? If the question is "What are the chances that, on this particular vacation, I'd be seated next to Dave?" then the coincidence is pretty remarkable. However, if I frame the situation as "What are the chances that on one of my many vacations over many decades that I'd encounter someone I know out of the thousands of people I've known throughout my life?" then I'm surprised it took so long for me to bump into an old friend on a trip. The frame is the key.

> IT WOULD BE BEST IF YOU DESIGNED YOUR INVESTMENT PORTFOLIO SO THAT IT CAN WITHSTAND IMPROBABLE OCCURRENCES.

Instead of being surprised by the improbable, it's better to expect that unlikely events are bound to occur. Things like terrorist attacks, earthquakes, tsunamis, pandemics, infestations of murder hornets, train wrecks, and flash stock market crashes that come out of the blue occur all the time. Knowing that, it would be best if you designed your investment portfolio to accommodate improbable occurrences, which is accomplished by diversifying across types of assets (stocks, bonds, real estate, private equity) and building in a margin of safety by having suffi-cient cash and low-risk assets.

THE MENTAL MODELS AND HOW TO APPLY THEM

As humans, we seek patterns that will help us predict the future and mit-igate uncertainty. Our brains are always working to develop explanations and attribute causes to events. Therefore, it behooves us to adopt mental models wherein we always question causation and fight the urge to jump to causation as the explanation for events. Remember:

1. It's risky to think that one thing has caused another. Coincidence can lead us to assume causation. Multiple factors often com-bine to create outcomes, so it's usually impossible to pinpoint a single cause.

2. Correlation does not imply causation. Just because two things are strongly correlated doesn't mean that one causes the other. Remem-ber that unrelated variables—like Bangladeshi butter production and the stock market—can be highly correlated.

3. Regression to the mean describes the phenomenon whereby extreme events are usually followed by ones closer to the average. Regression occurs whenever two variables are less than perfectly correlated, like child and parent heights. Regression to the mean explains why it may make sense to invest in underperforming funds and why outstanding performance is often followed by stumbles.

4. Beware of drawing conclusions based on small sample sizes. As sample sizes get smaller, variation from the mean increases expo-nentially. Ignorance of this statistical law has led to a lot of wasted time and money. Asking "what's the sample size?" is critical when-ever causation is asserted.

5. The final mental model in this chapter is that the highly improb-able happens all the time. Coincidences are not supernatural

miracles; they're just math. Being surprised by unlikely occurrences can leave us unprepared both in our portfolios and in our lives.

Be sure to apply these mental models when investing. Any decisions you make that assume causation where it doesn't exist will likely be poor ones. Because humans have a deep desire to explain, you'll often see cause where none exists. Knowing when one thing causes another is tricky and is especially difficult when observing highly correlated things because correlation makes it seem as if there's causation. Determining causation is further complicated because sometimes things occur just because the math says they will, as is the case with regression to the mean and small sample size observations. Finally, the highly improbable is not only probable, it's inevitable. It pays to be prepared for when the unlikely occurs, which it surely will, given a long enough period and a sufficiently large sample size.

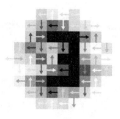

CHAPTER 3

THE STOCK MARKET IS NOT THE ECONOMY (OR WHAT TOILET PAPER CAN TEACH US ABOUT INVESTING)

*In investing, there is nothing that always works, since the environment is always chang-
ing, and investors' efforts to respond to the environment cause it to change further.*
—HOWARD MARKS, *MASTERING THE MARKET CYCLE*

Something curious happened during the early months of the COVID-19
pandemic: people across the country began hoarding toilet paper. From
February to March of 2020, toilet paper sales jumped 700 percent. Crazy,
right? Why would anyone need hundreds of rolls of toilet paper? And why
hoard toilet paper rather than, say, more things useful to survival like cans
of beans or jugs of water?

Who knows what triggered the massive surge in toilet paper purchases,
but once people started buying it in quantity, that led to a panic. Why?

Because if you see lots of people buying lots of toilet paper, it makes perfect sense to think that might lead to even more people buying more toilet paper, which in turn could lead to a toilet paper shortage. So, what to do? Go stock up on toilet paper.

Of course, at a system level, stockpiling toilet paper was nuts. But at the individual level, it was perfectly rational because no one wanted to be left behind (pun intended) without any toilet paper.

When I first heard about it, I thought hoarding toilet paper was bonkers. Then when I went to the drug store to pick up a prescription a few months into the pandemic, I saw only a few lonely packages of toilet paper on what looked to be a gapingly empty shelf, and I bought them, even though we had plenty at home. I knew I was being part of the problem, but I didn't want our household to run out. I sort of panicked.

> HOARDING TOILET PAPER IS A SPOT-ON ILLUSTRATION OF HOW COMPLEX SOCIAL SYSTEMS WORK: THE SMALL ACTIONS OF INDIVIDUALS CAN CAUSE BROAD IRRATIONAL OUTCOMES FOR THE SYSTEM.

Hoarding toilet paper is a spot-on illustration of how complex social systems work: the small actions of individuals can cause broad, disproportionate, and often irrational outcomes for the system. The toilet paper example is relevant to investing because the stock market, too, is a complex social system of millions of individuals interacting. Individual investment decisions combine to cause unpredictable system-wide effects. We'll delve into how toilet paper relates to investing later on in this chapter.

THE ECONOMY DOESN'T PREDICT THE STOCK MARKET

I felt I aged ten years during the Financial Crisis. The bad news just kept coming and wouldn't stop. There was legitimate concern that the recession could turn into a depression. I couldn't see how the global economy would stabilize and turn around.

The stock market bottomed on March 9, 2009, after dropping a whopping 57 percent from its peak on October 23, 2007. At the time, it didn't feel like a bottom because the economic news continued to be horrible. For example,

- A few days prior to the bottom, the US Bureau of Labor Statistics announced that February unemployment was 8.1 percent, up a full half-point from January.

- Unemployment eventually climbed to 10 percent by October and stayed around 10 percent for over a year.

- The economy was still contracting in March 2009, and it didn't reach the trough of the recession until June, four months later.

- Inflation was rising.

Yet, in the midst of all this bad economic news, the market stabilized in March 2009. The S&P 500 began to climb. Over the next eleven years, it would rise over 600 percent, including dividends.

As the market rebounded, there was still no sign we were out of the woods (see Figure 3.1). As spring turned into summer, and then fall, unemployment remained high; the health of large global banks remained a concern. Over the next few years, the European sovereign debt crisis intensified; there were increasing worries that the euro would collapse; S&P downgraded US Treasuries. As the market advanced after the March 2009 bottom, many investors thought that gains were merely a "dead cat bounce" and that the market would still fall to new lows. But it didn't. March 9th remained the bottom.

More recently, we experienced a similar situation in March 2020, during the COVID-19 pandemic. The stock market reacted to the economic impacts of COVID-19 by dropping 30 percent in twenty-two days—the fastest decline ever. As a comparison, during the Financial Crisis, it took 250 days for the S&P 500 to drop 30 percent; during the crash of 1929, the 30 percent drop took thirty-one days.

THE STOCK MARKET REBOUND DURING THE FINANCIAL CRISIS

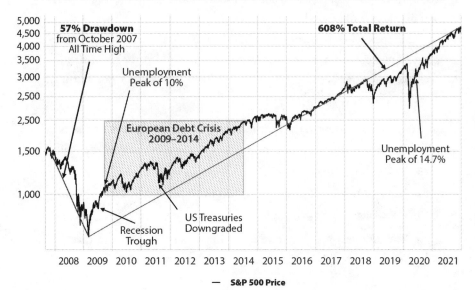

FIGURE 3.1

Like 2009, in 2020, after that 30-plus percent tumble, the market bottomed and then gained over 45 percent across the next three months. This rebound happened while COVID-19 cases and deaths were skyrocketing, the economy was contracting at a pace not seen since the Great Depression, and unemployment was spiking at a fearful rate.

These examples should inform the mental model for all investors: *the stock market is not the economy*; economic news does not predict what will happen in the market.

THE ECONOMY AND THE STOCK MARKET
ARE NOT CORRELATED

The stock market and the economy are *related*, but that doesn't mean they rise and fall in tandem. Just because the economy is contracting doesn't mean that the stock market will decline. History shows us that GDP growth is not a good predictor of future stock prices.

Figure 3.2 demonstrates the lack of relationship between annual stock market returns and GDP growth.

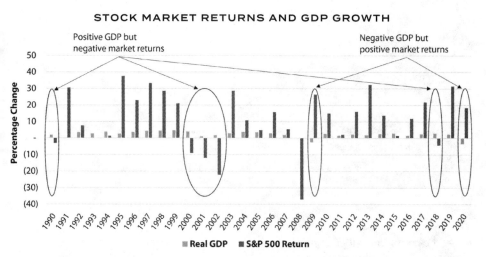

FIGURE 3.2

The thirty-year period shown in Figure 3.2 is typical. Over time, correlations between GDP growth and stock market returns hang around zero. From World War II to today, the correlation between GDP and stocks is a mere 0.03—basically zero.

The primary reason the correlations are so weak is that the stock market anticipates economic growth (or decline) and responds before the economy. This phenomenon becomes more apparent when we compare GDP growth to the prior year's stock market returns, which dramatically increases the correlations.

Figure 3.3 shows almost no correlation between current year GDP growth and stock market returns. It also illustrates that stock market returns have a stronger correlation with the following year's GDP returns, meaning that the stock market predicts what the economy will do—not the other way around.

Research published by Credit Suisse explains this effect: investor decision making tends to anticipate the economy's changed circumstances, and

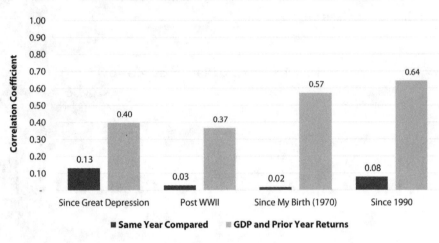

FIGURE 3.3

the empirical evidence supports this claim. Stock market fluctuations predict changes in GDP, but movements in GDP do not predict stock market returns. Over time, forward-looking predictions of economic change are incorporated in today's fluctuations in the stock market.[1]

Looking at stock market returns during years when GDP growth was negative also supports this conclusion (see Figure 3.4). Since 1930, the United States has experienced nineteen years of negative GDP growth. In twelve of those nineteen years (or about two-thirds of the time), stock market returns were positive; in most cases, well over 15 percent. And since 1945, the market has been up when GDP growth is negative a remarkable 80 percent of the time.

What does this mean for investors? When economic news is dire, know that the market has *already* absorbed it and priced it in. Surprises move markets, not expected news, because market prices reflect the range of expected news. So, if you're tempted to change your investments because of bad news, ask yourself these questions:

- Do you know something the market doesn't?

- Or are you weighting widely known news differently than everyone else?

- If so, do you have a good reason?

If the answers to these questions are *no*, then it's probably best to resist the urge to make portfolio changes (unless you are rebalancing based on your investment discipline).

During times of market volatility, even under the threat of a recession, your first step should be to continue to rely on the investment discipline you put in place when times weren't so scary. For most people, this means sticking with the asset allocation you established before the market turmoil and rebalancing according to that allocation.

POSITIVE STOCK MARKET RETURNS AND NEGATIVE GDP

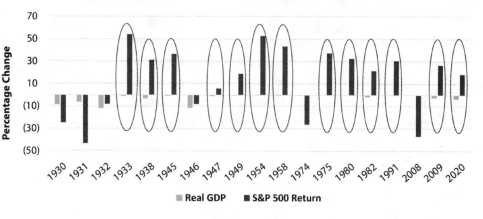

FIGURE 3.4

WHY THE STOCK MARKET DOESN'T MAKE ANY SENSE

It's not just the stock market's lack of correlation to the economy that confounds investors; the stock market's ups and downs often defy explanation. For example, for no apparent reason, the Dow Jones plunged 1,861 points (a 6.9 percent decline) on June 11, 2020. Pundits ascribed the drop to traders worrying about the uptick in COVID-19 cases in some states. But that doesn't adequately explain the 1,861-point drop because in the weeks prior it was reported that we could expect cases to rise as states reopened and as people gathered for Memorial Day. Nothing was reported that was revelatory or different about the number of COVID-19 cases in the days leading up to the drop. Yet analysts are supposed to explain market fluctuations (that's why they are called analysts) and people are inclined to believe them.

Stock market gyrations often defy explanation because the market is a complex adaptive system. In a complex adaptive system, understanding each component input doesn't mean we can understand the system's outputs. As with hoarding toilet paper during the pandemic, system-level results are often greater than the sum of the parts because the market consists of heterogeneous actors (called agents) that interact with each other in ways that make system-level predictions difficult or impossible.

In complex adaptive systems, intelligent agents learn and change their behavior accordingly—sometimes rationally, sometimes irrationally—as circumstances change. (Even though I had toilet paper and knew I didn't really need it, I still bought it, contributing my little bit to the perceived system shortage.) Changing behavior creates feedback loops as the output from one result becomes the next iteration's input. Feedback can amplify small actions into large and unexpected results. Positive feedback loops create system-wide results that aren't predictable by observing the actions of individual agents.

KEYNESIAN BEAUTY CONTESTS

A classic example of how intelligent agents act in a complex adaptive system is the so-called Keynesian Beauty Contest created by famous British economist John Maynard Keynes. In the 1930s, he described a newspaper game where participants submitted their picks of the six prettiest faces from one hundred photographs. The winner would be the player whose picks included the most popular choice overall.

According to Keynes, the winning strategy was this:

Each competitor has to pick not those faces that he finds prettiest, but those that he thinks likeliest to catch the fancy of the other competitors, all of whom are looking at the problem from the same point of view ... [Thus], it is not a case of choosing those [faces] which, to the best of one's judgment, are really the prettiest, nor even those which average opinion genuinely thinks the prettiest. We have reached the third degree where we devote our intelligence to anticipating what average opinion expects the average opinion to be. And there are some, I believe, who practice the fourth, fifth and higher degrees."[2]

Keynes's beauty contest is an accurate description of how financial markets work. Like hoarding toilet paper, it's me watching you; you watching me; me watching you watching me, and so on, multiplied by the millions. Each player in the market is trying to guess what the other players are guessing. It's like sitting at a poker table with millions of players holding cards.

We see complex adaptive systems throughout the social fabric of our lives. In their book *Complex Adaptive Systems*, John Miller and Scott Page write: "We turn away from crowded restaurants and highways, smoothing demand. We exploit the profit opportunities arising from patterns generated by a stock market and, in so doing, dissipate their very existence. Like bees defending the hive, we respond to signals in the media and market, creating booms, busts, and fads."[3]

In the stock market, such feedback loops amplify small actions and lead to cascading effects. Millions of actions by tens of millions of individuals aggregate to cause stocks to rise or fall, and then that rise or fall causes everyone to reassess what they should do in the future. In this way, individuals' small rational actions cause broad unexpected outcomes for the system that may appear irrational. Like the proverbial flap of a butterfly's wings in Brazil that leads to a hurricane in the Gulf of Mexico, small actions by a few individuals lead to cascading, disproportionate, and unpredictable effects.

Understanding that the market is a complex adaptive system explains why it can zoom along with little volatility for weeks or months then experience a drop like the 1,861-point decline we saw on June 11, 2020.

COMPLEX ADAPTIVE SYSTEMS CAN
GENERATE EXTREME RESULTS

When humans interact with each other in social systems, extreme outcomes occur that defy prediction. A prime example is the famous "Dutch tulip craze" of the 1600s.

Tulips, introduced to Europe from the Ottoman Empire in the mid-sixteenth century, became wildly popular in the Netherlands and other northern European countries. By the 1620s, a single bulb could fetch 1,000 Dutch florins. (The average laborer at the time made 150 florins a year.) By 1636, a single bulb was worth 15,000 florins.

People accepted them in exchange for livestock and land, and financiers invented futures contracts to trade them on exchanges. Indeed, tulip bulb contracts were among the first derivatives.

WHEN HUMANS
INTERACT WITH
EACH OTHER IN
SOCIAL SYSTEMS,
EXTREME OUTCOMES
OCCUR THAT DEFY
PREDICTION.

Tulip mania is an illustration of the "greater fool theory." Their prices didn't skyrocket because of their intrinsic value; the boom was a reflection of the idea that there would always be someone willing to pay an even higher price for them in the future.

The bubble burst in February 1637 as tulip traders could no longer realize insanely inflated prices for their bulbs and sold to lock in their gains. A panic ensued. Prices crashed, and thousands were ruined.[4]

Tulip mania is an excellent example of a complex adaptive system in action. People in the Netherlands watched each other watching each other buy bulbs. Rising prices created a positive feedback loop that caused more people to want them, further inflating the cost that, eventually, could not be sustained.

An example closer to our time occurred on October 19, 1987. Known as Black Monday, the Dow Jones Industrial Average plunged nearly 23 percent. Before Black Monday, such a massive drop in the market wasn't considered possible because statistics put such a decline at an impossibly rare twenty-two standard deviation event. Even during the stock market crash of the 1920s, the largest single-day decline was 13 percent, a large drop but way shy of 23 percent. Black Monday was unthinkable before it happened.

What caused the drop? While there's no one clear answer, and economists and investment strategists still debate the underpinnings of Black Monday, one widely acknowledged cause is the popularity of a derivative strategy known as *portfolio insurance*. The scheme involved using options to hedge a portfolio to enjoy gains when stocks went up and limit losses when they went down. It was dynamic trade, meaning that portfolio managers adjusted the hedges as the market gained or lost. In the years leading up to Black Monday, the use of portfolio insurance spread among Wall Street firms that used the strategy on tens of billions of dollars of investments.

On an individual basis, it made sense to implement portfolio insurance. Who wouldn't like to enjoy one's gains while limiting one's losses? However, on a system-wide basis, having tens of billions of dollars deployed using the same strategy was disastrous.

As market volatility increased in the days leading up to Black Monday, the portfolio insurance strategy led investment managers to sell holdings to raise money to increase their hedges. This selling generated losses, which caused the portfolio insurance algorithms to require the sale of even more assets to place more hedges. This feedback loop of losses generated still more selling, creating still more losses, leading to more selling, and so on. The next thing you knew, it was Black Monday.

In his book *A Demon of Our Own Design: Markets, Hedge Funds, and the Perils of Financial Innovation*, Richard Bookstaber, who in 1987 was head of risk management at Morgan Stanley, explained, "If one small portfolio uses this sort of strategy, liquidity will not be an issue. If everyone in the market is trying to do it, it can become a nightmare, a little like everyone on a cruise ship trying to pile into a single lifeboat: it won't float."[5]

What hoarding toilet paper, Dutch tulip mania, and the 1987 stock

... THE COMPLEX SYSTEM OF HUMAN INTERACTION CAN CREATE FEEDBACK LOOPS THAT RESULT IN EXTREME OUTCOMES.

market crash have in common (and should teach us) is that complex human interactions create feedback loops that can result in extreme outcomes. Who would have predicted in January 2020 that a global pandemic would cause Americans to hoard toilet paper? Likewise, the atmospheric rise of tulip prices was unpredictable before it happened, as was a 23 percent stock market drop in a single day.

WHY IT'S IMPORTANT TO UNDERSTAND THAT THE MARKET IS A COMPLEX ADAPTIVE SYSTEM

The fact that the stock market operates as a complex adaptive system is an essential concept to put in our toolbox of mental models. It means that many effects we see in the markets have no readily discernible cause; there's simply too much complexity generated between the various agents that interact and create feedback loops. As explained by author and investment strategist Michael Mauboussin in his excellent book *More Than You Know: Finding Financial Wisdom in Unconventional Places*, "Investors who insist on understanding the causes for the market's moves risk focusing on faulty causality or inappropriately anchoring on false explanations. Many of the big moves in the market are not easy to explain."[6]

Knowing that the market is a complex adaptive system goes a long way toward explaining why successful investment strategies don't remain successful indefinitely: agents within the system learn, adapt, and change until the strategy no longer works.

The rise and fall of hedge funds is illustrative. Hedge funds are a type of nonregistered alternative investment that uses various specialized strategies to earn returns for investors. They often use derivatives such as puts and calls, or tactics like shorting some stocks while buying (or going "long") other stocks.

Hedge funds had a nice run of outperforming the market around the millennium. From 1998 to 2002 they produced 9 percent of annual alpha, which is a measure of outperformance. But then their performance declined, drastically. From 2003 to 2007, hedge fund alpha turned to a negative 0.7 percent, and then from 2008 to 2012, alpha further declined to −4.5 percent.[7] Why did hedge fund returns fall off a cliff?

David A. Hsieh, a professor at Duke's Fuqua School of Business, provided an answer in research he published in 2006, before hedge funds really flopped.[8] Professor Hsieh determined that the amount of alpha available to the hedge fund industry as a whole was about $30 billion. This means, mathematically, that when the industry only managed $300 billion, which was the size of the industry in 2000, hedge fund managers could average about 10 percent above the market. After the industry ballooned to over $2 trillion of assets in 2007, $30 billion of alpha didn't cover the high fees the hedge funds charged investors, and alpha turned negative.

This sort of pattern has repeated itself over and over in the investment industry: an attractive strategy provides strong returns; it becomes popular, but once a certain amount of money flows into the strategy, it no longer works. Or, as Yogi Berra once (allegedly) said of a popular restaurant, "No one goes there anymore; it's too crowded."

ECONOMIC INDICATORS DON'T PREDICT THE STOCK MARKET

Thinking of the stock market as a complex adaptive system allows us to understand why economic and market indicators don't predict stock market returns. If there was a signal that investors knew could predict future market movements, they would change their behavior. Then, the indicator would no longer work.

This point is simply illustrated with an analogy. Assume an investment firm called Alpha Monkey discovered that when Treasury yields rise for fifteen consecutive trading days, the stock market declines 3 to 5 percent the next day. Knowing this gives Alpha Monkey the ability to short stocks on day fifteen and make handsome profits. As long as Alpha Monkey keeps this information to itself, it should continue to work (assuming it's not a spurious correlation).

However, if Alpha Monkey's secret leaks out, what happens? At first, when it's just a few other investors who know, shorting on day fifteen still makes money. But as more people find out about this indicator, their transactions on day fifteen will move the market because both buyers and sellers will know of the signal. So, to make profits, investors will need to make their move on day fourteen. And then, day thirteen. And so on, until the indicator is useless.

Supporting this hypothetical is the research study, "Does Academic Research Destroy Stock Return Predictability?" in which authors R. David McLean and Jeffrey Pontiff examined ninety-seven academic studies that claimed to find indicators that predicted future stock market returns. Their study found significant "post-publication decay in predictor returns."[9] Translated, that means that once indicators that could predict the market are known, their effectiveness either diminishes or disappears (or maybe the indicator's predictive ability was just a spurious correlation).

Common economic indicators followed by investors don't predict market returns. This conclusion is supported by a 2012 study by Vanguard. In the study, Vanguard analyzed stock market returns from 1926 to 2011 compared to various economic indicators and stock market signals to see if they could predict future returns.[10]

The study looked at price-to-earnings ratios (P/E ratios), government debt levels, dividend yields, GDP growth, corporate earnings, treasury yields, and trailing stock market returns, among others. Vanguard also added a dummy variable: the relationship between rainfall and returns.

What did the study find? None of the indicators showed any significant predictive ability in forecasting the next year's returns, and only P/E ratios had a meaningful predictive value for longer-term returns. Vanguard summarized the research as follows: "Even over longer time horizons, many metrics and rough 'rules of thumb' commonly assumed to have predictive ability have had little or no power in explaining the long-run equity return over inflation. Although valuations [i.e., P/E ratios] have been the most useful measure in this regard, even they have performed modestly, leaving nearly 60 percent of the variation in long-term returns unexplained."

How did rainfall do? It explained only 0.06 of the variation of the longer-term (ten-year) return. Pretty bad.

On the other hand, rainfall's 0.06 was better than the predictive ability of these commonly used indicators:

- Trailing ten-year stock market returns

- Trend GDP growth

- Trend corporate earnings growth

- Ten-year Treasury yield

- Corporate profit margins

- Trailing one-year stock returns

- Consensus earnings growth

- Consensus GDP growth

Figure 3.5 is from the Vanguard paper. Note that the y-axis shows R^2, which is a measure of how much one variable explains another.

At our firm, we refer to these economic indicators and market signals as being "right of rainfall," meaning that you should ignore them when making investment decisions. Even P/E ratios should not be used to time the market or shift allocations among asset classes because they only explain about 40 percent of the variation in long-term returns.

Academic studies confirm Vanguard's conclusions. For example, researchers from Emory and Yale examined common indicators similar to the ones the Vanguard study looked at and found that "not a single one would have helped a real-world investor outpredicting the then-prevailing historical equity premium mean. Most would have outright hurt. Therefore, we find that, for all practical purposes, the equity premium has not been predictable."[11]

COMMON INDICATORS HAVE LITTLE
OR NO PREDICTIVE ABILITY

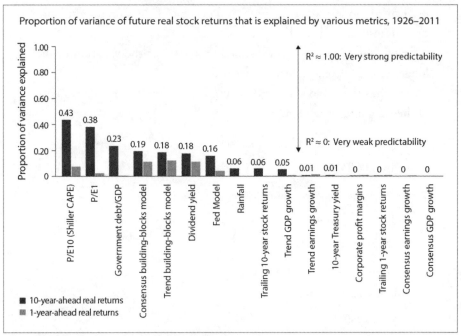

Source: © The Vanguard Group, Inc., used with permission.

FIGURE 3.5

The lesson of the Vanguard study and others like it is that investors should not use economic indicators to make investment decisions. As Vanguard states in its research, "This underscores a key principle in Vanguard's approach to investing: *The future is difficult to predict*."[12] Thus, rather than predicting the future, it is more fruitful to construct all-weather portfolios prepared for the unexpected.

THE MENTAL MODELS AND HOW TO APPLY THEM

In this chapter, we've learned some valuable mental models:

1. The stock market is not the economy. Economic growth and stock market performance are not correlated. The stock market commonly rebounds when economic news is bad and declines when it's good.

2. The stock market is a complex adaptive system, which is why it often seems to make no sense. Millions of intelligent agents are all watching each other, learning, drawing their own conclusions, and creating feedback loops, which makes predicting stock market movements nearly impossible.

3. Because the stock market is a complex adaptive system, economic indicators and market signals don't predict market performance. The market changes and evolves, and investors learn. Indicators that might be predictive of market returns will be destroyed once they are widely known by those millions of agents.

> THE LESSON OF THE VANGUARD STUDY AND OTHERS LIKE IT IS THAT INVESTORS SHOULD NOT USE ECONOMIC INDICATORS TO MAKE INVESTMENT DECISIONS.

Instead of looking to the economy to inform investment decisions, remember that the stock market is not the economy. Do not let irrelevant, external information change your investment behavior. Instead of trying to predict what the market will do, invest as if you don't know, which is rational, because you don't. Most of what is reported in the financial media and discussed by investment analysts is "right of rainfall."

Thinking of the stock market as a complex adaptive system that is constantly evolving and changing is difficult because humans are hardwired to find patterns and attach meaning to them. Accepting that the market is inherently unpredictable and often defies explanation is uncomfortable. Yet fooling yourself that the market can be reliably predicted will not make you a better investor. Instead, embrace your ignorance; realize that neither you nor anyone else can predict what will happen.

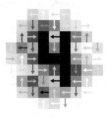

CHAPTER 4

MARKET CYCLES AND THE TWO AXIOMS OF INVESTING

What the wise man does in the beginning, the fool does in the end.

—WARREN BUFFETT

Swallowing the outlandish premises of some science fiction books can be hard, but periodically suspending one's disbelief can spark creativity. Personally, I had an epiphany about investing reading *The Dark Forest* by Cixin Liu.

Cixin Liu is widely considered China's greatest science fiction writer. American sci-fi fans call him China's Isaac Asimov. Like Asimov with his *Foundation* series, Liu is best known for a trilogy, *Remembrance of Earth's Past* (usually known under the umbrella *The Three-Body Problem*). The trilogy's plot is based on the physics problem in which one tries to solve for the movement and velocity of three bodies under Newton's laws of motion and gravitation.

The problem has no straightforward solution because there is no existing equation or rule to predict how three interacting celestial bodies will move about one another. Some orbits of three objects repeat while others are chaotic. Physicists have been searching for a mathematical solution to the three-body problem for over 300 years, but the orbits of three celestial bodies defy prediction.

The Three-Body Problem, book one of the series, introduces the reader to an alien race that inhabits a planet that orbits three stars (due to the planet orbiting three stars, humans dub them "Trisolarans"). Due to the three-body problem, their planet's orbit is unpredictable. As a result, sometimes their planet is too close or too far from one of its stars so that the race must do something akin to hibernation to survive the heat or cold. Other times the planet's orbit is in the goldilocks zone, and the Trisolarans can live comfortably.

As one might expect, life under these conditions is difficult, and the Trisolarans want to find a new home planet. They discover Earth and set out to conquer it. Humanity learns that they're on their way about 200 years before they arrive. The Trisolarans' technology is way ahead of ours, and even given a two-century heads up, humanity's fate seems dire.

The second book of the trilogy, *The Dark Forest*, focuses on humanity's attempts to defend against the impending alien attack. *The Dark Forest's* main character is one of three chosen to spearhead humanity's defense. A key to his strategy rests on "the two axioms of cosmic sociology":

First: Survival is the primary need of civilization.

Second: Civilization continuously grows and expands, but the total matter in the universe remains constant.[1]

These axioms create opposing tension: all civilizations grow and expand, but the number of habitable planets is limited. This conflict suggests that alien civilizations will hide from each other because if another more advanced alien race discovers them, they risk invasion and destruction.

Consequently, the Universe (in Liu's imagining) is like a dark forest where, depending on what creature one encounters, it can be either predator or prey—a pretty dangerous and unpredictable situation in which keeping a low profile makes a lot of sense. Survival depends on engaging only with civilizations weaker than yours.

Reflecting on *The Dark Forest*, I realized that investing has two axioms that, like Liu's, create opposing tension:

First: Markets move in cycles.

Second: Market cycles cannot be consistently timed profitably.

These two axioms cause investors and advisors a lot of angst. While it seems *crazy* to ignore the ebbs and flows of the market, it is also *senseless* to invest in a manner that relies on predicting them because (as has been proven over and over) that just doesn't work.

Let's explore some critical mental models that will help navigate the uncomfortable tension between the inevitability of market cycles and their unpredictable nature.

STABILITY LEADS TO INSTABILITY

The stock market and the economy both move in cycles. Boom is followed by bust followed by boom, seemingly forever. The market often declines during recessions (but not always—a notable exception being 2020), but it can also drop when there is no recession. Nobel Prize–winning economist Paul Samuelson's quip that "the stock market has predicted nine of the last five recessions" is apropos. As discussed in Chapter 3, the stock market and the economy are not correlated; the stock market often drops when the economy is healthy and rises when the economic news is dire.

Historically, economic and market cycles have fluctuated around a longer-term secular trend, and fortunately, that trend has been up. That means that over full cycles, the economy grows, and, likewise, the stock market generates positive returns.

Compared to the economy, the stock market is more volatile as it moves through its cycles of ups and downs. Between 1970 and 2020, the S&P 500 Index averaged about a 10 percent annualized return, but that's an average that disguises much greater volatility: in reality, only three of those fifty-one years (about 6 percent of the time) showed a return between 8 percent and 12 percent. In contrast, the market spent about one-fourth of the years more than 20 percent off that 10 percent average (meaning it was up over 30 percent or down over 10 percent). And that 20 percent is another average; sometimes it was more than 30 percent off. In other words, you can spend decades in the market and never see a year close to a 10 percent return—returns are almost always much higher or lower than the average.

While the stock market bounces around and can experience declines when the economy is healthy, the most severe drops typically happen as the economy heads toward recession. Thus, recognizing economic cycles and what causes them can be useful, especially if you can identify what stage of the cycle the economy is in.

Hyman Minsky's financial instability hypothesis provides a crucial model for why the economy cycles through boom and bust and a framework for estimating where we are in the cycle.

MINSKY'S FINANCIAL INSTABILITY HYPOTHESIS

Sometimes artists, musicians, and philosophers don't achieve fame for their works until after they die. The same can be true for economists, particularly Hyman Minsky who was a professor at Washington University in St. Louis. Now known for his "financial instability hypothesis," which has become quite popular in economic and investment circles since the Financial Crisis of 2008, Minsky was criticized and even ridiculed for his theory during his lifetime.

Classical economic theory assumed that the economy is fundamentally stable. As excesses occur, rational market actors see them and act to make money or avoid losing it, and thereby move the economy back toward equilibrium. In this view, bubbles and crashes are caused by external shocks to the economy such as technological advances, disease, wars, and commodity surpluses or shortages. While external shocks, such as the OPEC oil embargo of the 1970s or the COVID-19 pandemic, certainly have significant economic effects, they don't adequately explain all the cycles of booms and busts. External shocks didn't cause the dotcom bust of 2000 or the financial crisis of 2008.

Minsky swam against the tide; he didn't believe that the economy was fundamentally stable and was knocked off course only by external shocks. Instead, he thought that the economy sometimes creates *its own* bubbles and crashes. The gist of his theory was that stable economies sow the seeds of their own destruction because stability, seemingly safe, encourages businesses and individuals to take risks, which creates instability that eventually results in panic and crisis.[2] This important point bears repeating: stability itself is destabilizing because, during times of economic stability, healthy investments lead to speculative euphoria, increasing financial leverage, and over-extension of debt. This eventually results in a "Minsky moment," the point where everyone realizes there are problems—and panic ensues. At this point, a recession or even a financial crisis occurs. Then the whole cycle starts over (see Figure 4.1).

THE MINSKY CYCLE

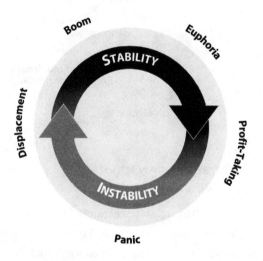

FIGURE 4.1

Unfortunately, Minsky's hypothesis was not taken seriously during his lifetime. He died in 1996, before the dotcom bubble and the Great

Recession, both of which—downturns in the absence of external shocks—gave credence to his ideas. The economic establishment now accepts his theory as a primary explanation for boom-and-bust cycles in the economy, and lists of the greatest economists of all-time now include Hyman Minsky.

THE EMOTIONS OF THE MARKET CYCLE

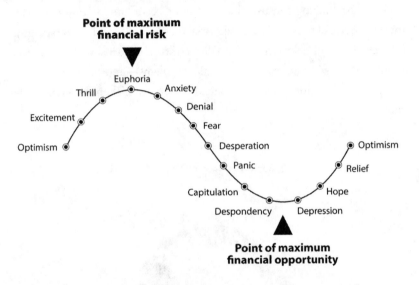

FIGURE 4.2

HOW MINSKY'S INSIGHT CAN HELP
US BE BETTER INVESTORS

As we move through market cycles (see Figure 4.2), we can't know when the next phase will happen because the tops and bottoms of market cycles are only known in retrospect. A confounding factor is that the euphoria and panic stages tend to last longer than most people expect. Yet, it is possible to roughly know where we are in the cycle, and we can use that knowledge to inform good strategies. Legendary investor Howard Marks says the goal of understanding market cycles is to "predict the present"—to understand where we are currently rather than try to predict the future. "I don't even think about the timing," he says. "In the investment business, it's very hard to do the right thing, and it's impossible to do the right thing at the right time."[3]

Specifically, as the economy moves from boom to euphoria, investors need to build in a healthy margin of safety in the form of cash and high-quality bonds to withstand (and thrive during) the coming panic. Similarly, smart businesses will shore up their liquidity and resist the temptation to take on more debt in the euphoric part of the cycle. When profit-taking and panic occur, both investors and businesses can redeploy their safety margin into assets that have declined in value.

There's another paradoxical point to Minsky's model: the most significant risk in investing occurs when everything seems to be going well, while the panic found deep in a bear market or recession often provides the best investment opportunities. Thus, waiting until everything seems relatively safe and the economy is healthy is *not* a profitable strategy.

A 2012 study from J.P. Morgan underscores this by simulating an investor "waiting for a clear turn in the business cycle before adopting normal investment positions."[4] The study examined two different portfolio investment strategies:

> WAITING UNTIL EVERYTHING SEEMS RELATIVELY SAFE AND THE ECONOMY IS HEALTHY IS NOT A PROFITABLE STRATEGY.

1. Stay fully invested through good times and bad; or

2. Only invest when the "coast is clear."

The definition of "the coast is clear" is when the stock market's valuation is reasonable, unemployment is low or falling, the economy is expanding, and inflation is below 4 percent or declining. If the economy meets all these factors, then "the coast is clear" to invest in the stock market; if not, the portfolio is moved to cash.

How did the two portfolios do? The "coast is clear" portfolio was less volatile but sacrificed a lot of return: from 1948 to 2011, "the always-invested portfolio" beat the "coast is clear" portfolio by nearly three times, and between 1980 and 2011, its returns were more than double.

The lesson to take from Minsky's hypothesis (and the J.P. Morgan study) is not to capitulate to the fear that comes with the panicky part of the cycle or indulge in the greed that accompanies the euphoria. While it's not possible to accurately time the market's tops and bottoms, understanding the cycle and knowing roughly where you are can help you maintain a sane investment strategy when everyone around you is going nuts.

THE FUTILITY OF MARKET TIMING

In November 2006, I attended an investment conference where a moderator interviewed Alan Greenspan, who had retired as Chairman of the Federal Reserve nine months earlier. When asked about issues popping up in the housing market—and specifically about the concerning weakness in the subprime mortgage sector—Greenspan replied that he wasn't worried. He said that while "the housing market wasn't out of the woods yet, it wouldn't worsen" and that subprime mortgages, making up just a tiny fraction of the housing sector, wouldn't cause material harm to the broader economy. His forecast was for a soft patch of lower growth for the US economy for a few quarters before it returned to growing at a good clip. Basically, he thought the economy was fine.

That was reassuring because I'd been worried about reported subprime loan defaults. And why wouldn't I listen to Alan Greenspan? He was hailed at the time as one of history's greatest central bankers. Even Bob Woodward wrote a biography of Greenspan titled *Maestro* that lauded his deft handling of the economy during his nineteen years as Fed chairman.

Of course, Greenspan was grotesquely wrong. Even as he was going on about soft patches and a sunny future, the economy was just a year away from the worst financial crisis since the Great Depression, sparked by high levels of defaults on subprime mortgages. After the crisis, Greenspan was lambasted for not having detected the economy's weakness and contributing to the mayhem by keeping interest rates too low for too long.

But how hard can we be on Greenspan? Forecasting the future is a mug's game. And he wasn't alone in missing the warning signs. The entire economics profession and the vast majority of investment managers didn't see what was going to hit in 2008.

WHAT IS MARKET TIMING?

Usually, when people clear their throats and begin, "With all due respect," they're about to say something disrespectful. Starting a sentence with "No offense, but . . ." is a sure sign that someone is about to offend you. Or, if someone starts a discussion by saying, "You know I think the world of Carl, but . . ." they're almost certainly preparing to criticize him. The same thing is true in investing. When someone says, "I'm not a market timer, but . . ." you can bet they're going to make an investment decision based on market timing.

We commonly think of market timing as calling the tops and bottoms. That's the most obvious definition. More commonly, investors succumb to the siren song of market timing incrementally by making changes to their portfolios based on insights they think they possess about how stock returns will play out in the future. In other words, you're market timing when you tinker with your portfolio based on what you think will happen in the markets.

WHY SHOULDN'T WE TRY TO TIME THE MARKET?

Loads of academic studies confirm that it's impossible to consistently profit from timing the market. Sometimes you'll get lucky; more often you won't. This, of course, makes perfect sense. If something or somethings consistently signaled market tops and bottoms, everyone would know it;

buyers and sellers would use the information to set their prices accordingly. And there ends the utility of those signals.

For example, if investors knew that when the P/E ratio for the S&P 500 reached twenty times the market was at a peak—then everyone would want to sell. But potential buyers would also know that a 20x P/E ratio signaled a peak and wouldn't want to buy at that level. So, as soon as the 20x P/E peak becomes widely known, it no longer works as a profit maker. To successfully time the market, you need to know something that predicts the market that *isn't* widely known. And good luck with that in the information age.

At an investment conference a few years ago, I led a roundtable discussion about where investment opportunities might lie ahead in the coming year. Our roundtable included me and ten others, each of whom was an investment executive for a large corporate pension plan or a sizable university endowment. It was an impressive group of investors, and well over $100 billion of investment assets were represented at the table.

As the discussion moved to what types of investments might be attractive or unattractive, I asked whether anyone at the table employed "tactical portfolio shifts." A tactical shift is making portfolio changes based on what you think various parts of the global stock and bond markets will do in the future. For instance, if you believed that international companies' stocks would do well soon, you'd increase your allocation to those stocks. On the flip side, you'd reduce your exposure to areas of the market you didn't think would provide healthy future returns. Tactical shifts are a form of market timing.

Only one participant at our table, the chief investment officer of a big pension plan, said that she used tactical shifts. Nobody else changed their institution's portfolio based on their thoughts (or expert insight) about what the market would or would not do. Instead, they followed a discipline whereby their preset allocations dictated their buys and sells. For example, if their strategy called for having 30 percent of the portfolio in US stocks, and if, due to robust performance, the allocation rose to 35 percent, they would sell some of the stocks to bring the percentage back down to 30 percent and use those funds to buy other investments that hadn't done as well. These portfolio tweaks are based on math, not on timing, not on predictions.

Interestingly, all the professionals around the table had once employed tactical shifts but had changed because the results were disappointing. Understand: these pensions and endowments all have large staffs of professionals researching the markets. Many of them employ sophisticated investment consulting firms on top of that. They each have relationships with global investment firms that provide them with data, news, and market views. And even with all these resources, they found that trying to time the market just ... didn't ... work.

The roundtable participants' conclusions about trying to predict market returns are consistent with the disappointing returns of hedge funds that follow an investment strategy called *global macro*. Global macro funds can invest in anything they like based on their views of where global financial markets are headed. Their portfolios often include stocks, bonds, currencies, commodities, and derivatives (e.g., put and call options). When you invest with a global macro manager, you trust them to use their vast access to information and sophisticated analytical techniques to deftly navigate the opportunities and pitfalls in the global markets. Call it market timing on steroids.

So how do these market-timing hedge funds do? With rare exceptions, not well. Over the past ten years, global macro funds have returned about half the global stock market. Speaking about the lackluster returns posted by global macro funds over the past ten-plus years, Effie Datson, head of hedge funds at Union Bancaire Privée, a Swiss private bank, said in 2019:

> Global macro, especially discretionary global macro, looks like something that is just not there anymore. There used to be a day when George Soros [a famous global macro hedge fund manager] knew everybody personally up and down the Fed and could have lunch with them and would get insight as to what rate policy was going to be. That's gone. There's full transparency now. There are tons of data. If you add in all the alternative data sets, what are you arbitraging?[5*]

* Reprinted with permission of *Barron's*, Copyright © 2019 Dow Jones & Company, Inc. All Rights Reserved Worldwide. License number 5357791428850.

If high-priced global macro hedge funds can't market time successfully, what are the chances that you (or your broker) are going to make profitable tweaks to your portfolio?

BEING RIGHT ONCE IS HARD. BEING RIGHT TWICE IS HARDER

Another major problem with timing the stock market is that you must be right twice to be successful once. Just getting out near the top isn't enough. You also need to get back in near the bottom.

Here's an illustration: During the first week of March 2020, I had my last face-to-face client meeting before the COVID-19 shutdown. The stock market was in free fall and my client was trying not to panic. At some point in the conversation, she said, "Nobody could see this coming." I told her I disagreed. Since early January, I'd been reading articles and blog posts by infectious disease experts who said there was no doubt that the SARS-CoV-2 virus (which causes COVID-19) would make its way to the United States. Because the US wouldn't lock down the way China did, the virus would spread far and wide here with devastating effect. So, we were warned.

She looked at me incredulously and asked, "Well, then why didn't you do something? Why didn't you have us get out of the market?"

I told her that we didn't advise our clients to sell because we wouldn't know when to tell them to get back in. By going to cash, our clients likely would miss the rebound when it came. Once you're in cash, it's psychologically a lot harder to put it to work when things are scary than it is to stay invested. Take a look at Figure 4.3, which depicts the S&P 500 in 2020, along with some of the important economic and pandemic-related events. Notably, no event signaled the market bottom on March 23, and there was a lot of bad news that came after it did.

Had we moved our clients to cash in mid-February, what would have been our signal to get back in? As discussed in Chapter 3, the market often rebounds while the news is still terrible. Only in retrospect did we know

S&P 500 INDEX IN 2020

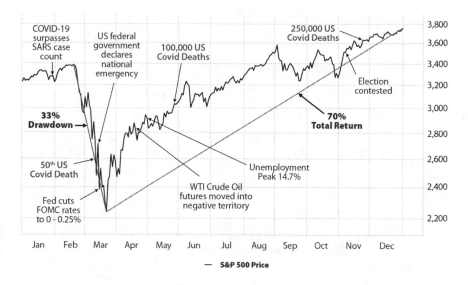

FIGURE 4.3

that March 23 was the market low; at the time, the stock market seemed to be in free fall. Fortunately, things turned out well for that client and our other clients. They didn't sell out of the market, and they fully participated in the market's recovery.

IT'S OKAY TO INVEST (OR STAY INVESTED) IN ADVANCE OF A BEAR MARKET

History has shown that investing in advance of a bear market (or remaining invested) is not as bad as you might think, and sometimes it turns out great. Unless you call market tops and bottoms correctly, which (as you've been reading so far) is nearly impossible, you're better off investing in advance of a bear market (assuming you're investing in a diversified and disciplined manner) rather than trying to time the markets. This statement may seem counterintuitive, but consider a study my firm did of how different start-ing points affect long-term portfolio value. Our study assumed an investor started with $20 million of cash and invests in a diversified portfolio (about 70 percent stocks and 30 percent bonds), which is rebalanced quarterly (meaning that investments are bought and sold to bring the portfolio back to its 70/30 allocation). The study varied when the $20 million was invested to see the effects of investing in advance of bear and bull markets.

For the first iteration, we analyzed investing around the dotcom bubble, assuming investment of the $20 million on January 1 of 1998, 1999, 2000, 2001, 2002, or 2003 (generating six different scenarios). As a point of reference, the S&P 500's high was on March 24, 2000, falling thereafter by 49 percent, then bottoming on October 9, 2002. Table 4.1 shows the results of the first iteration of the study.

VALUE AS OF 12/31/2021 OF SIX PORTFOLIOS WITH DIFFERENT STARTING POINTS AROUND THE DOTCOM BUBBLE

Rank	Date of $20 Million Investment	Value on 12/31/2021	Years from Market Top/Bottom
1	January 1, 1998	$100.3 million	2¼ years prior to market top
2	January 1, 1999	$89.9 million	1¼ years prior to market top
3	January 1, 2003	$89.4 million	¼ year after market bottom
4	January 1, 2002	$82.2 million	¾ year prior to market bottom
5	January 1, 2001	$78.8 million	¾ year after market top
6	January 1, 2000	$78.5 million	¼ year prior to market top

TABLE 4.1

A few notable things: First, the top two portfolios were invested *prior* to the bursting of the biggest stock market bubble since the 1920s—better than waiting until after the stock market bottomed. Second, under all scenarios, the $20 million more than tripled.

We ran the analysis again, this time investing around the Financial Crisis. As a point of reference, the S&P 500's high was on October 23, 2007, falling thereafter by 57 percent, then bottoming on March 9, 2009. Table 4.2 shows the results of the second iteration of the study.

VALUE AS OF 12/31/2021 OF

SIX PORTFOLIOS WITH DIFFERENT STARTING POINTS

AROUND THE FINANCIAL CRISIS

Rank	Date of $20 Million Investment	Value on 12/31/2021	Years from Market Top/Bottom
1	January 1, 2009	$65.2 million	¼ year prior to market bottom
2	January 1, 2006	$58.4 million	1¾ years prior to market top
3	January 1, 2010	$52.2 million	¾ year after market bottom
4	January 1, 2007	$50.6 million	¾ year prior to market top
5	January 1, 2008	$47.6 million	¼ year after market top
6	January 1, 2011	$46.2 million	1¾ years after market bottom

TABLE 4.2

This second iteration shows that if you happened to invest money in the market close to the bottom (in this case, January 1, 2009, which was just over two months before the market bottom), you were best off. But, investing on January 1, 2006, less than two years from the market top, was the second-best outcome. Waiting for an "all-clear signal" and delaying investment until 2011 provided the worst outcome (and in reality, there was no "all clear" signal in 2011—in August of that year US Treasuries were downgraded). Just as J.P. Morgan's research concluded, investing only when the economy appears all clear is a losing strategy.

Over the past quarter century, I've lived these scenarios with clients as they've struggled to decide to invest (or stay invested) when it seemed like we were at a market top or when the market appeared to be in free fall. Both experiences are gut-wrenching, but the clients who invested have done better over time than those who tried to time the markets.

THE MARKET CAN STAY IRRATIONAL LONGER THAN YOU CAN STAY SOLVENT

Of the fifty-two years I've been on this planet, 1999 sticks out. We had our first child; Y2K was coming to a boil; the dotcom bubble was about to burst. In hindsight there were signs of a speculative bubble. For example, in 1999, seventeen internet companies, most of them unprofitable, purchased insanely expensive Super Bowl ads. From Wall Street to Main Street, everyone was over the moon about all the money they were making in tech stocks. Companies with no earnings, but dotcom in their name, were skyrocketing in value. Stay-at-home parents were day trading, as were office workers during their lunch breaks. There was (people said) a "new economy" in which the real currency was clicks and networks, not dollars and earnings.

Of course, we all know how that story ended. After Super Bowl XXXIV (St. Louis Rams 23, Tennessee Titans 16) on January 30, 2000, the market continued to climb, peaking in March, whereupon it turned around and fell 49 percent over the next two-plus years. Growth and tech stocks declined precipitously. When all was done and dusted, the tech-heavy Nasdaq had fallen 77 percent. It didn't recover its peak for fifteen years.

In a seemingly prescient speech in December 1996, Alan Greenspan warned investors of "irrational exuberance" in the stock market. Unlike in late 2006 (when he missed the signs of the coming Financial Crisis) his warning was prophetic. The problem was that it was way too early; the S&P 500 more than doubled between his warning in 1996 and the market top in March 2000. The Nasdaq gained nearly 300 percent.

Greenspan's too-early warning highlights a concept called *the limits of arbitrage* and is commonly known by the adage "the market can stay irrational longer than you can stay solvent." It doesn't really matter if you're right; it matters if you're right *at the right time.* Being correct too early is indistinguishable from being wrong.

Greenspan didn't coin the phrase "irrational exuberance"; economist Robert Shiller did. In fact, in 2000 he wrote a book about it, titled *Irrational Exuberance*, predicting the 2000 dotcom crash, and warning that a real estate bubble could cause a financial crisis (as it did in 2007). In 2013, Shiller was awarded the Nobel Prize in Economics for his work on asset price bubbles. In short, Shiller is one of the world's foremost experts on asset bubbles. When he talks, it makes sense to listen.

In 2017, he was asked whether he saw any bubbles in the financial markets. "The best example right now is Bitcoin," he replied. When he said this, Bitcoin was trading at $4,200 per coin. Since then, Bitcoin's performance has been breathtaking. In March 2021 it hit $60,000 per coin—a 1,400 percent increase from Shiller's Bitcoin bubble call. As I write this chapter, I don't know if Shiller will be proven correct over the long term. Maybe he will, maybe he won't. What we do know is that if you had bet against Bitcoin when he declared it a bubble in 2017, you'd be out a lot of money right now. Even Nobel Prize–winning bubble experts don't always call bubbles correctly.

THE MENTAL MODELS AND
HOW TO APPLY THEM

The mental models detailed in this chapter include:

- Markets move in cycles. Boom followed by bust followed by boom. Cycles vary in duration as well as the height of their peaks and the depth of their valleys, but there are no permanent plateaus. Knowing roughly where we are in the market cycle can help you practice good investment behavior by not getting caught up in the greed of market tops or the panic that accompanies market bottoms.

- Economic stability creates instability. Times of apparent stability are the riskiest; the best opportunities often occur when everyone else is going cuckoo.

- Market timing doesn't work. There are no established indicators that signal to investors that the market is about to turn. Plus, successful market timing requires being right twice (knowing when to get out and then back in), which is extremely difficult.

- Waiting to invest until the coast is clear is not a sound strategy. Even if you invest just a few years in advance of a bear market, your portfolio will likely do fine if you don't panic and if you follow a disciplined strategy.

- Being "right" doesn't mean you win because the market can stay "wrong" for a long time. Being right at the right time is what matters.

While the market indisputably moves in cycles, it's impossible to consistently time market cycles profitably. Understanding these two opposing axioms of investing gives you the freedom to shut out most of the market's noise and focus on your behavior. Instead of trying to guess what the economy or stock market is going to do, resist the greed—or irrational enthusiasm—that accompanies booms, as well as the panic that comes with busts. Keep calm, carry on, and avoid the urge to tinker with your portfolio.

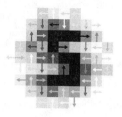

CHAPTER 5

BEWARE EXPERTS BEARING PREDICTIONS

The only function of economic forecasting is to make astrology look respectable.

—JOHN KENNETH GALBRAITH

In February 2009, the global economy was deep in the throes of the financial crisis and the stock market was in free fall, having dropped nearly 50 percent from its 2007 peak. I was a wealth manager and desperate to find somebody who could make sense of what was going on. I arranged a call with a New York City–based hedge fund manager. Let's call him Tom. I'd met him in 2007 at an investment conference where he'd impressed me greatly. Because of his deep experience, and his hedge fund's excellent track record, I was hoping to gain some insight into this rolling nightmare.

The call was not reassuring.

Tom told me, "If you think things are bad now, just wait. There's worse news coming that will make what we've experienced so far seem like an appetizer to a four-course meal of misery."

His firm was predicting that the stock market would decline at least another 50 percent, and they thought there was greater than a 50/50 chance that the entire global financial system would collapse. As he listed the reasons for why we were all doomed, I felt progressively worse. I asked him how confident he was in his predictions.

"Well, we've moved nearly all of our $3 billion fund to cash and gold, so I guess you could say we're just about 100 percent confident."

In fact, Tom was so convinced everything was about to collapse that he'd bought farmland in New Jersey. He was stocking up on guns, electric generators, and supplies. He'd stashed gold coins in the safe in his apartment, so he could buy his family's safe passage out of New York City.

Tom was preparing for the apocalypse.

I thanked him for his insights, hung up, turned off the lights in my office, laid down on the floor, and began doing deep breathing exercises.

Tom was a superstar, and his vision, while extreme, wasn't that far out of line with what I'd been hearing and reading. So, forgetting my own family for the moment, I thought of our clients. *What should we be doing for them? Should they sell out of the markets? Should they buy gold, farmland, and guns?*

Of course, Tom was wrong. The stock market bottomed a few weeks after our call, and as I write this chapter, has returned over 600 percent from its March 2009 lows. We didn't, in fact, take our clients out of the market. Tom did convince me of one thing: even the most esteemed and successful financial experts have no more idea what the future holds than any of us do. Today, whenever I hear someone making a prediction that sounds eminently reasonable, I imagine Tom sitting in a storm cellar somewhere in New Jersey, scowling and eating peaches from a can, shotgun across his lap.[1]

HOW GOOD ARE EXPERTS AT PREDICTING THE FUTURE?

POLITICAL PREDICTIONS

For the past fifteen years, I've regularly attended an investment conference that features a leading political consultant. He's a mesmerizing speaker, and each year he predicts what will happen in major elections, how US policy will shift, what global geopolitical events will occur, and how they will impact the country. He always receives a standing ovation, and everyone leaves feeling in-the-know.

I always learn a lot from his talks. But over the years I've kept track of the predictions he makes and, honestly, he's a lousy forecaster. From Hilary Clinton's inevitable landslide victory to predicting that the estate tax exemption would go down when it went up, he's wrong a lot. How could such a smart, knowledgeable, confident guy be so consistently off base? It turns out that confident experts usually have poor batting averages when they try to predict the future.

Since the early 1980s, Philip Tetlock, a sociologist at the University of California, Berkeley, has collected over 80,000 political predictions, including whether the Soviet Union would collapse, whether there would be a nonviolent end to Apartheid, whether the US would go to war in the Gulf, and whether Canada would split apart, as well as many others.[2] Analyzing all these predictions, Tetlock found that:

- Expert political predictions provide almost no value. They barely outperform control groups of college students, and they underperform simple formulas that equal-weight various outcomes. Almost nobody predicted the collapse of the Soviet Union, including Soviet experts at the CIA and top political scientists.

- Knowing a bit about a topic increases prediction ability over someone who knows nothing, but specialists with a significant amount of knowledge don't do any better than nonspecialists with general knowledge. The point of diminishing returns for knowledge that's useful in predictions is reached relatively quickly.

- The more confident an expert is, the less accurate the predictions. A related finding was that being confident in predictions helped experts get quoted in the news and interviewed on TV. This means the experts we hear from most are simply the most confident ones, not the most reliable ones.

- Like all of us, experts are subject to confirmation bias. They seek out facts that support their views and tend to dismiss facts that don't.

- Over the course of Dr. Tetlock's studies, events classified by experts as having "no chance of happening" occurred about 15 percent of the time, and things experts declared were absolutely going to occur failed to materialize 25 percent of the time.

INVESTMENT PREDICTIONS

Predictions by investment experts are just like those of political pundits: that is, nearly worthless. The predictions for the stock market and economy for 2020 (the year COVID-19 hit) are prime examples. Going into the year, forecasters predicted a stable, growing economy and single-digit stock market returns. According to the *New York Times*, "In December 2019, the median consensus on Wall Street was that the S&P 500 would rise 2.7 percent in the 2020 calendar year."[3]

Specifically, these were some of the predictions of the biggest Wall Street firms:

- Citigroup: "We are not forecasting a global (or U.S.) recession in 2020" as the "global economy appears to be stabilizing." For the US stock market, Citi predicted "upper single-digit returns" and said that "value stocks are largely expected to outperform their growth counterparts."[4]

- J.P. Morgan predicted that there was little chance of extreme market swings and that we'd see "mid-to-high-single-digit returns for stocks." Like Citigroup, J.P. Morgan recommended that investors overweight value stocks as they would outperform growth stocks.[5]

- Goldman Sachs expected a 3.4 percent increase in GDP and "continued labor market improvement." Goldman strategist David Kostin predicted that "a durable profit cycle and continued economic expansion will lift the S&P 500 index by 5 percent to 3,250 in early 2020. However, rising political and policy uncertainty will keep the index range-bound for most of next year."[6]

- Morgan Stanley forecasted 2.3 percent economic growth and that active managers would outperform the indices. It also predicted about a 4 percent market decline in 2020 and that international stocks would outperform US stocks.[7]

Wrong. Wrong. Wrong and wrong. Here's what actually happened:

- Market returns: The 2.7 percent consensus forecast undershot the 2020 stock market price return by more than 15 percent.
- Value versus growth: Not only did value underperform growth, but growth stocks outperformed value by nearly 40 percent. An investor following J.P. Morgan's and Citigroup's advice to overweight value would have found it very costly.
- International versus domestic stocks: US stocks continued their dominance, outperforming non-US stocks by nearly 10 percent. So, if you followed Morgan Stanley's advice to shift funds from domestic to international stocks, you missed a lot of potential gains.
- Active versus passive: Active managers struggled in the face of the market volatility, and most trailed the index. Predictions that active managers (those who pick stocks to try to beat the market) can better navigate choppy waters have yet to be realized.
- Economic growth: None of these firms predicted the global recession or that the Fed would cut rates or offer a massive monetary stimulus.

We might forgive forecasters for not predicting a global pandemic, but once they knew what was happening, their revised forecasts confirm how truly useless market predictions are. When the economic effects of the pandemic were becoming evident in April 2020, a survey by Bloomberg found that forecasters had reduced their 2020 year-end prediction for the S&P 500 to an average of −11 percent, totally missing the 70 percent tear the market went on from March 23, 2020, to the end of the year.

Wrong, and expensively so. We saw a similar situation heading into 2022. Experts who predicted that the strong global economic recovery would continue unabated had to dial back their predictions when Russia attacked Ukraine.

We can draw two lessons from all this:

1. Trying to predict the future is a waste of time and breath because unexpected events such as global pandemics, wars, and natural disasters occur all the time.

2. Even when unexpected events become known, predicting how the stock market will react is problematic. It's like throwing darts at a dartboard blindfolded.

The preceding 2020 stock market predictions are consistent with the poor track record of expert predictions in previous years. The wrong-headed predictions of 2020 were not outliers; 2020 was not special; market predictions are always toss-ups.

Don't believe me? Figure 5.1 shows how far off the consensus S&P 500 prediction was from the actual return by year.

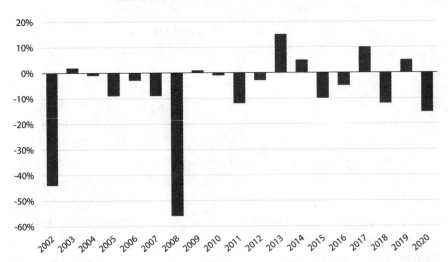

DIFFERENCE BETWEEN S&P 500 PROJECTIONS AND ACTUAL RETURNS

FIGURE 5.1

I draw three conclusions from the data on stock market predictions versus reality in Figure 5.1:

1. The correlation between analyst predictions and what happens is a mere 0.15. In other words, expert stock market predictions and what actually occurs bear almost no relationship to each other.

2. The predictions were mainly too bullish; the difference is negative in twelve of the nineteen range years, or about two-thirds of the time.

3. Expert market predictions are wrong when we need them most. Their biggest misses were in not predicting the bear markets in 2002 and 2008, missing what the S&P 500 actually returned by more than 40 percent and 50 percent, respectively.

The third point—that investment experts are most wrong when we need them most—reminds me of a story Tom Nichols tells in his book *The Death of Expertise*:

> There's an old joke about a British civil servant who retired after a long career in the Foreign Office spanning most of the twentieth century. 'Every morning,' the experienced diplomatic hand said, 'I went to the Prime Minister and assured him there would be no world war today. And I am pleased to note that in a career of 40 years, I was only wrong twice.' Judged purely on the number of hits and misses, the old man had a pretty good record.[8]

Of course, the diplomat's batting average is irrelevant. The only two times his prediction mattered were the two times he was wrong.

ECONOMIC PREDICTIONS

Economists also have a poor track record of making predictions. In 2007, not only did economists not foresee the Financial Crisis, but most economists also didn't even think such a crisis was possible. In 2009, writing in the *New York Times*, Nobel Prize–winning economist Paul Krugman explained why his colleagues were so wrong:

> The economics profession went astray because economists, as a group, mistook beauty, clad in impressive-looking mathematics, for truth. They turned a blind eye to the limitations of human rationality that often lead to bubbles and busts; to the problems of institutions that run amok; to the imperfections of markets—especially financial markets—that can cause the economy's operating system to undergo sudden, unpredictable crashes; and to the dangers created when regulators don't believe in regulation.[9]

Krugman makes an important point: the economics profession is overly focused on finding mathematical models that will predict our financial future. Economic and financial research papers are usually stuffed full of highly complex formulas and models. Professor Andrew Lo of MIT in his book *Adaptive Markets: Financial Evolution at the Speed of Thought* suggests that economists have physics envy. They want to explain the economy and markets with hard and fast rules akin to Newton's Laws of Motion. The problem is that economics is not like physics with its immutable laws. Instead, economics is more like biology with its complex and changing relationships among plants and animals and constantly evolving organisms. Professor Lo explains:

> Physicists can explain 99 percent of all observable physical phenomena using Newton's three laws of motion. Economists wish we had three laws capable of explaining 99 percent of all observable behavior in our professional purview. Instead, we probably have ninety-nine laws that explain 3 percent of all economic behavior, and it's a source of terrible frustration for us. So we sometimes cloak our ideas in the trappings of physics. We make axioms from which we derive seemingly mathematically rigorous universal economic principles, carefully calibrated simulations, and the very occasional empirical test of those theories.[10]

As discussed in Chapter 3, the economy and stock market are complex adaptive systems that are based on human interaction plus reaction to external stimuli—me watching you watching me—creating feedback loops that lead to unpredictable results. Lo summarizes this concept by quoting Nobel Prize–winning physicist Richard Feynman who once said, "Imagine how much harder physics would be if electrons had feelings."[11]

The lesson is that your first reaction should be skepticism, not reliance, when you hear an economic or market forecast.

WHY EXPERTS MAKE PREDICTIONS EVEN THOUGH THEY AREN'T GOOD AT IT

You'd think that after being wrong over and over again, the experts might say to themselves, "Wow, I really stink at this, so I'm going to stop predicting stuff." Some experts come to this realization, but many continue to predict anyway, results be damned. Why do experts make predictions even though the data shows they aren't good at it? It boils down to human nature.

OVERCONFIDENCE

One of the reasons experts keep making predictions even though they're clearly bad at it is overconfidence (which is a topic we hit in depth in Chapter 9). We're all overconfident. It's an ingrained human trait and is the primary reason experts persist in making forecasts of future events even when their predictions aren't good. For example, in 2004, undergraduates and investment professionals were asked to select one stock from each of twenty pairs of stocks—all blue-chip companies. The participants' goal was to pick the stock in each pair that would outperform the other. The participants were given information about the stocks, including past performance and analyst research. The researchers also asked how confident the players were that their chosen stocks would outperform those they didn't select.

The results? The students picked outperforming stocks 49 percent of the time, basically a coin flip. In fact, many students said that's what they did to pick their stocks. Not a great result. But the students outperformed the professionals, who only had a 40 percent success rate (i.e., they'd have been better off flipping a coin). In terms of confidence, the students on average were 59 percent confident in their stock-picking abilities, while the fund managers averaged 65 percent confidence. And the more confident the professionals were, the worse they did; professionals who were 100 percent confident in their picks were right less than 12 percent of the time.

The study results—that confidence is inversely related to the ability to predict the future—have been replicated many times in various areas, including sports betting, economic forecasts, and political predictions.

We should always be wary of overconfidence. While we're wired to crave confident-sounding predictions, we need to train ourselves not to listen to them. It's hard. The first step is knowing that confidence and prediction ability are inversely related. Instead, we should embrace the inherent uncertainty of the future and learn to sit in our discomfort. Making changes to our portfolios or other aspects of our lives based on our confidence in our predictive abilities is likely to turn out badly. This is tough to do. Our regular advice to our clients in the face of uncertainty is to do nothing, which I know is frustrating. When the markets are volatile and our fight-or-flight response has kicked in, we are primed to take action.

> INSTEAD, WE SHOULD EMBRACE THE INHERENT UNCERTAINTY OF THE FUTURE AND LEARN TO SIT IN OUR DISCOMFORT.

THE ILLUSION OF VALIDITY

The 2001 St. Louis Rams were a juggernaut. Led by Hall of Famers Kurt Warner, Orlando Pace, Isaac Bruce, and Marshall Faulk, the Rams were stacked. Their prolific offense, known as the "Greatest Show on Turf," was a scoring machine, and they were the first team to tally more than 500 points a year in three consecutive seasons. They only lost two games all year, and in the playoffs they blew out the Green Bay Packers, won a slugfest against the Philadelphia Eagles, and entered Super Bowl XXXVI as two touchdown favorites over the 11–5 New England Patriots.

The Patriots were underdogs, partly because their star quarterback, Drew Bledsoe, had been knocked out for the season earlier that year. Now the Patriots were led by a second-year, sixth-round draft pick named Tom Brady. While Brady had done well filling in for Bledsoe, pundits thought the Super Bowl would be a high-scoring game and that Brady and his offense wouldn't be able to keep up.

The Rams outgained the Patriots during the game 427–267 in total yards. But the game was tied with 1:30 remaining when the Patriots got the ball for the final drive. Everyone expected the Patriots to run the ball a few times and send the game into overtime, but with no timeouts left, Brady completed five key passes and moved his team into field goal range. The Patriots then kicked the game winner as the clock expired.

I attended Super Bowl XXXVI and, as a die-hard Rams fan, I was devastated. I paid a ton of money for the tickets, drove ten hours from Saint Louis to New Orleans, and slept on the floor of a hotel room with ten other people because hotel rooms were so scarce. I had fun, but the upset cast a pall.

After the game, I was at a bar commiserating with some fellow Rams fans. I mentioned that, including the Super Bowl, I'd attended just three Rams games that year, and those were the only three they'd lost. Everyone at the table was stunned, wondering if anyone else had only attended their losing games. My record of attendance was unusual: typically, if you were a big enough fan to go to the Super Bowl, you'd have gone to more than just two regular season games. Soon, people started joking, blaming me for the loss. Then, some actually started to get mad at me. (To be fair, we were at a bar, and everyone was drinking.)

And it didn't end there. Back in Saint Louis, some of my friends begged me not to go to any Rams games the following season. I ignored them and went to the first two. They lost. Wow. I went to a total of five games over two years and they lost every one—the only five the Rams had lost over the previous twenty-two. The cries for me to stop going grew louder. Even though I knew better, I was starting to feel a bit paranoid about my bad luck.

Of course, it's ridiculous to think that one fan has any influence on a team winning or losing, but we've evolved to think this way. As discussed in Chapter 1, one of our key survival advantages is our ability to recognize patterns. Our brains are constantly looking for patterns to guide our way through the world. When we recognize one, we want to explain it.

The problem is that many of the patterns we see are meaningless—like the pattern of my Rams game attendance. But our brains insist on finding coherence—a narrative when there is none.

This drive to discover patterns and explain them is a major factor in overconfidence. It's why we think we're better at predicting outcomes than we are. As long as the explanation we construct is coherent, we trust it. We can't help it. Explanations give us confidence that we understand the world, and that makes us feel safe. As social psychologist David Dunning says in his article, "We Are All Confident Idiots," "we are unbridled pattern recognizers and profligate theorizers."[12]

One of my favorite examples of overconfidence at work was an experiment that pitted students at Yale against a rat in their ability to find food at the end of a maze. In the first part of the experiment, a rat was put in a simple T-shaped maze (see Figure 5.2) with a food reward on one side or the other. The food was on the right side 60 percent of the time and on the left 40 percent of the time. Otherwise, the distribution was random. How did the rat do? After some runs, it figured out that the food was more often on the right side, and it turned right every time, resulting in the rat being correct nearly 60 percent of the time.

DIAGRAM OF A T-MAZE

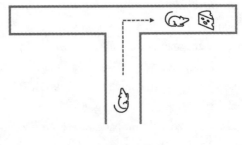

FIGURE 5.2

In the second part of the experiment, the students were given the same problem, with the same distribution of food (even though putting college students in a physical maze sounds like fun, a computer-simulated maze was used for the students). How did the Yalies do? They chose correctly 52 percent of the time. Why did the students fare more poorly than the rat? Because they were overconfident in their ability to recognize patterns. They simply couldn't accept that they should throw in the towel and select the right side of the maze each time. As noted by Philip Tetlock about this rat versus Yale student study, "Our reluctance to acknowledge unpredictability keeps us looking for predictive cues well beyond the point of diminishing returns."[13]

Even when they're not there.

Experts who make forecasts are just like the rest of us: they fall prey to the illusion of validity. They see patterns and seek to make sense of them, even when the patterns are meaningless, and their explanations are wrong. The stock market and economy provide a vast array of data, and our pattern-seeking brains can't help but imagine relationships between things that are only noise.

TOO MUCH INFORMATION

In 1956, George Miller published one of the most famous papers in the history of psychology called "The Magical Number Seven, Plus or Minus Two: Some Limits on Our Capacity for Processing Information."[14] In the paper, Dr. Miller described the phenomenon of us being able to only store five to nine items of information in our working memory (or "seven plus or minus two"). Working memory has a duration of about ten to fifteen seconds and contains information that helps us move from one thought to the next and allows us to do quick and dirty calculations. It's where we do our thinking.

A 2005 study out of the University of Queensland in Australia suggests that Miller's five to nine items may actually be too high. It found that humans can only consider four variables at a time. Where we're exposed to five variables or more, our brains tend to "revert to a simplified version of the task that does not take all aspects into account and therefore may make the wrong decision."[15]

This means our working memory serves as a severe bottleneck to our ability to process complex information. We can only juggle a handful of items of information at a time. This is why we can't actually multitask. When we think we are multitasking, we're really just quickly moving from one thing to another and back again.

As we move through our lives making decisions and guessing what the future holds for us, we don't usually think about the limits of our working memory. Typically, we like to have more information, not less. This is especially true when faced with uncertainty because a primary strategy for battling uncertainty is collecting more information. But possessing more information can increase our confidence without improving our predictive or decision-making ability.

For example, researchers from the University of Chicago and the University of Toronto tested college football fans' ability to predict the outcome of games by using differing amounts of information.[16] In the experiment, team names were replaced with letters (e.g., Team A, Team B, etc.). In the first round, the fans were given six items of information about each team and asked to predict winners. This was repeated for a total of six rounds, but at each round, the subjects received six more items of information about the teams (i.e., in round one there were six items of information, in round two there were twelve, and so on).

How did the fans do? Pretty well. They picked winners about two-thirds of the time. However, that success rate hardly budged throughout the six trials. Having additional information didn't give them any significant advantage. What did increase with each round, however, was their confidence in their predictions (see Figure 5.3). Sound familiar?

The same thing happens in the investment realm. More information leads to more confidence, but after a certain point it harms the ability to make decisions. For example, a study of venture capitalists found, "the more information about the venture provided to the [venture capitalists], the less able they were at predicting outcomes."[17]

ACCURACY AND CONFIDENCE OF PREDICTIONS FROM PARTICIPANTS

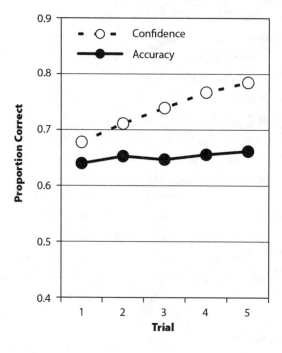

FIGURE 5.3

EXPERTS MAKE PREDICTIONS BECAUSE WE WANT THEM TO

A few years ago, I fell ill with some sort of cold or flu. After I'd been languishing on our basement couch for a few days, my wife convinced me to call my doctor. I described my symptoms, and my doctor said that he'd seen these same symptoms in other patients. He offered to call in a prescription for an antibiotic, which set off a warning bell. A few years prior to this, I'd read a book about the importance of our microbiome—the trillions of bacteria in our gut. The book said that these "good" bacteria are destroyed when we take antibiotics, which can damage our long-term health. So, I asked my doctor about it.

"Are you sure that my sickness has a bacterial origin?"

"No, it's probably not bacterial. It's almost certainly viral," he said.

When I asked him why he would prescribe an antibiotic for a viral illness, his answer disturbed me.

"In over thirty years of practicing medicine, you're the first patient to push back. Most patients demand an antibiotic whenever they're ill. I just assumed you'd want me to prescribe something."

I was disappointed in my doctor. While I appreciated his honesty, I didn't trust him as much after this experience.

But I also sympathized with him because I've been in similar situations with clients. When things are scary in the stock market, some clients want to take some sort of action. They want to *do* something. They want me to tell them what's going to happen and recommend a change to their portfolio; just sitting still and doing nothing is hard. Giving the right advice—that they shouldn't make emotional changes to portfolios when the stock market is topsy-turvy—is hard because advisors are conditioned to give clients what they want. Many investment experts know they can't predict what the stock market is going to do, but they feel pressured to do so anyway.

At an investment conference I attended a few years ago, the keynote speaker was the chief investment officer of a large investment advisory firm, and he presented his firm's forecast of domestic and international markets for the coming years. He suggested that investors over-weight some areas of the market and under-weight others based on these predictions. It was an impressive presentation with a plethora of supporting charts and data.

A few hours later, I sat next to him at the hotel bar, and after we both had a few Manhattans, I asked him how he invested his own money. He said he was mainly in index funds, only looked at his portfolio about once a year, and tried not to tinker. Given his talk about making portfolio shifts based on market forecasts, I was a bit surprised and said so. He explained that he didn't think anyone could predict the market; he only attempted to do so because clients weren't happy unless he gave them predictions along with recommendations for tweaking their portfolios.

He said he made peace with his conscience by only recommending small tweaks and thus limiting the harm of making changes. I've heard other investment professionals say the same things . . . off the record. Of course, I also know a lot of investment professionals who believe that they *can* predict the market, just as I'm also familiar with their excuses when they're wrong.

Expert predictions are hard to resist. Even though I know that stock market predictions are worthless, I find myself reading them anyway. Just the other day, I clicked on an article that quoted a famous investment guru who was calling a market top and advising everyone to lighten their exposure to stocks and move to cash. I had to stop and remind myself not to get caught up in his predictions.

It all boils down to our dislike of uncertainty. We seek predictions because we don't like not knowing what the future holds. When we don't know, we're stressed and want relief in the form of certainty. Of course, investing in the stock market necessarily involves uncertainty, so seeking expert opinions is a way to trick ourselves into thinking we're addressing our discomfort. This feeling of relief persists even when the prediction turns out wrong.

DO EXPERT FORECASTERS LEARN FROM THEIR MISTAKES?

Who do you think is better at making accurate predictions: weather forecasters or financial analysts? While we like to poke fun at weather forecasters for being wrong so often, they generally do a better job. Which makes sense. The weather is, within limits, predictable. Summer is hotter than fall; spring is usually the rainiest season; hurricanes most often occur during late summer and autumn; it almost never snows except in winter. To the contrary, financial markets do not follow reliable patterns. The stock market often changes without warning or apparent reason. A very good month can be followed by a horrible one. But, in Maine, it's not hot in January.

In a study from 2002, researchers had weather forecasters and financial analysts make predictions for the following month. The weather forecasters predicted the average temperature, and the financial analysts forecasted the return in the stock market. The weather forecasters were correct two-thirds of the time; the financial analysts one-third of the time.[18]

That the weather forecasters are better forecasters than financial analysts is interesting on its own, but the main point of the study was to examine the excuses each group gave when they were wrong. When asked about their failed predictions, weather forecasters were much more likely than financial analysts to admit that it's hard to predict the future. They were like, "Hey, it's the weather. It changes, and it's hard to predict." They understood that the weather was inherently changeable. To the contrary, financial analysts tended to explain their errors by referencing some sort of unforeseeable event that sabotaged what would otherwise have been a sterling prediction.

I've repeatedly run into this same excuse from investment experts. For example, an investment manager of international stocks that our firm works with positioned their portfolios in late 2010 to overweight Japanese stocks. They saw them as relatively cheap and poised to perform strongly. Then on March 11, 2011, a major earthquake eighty miles offshore slammed a fifty-foot tsunami into the Japanese coastline, which caused the meltdown of the Fukushima Daiichi nuclear power plant reactors. It was the worst nuclear power disaster since Chernobyl in 1986. The Japanese economy suffered severely, and the disruption tanked the stocks in which our investment manager had invested. When we had a call with this manager after the Fukushima disaster, they said their analysis was correct and their fund would have done well but for the tsunami. During the call their attitude was "we're still great at what we do. It's not our fault that we can't predict natural disasters."

Here's the thing: unpredictable events happen all the time. You don't get a mulligan because a tsunami, pandemic, or terrorist attack occurred. These unpredictable events are part of the fabric of life and constitute a major part of the uncertainty that makes predicting the future so hard.

Other excuses that financial experts commonly give when their forecasts are wrong include:

- I was early in predicting the event.
- I was almost right.
- You can't judge me on a single prediction (suggesting that they are usually correct).
- I was wrong, but for the right reasons (e.g., the market acted irrationally).

Keep an eye out for these excuses. They indicate that the expert hasn't learned anything from their failed predictions and that they're likely to plow ahead and continue to try to predict the future even though they aren't good at it.

The study also concluded that the financial analysts were much more confident in their predictions than the weather forecasters. This finding is consistent with the other research that confidence and predictive ability are negatively correlated. More importantly, the financial analysts didn't lower their ratings of themselves as forecasters when they were wrong, whereas the weather forecasters did.

Why didn't being wrong shake the financial analysts' confidence? One reason is that their clients want them to remain confident. Confidence is part of what clients are paying for. The study's authors speculated that the difference between the analysts and weather people may have to do with the type of clients that each set of experts is serving:

> Most people who listen to weather forecasts are happy if the forecast is not hopelessly inaccurate. But . . . if the reality of the [financial analysts'] predictions is even slightly below their expectations, investors can be very unhappy. Therefore, in order not to lose their clients, financial analysts must be quite sensitive about their reputations and better skilled than weather forecasters in formulating excuses for their errors.[19]

WHERE PREDICTIONS ADD VALUE

In the fall of 2020, while I was running, I stepped on something and twisted my right ankle. It was horribly painful. Due to an old injury, my right ankle is a mess. I've had two prior surgeries on it, so injuring it again was worrisome—and with good reason. After a few weeks, my ankle wasn't getting better, so I went to see my orthopedic surgeon. He ordered an MRI, which revealed cartilage damage, edema, bone spurs, scar tissue, and progression of my existing post-traumatic arthritis. My doctor recommended surgery, and then he did something amazing: he predicted the future. Accurately. He said that after surgery I'd be non–weight bearing for about five days. Then I'd be able to tolerate weight with crutches, then a cane, and everything would gradually improve over the next few months, helped along by physical therapy. And that's exactly what happened. He predicted my future so accurately because he's seen thousands of injuries like mine over his career and performed thousands of ankle surgeries.

There *are* areas where recognizing patterns helps us predict the future, which is why humans evolved to be pattern-recognizing machines. In sufficiently regular environments (not complex adaptive systems or ones commonly subject to unexpected disruptions like the economy and the stock market) that give us time to learn about them, predictions can be quite accurate. For example, chess masters can look at a board and see how the next moves are likely to play out. The chessboard always has the same number of black and white squares. There are many possible moves, but a finite number of possible next moves. My ankle is built like any other ankle. A lot of elements come into play in its functioning but, over time, and with experience, a doctor can learn how it can go wrong and how to fix it.

So, we shouldn't disregard all predictions about the future: just those in areas that are not amenable to prediction . . . like the financial markets.

THE MENTAL MODELS AND
HOW TO APPLY THEM

If you take one thing away from this chapter, it's that forecasts—particularly from geopolitical, investment, and economic experts—are highly questionable at best.

The biggest investing misconception is that forecasting is a key component of successful investing. It's not. It would be nice to have a crystal ball, but they don't exist. At first, this may sound depressing. But accepting this reality is freeing. Forget about trying to sift through the torrent of daily financial information. Don't try to find some mythical investment guru who can see around corners and predict the future. Instead, look for help from an experienced (and humble) guide who can explain the myriad types of investments and advise you on portfolio construction and their tax implications. That's essential, that's useful, and it's a whole lot better than depending on someone who claims to have an infallible crystal ball in their closet.

Using market predictions to inform investment decisions is like preparing your boat to go to sea based on weather forecasts that someone made up. Either you'll be unprepared for a storm or weighed down with life rafts and safety gear when you could be fair-weather sailing. It would be better to prepare your boat well for both storms and fine weather. That's how it is with investing.

> IT WOULD BE NICE TO HAVE A CRYSTAL BALL, BUT THEY DON'T EXIST.

As Nassim Taleb says in his book *Antifragile: Things That Gain from Disorder*, "Not seeing a tsunami or an economic event coming is excusable; building something fragile to them is not."[20] Since we can't predict what the markets will do, we should be well prepared for up and down years.

CHAPTER 6

SKILL AND LUCK
IN INVESTING

Success = talent + luck
Great success = a little more talent + a lot of luck.
—DANIEL KAHNEMAN, *THINKING, FAST AND SLOW*

THE ONE-STOCK CHALLENGE

In 2017, a group of investment professionals of which I'm a member held a One-Stock Challenge. The rules were simple:

1. Choose a stock.

2. Provide a rationale for choosing it.

3. After five months, the stock with the highest price appreciation (and the person who picked it) would be declared the winner.

The prize would be massive street cred.

I thought this sounded like fun, not because I imagine I'm particularly skilled at picking stocks, but because I saw it as a chance to conduct a little skill versus luck experiment. Instead of diligently researching my pick, I used a random stock pick generator on the Web. This was like closing your eyes and throwing a dart at a board full of ticker symbols.

The random generator gave me New York & Company, a women's clothing retailer. I'd heard of it, but I didn't know anything about it. I found out that New York & Company was down 42 percent year-to-date compared to the S&P 500's 12 percent positive return. The stock had been on a down escalator since its high in 2004, losing over 90 percent of its value. Ugly. I considered asking the website for another random pick, but, hey, random means random, so I went with it.

Twenty-seven of us participated in the challenge. The other participants said they submitted picks based on analysis and research, which they detailed with their selection. I said my pick was "selected using a random stock picker program on a website." I wanted, I wrote, "to see how a random, uninformed pick works out."

Some picks were familiar—Hertz, Facebook, Blue Apron—but I'd never heard of others: Osisko Royalties, Immuron.

After five months, the results were announced. The winning stock had gained 168 percent (Zogenix), and the worst performer had declined 65 percent (Blue Apron). Forty-four percent of the contestants beat the S&P 500; 56 percent did worse. The median picker returned just 3 percent compared to the index's 9 percent performance over the contest period. So, as a group, you could say our results were less than stellar.

How did my pick do? New York & Company (and I) came in fourth with a 68 percent return.

As I read through the results, I wondered how the other participants felt. Did the top-performing pickers feel good about themselves? Did they think their strong results were due to their brilliance and skills? Did the losers preserve their egos by saying things like, "I was too far ahead of the curve, and the stock will do well later," or "The contest period was too short to be meaningful"?

Me? Given that my pick was randomly generated, I didn't feel particularly proud to come in fourth. I knew that my pick could have just as easily come in tenth or twentieth or last. But I happened to do well because luck plays a big role in investing results, and I got lucky.

ONE HUNDRED SWIM RACES

Let's compare the stock-picking contest with another type of competition: swimming. During my thirties, I was obsessed with triathlons. I read books about triathlon training, followed detailed, science-backed training plans, and even hired a personal swim coach. I typically trained twice a day, six days a week: a morning run or bike ride, followed by a swim or weight training over lunch.

After about a year, I met Al, another triathlete who became my swim buddy. We met at the pool a few days a week and trained together for years. Al had been on his high school and college swim teams. He was on a whole different level.

During our training sessions we'd often race, sometimes a 50-yard sprint or maybe a longer distance like 400 yards. Over the years, I probably raced Al one hundred times and he beat me every single time. I was a decent swimmer, but not only was Al taller and built better for swimming, but his years as a competitive swimmer also meant he had thousands of hours more practice.

Unlike picking stocks, where luck plays a significant role, swim races are determined by skill. Because Al was more skilled, I never really had a chance.

SKILL AND LUCK AS OUTCOME DETERMINANTS

My favorite investment book is *The Success Equation: Untangling Skill and Luck in Business, Sports, and Investing* by Michael Mauboussin.[1] In the book, Mauboussin describes what he calls the "skill-luck continuum", a way of thinking about whether an activity's results are based on skill or luck (see Figure 6.1). The outcome of some activities like roulette, slot machines, and the lottery is entirely due to luck, and they fall on one side of the continuum. Others, like chess, are altogether skill-based and are at the opposite end. Most activities fall somewhere in between.

THE SKILL-LUCK CONTINUUM

Skill-Based
Outcomes

Luck-Based
Outcomes

FIGURE 6.1[2]

Most sports incline toward the skill-based end of the continuum; the more skilled players and teams usually win. But not always. For example, the other night, I watched my hockey team, the St. Louis Blues, lose a game by one goal. But three of their shots hit the goalposts. If any of those shots had been an inch to the inside, the game likely would have had a different outcome.

In *The Success Equation*, Mauboussin highlights a few questions that can help establish the relative contribution of skill or luck in determining outcomes. The first question is "Can an amateur beat a pro?" and if so, how often?

The more feasible it is that an amateur can win, the bigger role luck has in the outcome. For example, at the roulette table, experience doesn't matter. A first-time player and grizzled casino veteran can have the same results on an individual spin of the wheel because where the roulette ball falls is entirely random. But if an amateur sits down at a poker table where professionals are playing, she might win a hand occasionally, but skill and strategy are factors, and the professionals should win most hands, albeit not all the time.

The second question is "Can you lose on purpose?" Activities in which outcomes are skill-dependent can be lost on purpose. Al could have chosen to lose to me in one of our swimming races the same way I choose to lose the races to my four-year-old nephew that he challenges me to every time we're together (I'm way faster than a four-year-old). Likewise, I have a family member who's very skilled at chess, and I've seen him lose on purpose to make his opponent feel good.

At the other end of the continuum, where luck mainly determines the results, one can't usually lose on purpose. You may not win, but you can't guarantee that you'll lose. For example, you can't intentionally lose when playing a slot machine or buying a lottery ticket. You won't win much, but you can't be sure you'll lose.

Now let's apply the two questions to investing. First, can an amateur beat a pro? Yes, as my One-Stock Challenge story illustrates. Another amusing example is that in 2020, of the over $13 billion and hundreds of portfolios my firm oversees, the top-performing portfolio belonged to a middle-school-aged child of a client who'd picked her own stocks. She owned Apple (because she loves her iPhone), Netflix (because it's how she watches her favorite TV show), and Tesla (because her friend's father owns a Tesla, and she thinks that's cool). It just so happened that those three stocks were among the best performing US stocks in 2020. Over a more extended period, like a decade, it's still possible (but much less likely) that the middle-schooler's portfolio will be tops at our firm.

Next, how about losing on purpose? Can you intentionally pick a stock that will go down? Not really. If you could consistently choose losing stocks, you could make a lot of money by shorting them. But making money shorting stocks is pretty much impossible over the long term. There are no famous "short only" managers (i.e., those who make money by picking stocks that will decline in value) due to how hard it is to choose a lousy stock in advance. My pick of New York & Company demonstrates that. My random selection of a struggling company ended up with a 68 percent positive return.

The answers to the two questions illustrate that investment results have a significant luck component. Skill matters, but a highly skilled stock picker can have bad outcomes due to bad luck, and someone with no stock-picking skill can do well due to good luck.

IT'S HARD TO BEAT THE MARKET

Proof that luck plays a major role in investment results is found in how hard it is to beat the market. S&P keeps a scorecard of how actively managed funds do against the market, and their 2021 report found that 90 percent of actively managed US funds underperformed the market net of fees over the last twenty years.[3] Shorter periods have similar results: 86 percent underperformed for the previous ten years and 75 percent over the preceding five years.

Whether a high-performing investment manager can repeat his or her performance is known as *persistence*. Very few stock pickers have persistence. For example, a study led by Economics Nobel Prize–winner Eugene Fama analyzed the returns of active managers and found that only 3 percent of them displayed persistent skill.[4] The other 97 percent performed no better (and often worse) than chance would dictate. Similarly, a 2014 report by consultancy Hewitt EnnisKnupp, which is in the business of finding and recommending investment managers, found that less than 2 percent of managers generate alpha (a measure of outperformance) beyond their fees.[5]

We can see that persistence is rare if we rank investment manager returns from highest to lowest over a period and then look at their performance over the next period. Figure 6.2 shows the relative performance of 292 large-cap mutual funds compared to the S&P 500 over the five years ending December 31, 2005. Figure 6.3 shows the relative performance of those same investment managers in the same order over the following five-year period.

A comparison of the two charts shows no discernable correlation or pattern. Past returns don't inform what an investment manager will return in the future.

MUTUAL FUND PERFORMANCE 2001–2005

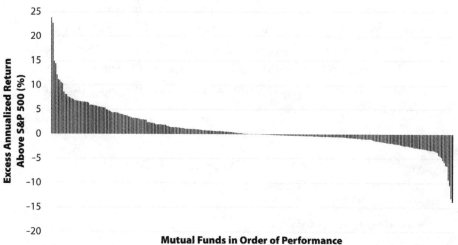

FIGURE 6.2: FIRST FIVE-YEAR PERIOD

MUTUAL FUND PERFORMANCE 2006–2010

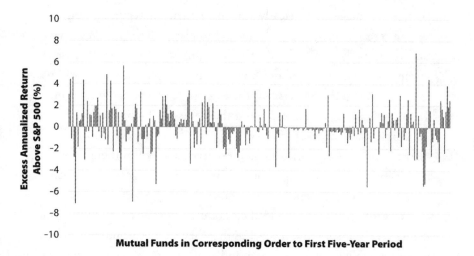

FIGURE 6.3: SECOND FIVE-YEAR PERIOD

The takeaway from studies on this topic and the preceding charts is that there's little to no persistence of public stock investment manager returns from one period to the next. The poor or sterling performance of most managers is in line with what chance would dictate, and only a relative few display persistence. This is because luck plays a significant role in investment returns. Hiring an investment manager with good past returns is no guarantee of future success.

WHY LUCK PLAYS SUCH A BIG ROLE IN INVESTMENT RESULTS

THE PARADOX OF SKILL

Over the past few decades, I've met with hundreds of investment management firms, but one meeting early in my career stands out because of what I learned. The representatives from the investment firm were incredibly impressive. An attractive and personable head of business development led the meeting, supported by a seasoned and confident portfolio manager who clearly explained their strategy; a young and earnest research analyst gave detailed examples; and their head of quantitative strategy, who had a doctorate in statistics and a thick Eastern European accent, talked about how they used sophisticated algorithms to narrow down the universe of stocks to those that would outperform. The presentation was fantastic, and there was no doubt that they were incredibly knowledgeable and skilled. Plus, their past performance was market-beating. Given their radiant expertise and skill, I thought they'd be a great addition to our stable of investment managers and that we should invest client money with them.

For various reasons, we ended up not using them. Still, I kept tabs on them over the years and was shocked that they massively underperformed in the years following our meeting, and all the people I'd met left the firm for greener pastures. They were so impressive. How could they have delivered such poor returns?

The answer lies in understanding a vital aspect of the skill-luck continuum. Even though investing is toward the luck-based end of the skill-luck continuum, it doesn't mean that investment professionals are unskilled. On the contrary, the skill level of investment managers has risen to very high levels across the financial industry, which (counterintuitively) means that luck is a more significant factor in investing than ever before. That's a paradox that in *The Success Equation* Mauboussin calls the "paradox of skill," writing that "as skill improves, performance becomes more consistent, and therefore luck becomes more important."[6]

To illustrate, suppose Alabama's Crimson Tide, winner of five of the last ten college football championships, plays an unranked team like New Mexico State. In that case, they'll almost certainly win, given their much greater skill level (which is what happened in 2021: Alabama rolled the Aggies 59–3). However, luck can play a considerable role when Alabama plays a similarly skilled competitor, as they did in the 2014 Sugar Bowl against the Oklahoma Sooners. In the 2014 game, Alabama had three turnovers—two interceptions and a fumble—and it missed a field goal. The Tide lost 45–31. Alabama's problem wasn't a lack of skill; it was poor execution along with a big dose of bad luck.

We see this all the time in sports. A player or team with a lot more skill usually beats a lesser-skilled player or team. Still, when two similarly skilled players or teams compete, the result often hinges on luck: the ball doinks off the uprights on a field-goal attempt, an outfielder trips and the ball goes over his head, a putt hits a spike mark and lips out on the first hole of a playoff.

The paradox of skill is relevant in the investment world because the skill level of investors has increased dramatically over the past few decades. Ever more lucrative rewards have attracted brilliant and analytically sophisticated students who might previously have gone into engineering, physics, or math. I read about an astrophysics professor at a top university who was meeting with one of his postdoctoral students to discuss his various job offers. The professor assumed they'd discuss offers from NASA, Cal Tech's Jet Propulsion Lab, or Lockheed Martin. Instead, the student was having trouble deciding between a hedge fund and a few large investment banks.

Evidence of the high and increasing skill level in the investment industry can be found in the rising number of chartered financial analysts (CFA), the investment industry's top designation. Gaining a CFA certificate is grueling, typically takes three to five years, and requires thousands of hours of study. A few decades ago, a CFA was a significant differentiator, but that's less true today. There are nearly 180,000 CFAs now compared to about 20,000 in the mid-1990s, a nine-fold increase (see Figure 6.4).

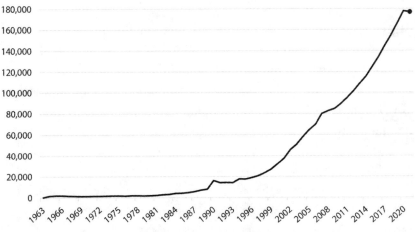

HOW THE CHARTERED FINANCIAL ANALYST DESIGNATION TOOK OFF (1963–2021)

Numbers until 1990 show number of annual examination candidates; numbers from 1990 show number of CFA charterholders.

FIGURE 6.4: CFA CHARTHOLDERS[7]

The sky-high skill level across the industry means that chances are most every investment manager you'll meet will be impressive. At our firm, we often say that after meeting one manager—and if they were the only one you'd ever met —you'd want to give them all your money.

Again, to use a football analogy: if you meet just one NFL wide receiver, you'll be stunned by his physical attributes—tall, fast, agile, strong—and you'll assume he'll lead the league in catches. But after meeting scores of NFL wide receivers, you'll realize that all of them are fast, agile, and strong. This, again, produces the paradox of skill: as the level of skill increases, so does the role of chance in outcomes.

THE SKEW: MOST STOCKS UNDERPERFORM THE MARKET

The paradox of skill isn't the only thing that makes beating the market so hard. Another difficulty is that investment managers are picking from a universe of stocks where most underperform the market.

Figure 6.5 is from Craig J. Lazzara at S&P and shows the cumulative returns of the 1,012 stocks that constituted the S&P 500 from 1999 through 2019.

INDIVIDUAL STOCK RETURNS 12/31/1999–12/31/2019

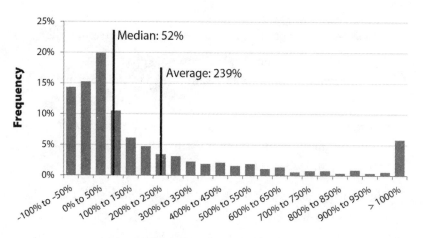

FIGURE 6.5: CONSTITUENT RETURNS FOR
THE S&P 500 ARE HIGHLY SKEWED[8]

Over these twenty years, the average (or mean) return of the S&P 500 was a cumulative 239 percent, equivalent to a 6.29 percent annualized return. The cumulative return for the median S&P stock was 52 percent, equating to a mere 2.12 percent a year. The fact that the average is higher than the median is important; while every stock has a 50/50 chance of being above the median, each has a much lower chance of being above average. From 1999 to 2019, only 26 percent of stocks outperformed the 239 percent average. Figure 6.5 shows that relatively few high-performing stocks pull up the average, while most stocks (almost three-quarters) underperform (think of this as the trivial many versus the vital few, a concept we hit in depth in Chapter 8).

And the longer the time frame, the worse the chances of an individual stock outperforming the market. A study of the returns of the over 25,000 publicly traded stocks that existed between 1926 and 2016 found:

- The mean annual return of all stocks between 1926 and 2016 was 14.74 percent, while the median was a mere 5.23 percent.

- Over half the stocks delivered negative returns during their lifetimes.

- Only 42 percent outperformed the three-month Treasury Bill.

- Just five stocks (Exxon, Apple, Microsoft, GE, and IBM) account for 10 percent of all wealth created by the stock market during that time.

- Just 4 percent of all stocks accounted for all the wealth created by the stock market from 1926 and 2016.[9]

Thus, buying and owning a few individual stocks will usually lead to poor performance. For the same reason, the odds are against active managers outperforming the overall market if they have concentrated portfolios.

This phenomenon of the average being above the median is called a *positively skewed distribution*, in this case, of returns. The skew occurs because while the most a stock can lose is 100 percent, it can gain well above 100 percent. The skew also happens because, mathematically, the compounding of random returns, even if symmetrically distributed, creates a skewed distribution of returns over time.

Here are the top ten performing stocks in the S&P 500 and their cumulative returns for the previously examined 1999–2019 period:

1. Apple, Inc., 9,092 percent
2. UnitedHealthcare Group, 5,073 percent
3. Humana Inc., 4,740 percent
4. Sherwin-Williams Co., 3,800 percent
5. Amazon.com, Inc, 3,785 percent
6. AutoZone, Inc., 3,587 percent
7. Aetna, Inc., 3,462 percent
8. Ball Corporation, 3,077 percent
9. TJX Companies, Inc., 2,901 percent
10. Lockheed Martin Corp., 2,821 percent

This list may surprise many investors as only two tech favorites, Apple and Amazon, are in the top ten. The rest are in health care, aerospace, specialty chemicals, apparel, automotive, and containers and packaging. Picking the high performers requires more than just focusing on a hot industry or sector.

Ultimately, the cold, hard reality of the skew means that picking an individual stock is like flipping a weighted coin where you lose most of the time. But when you win, you can win very big, so the temptation to pick individual stocks is strong. The skew doesn't mean that you shouldn't ever own individual stocks, but rather that you should know the odds are against you. It also means that if you invest in a concentrated fund (meaning one that owns relatively few stocks), you should expect that, given the odds, it will probably underperform the market. But the fund also may outperform and do so in a big way. Thus, it's very tempting to try to find those star investment managers.

Another thing to keep in mind is that even if you pick a stock that will outperform over the coming decades, it may be hard to stick with it. Why? Because even high-flying stocks experience many deep troughs, or drawdowns. If you'd owned some of the high-flyers of the past decade or two, you would have had incredible overall success. However, there would have been times that tried your patience and strongly tempted you to bail out. For instance:

- Facebook experienced drawdowns of 50 percent+, 40 percent+, and two more of 20 percent+.

- Amazon experienced a drawdown of 90 percent+ in the tech bubble and, after recovering, had five more 25 percent+ declines.

- Netflix has experienced four separate drawdowns of over 70 percent, another over 50 percent, and four more of 25 percent+.

- Google experienced a drawdown of 65 percent during the 2007–2008 financial crisis and had two more of 20 percent+.

WHAT MONKEYS CAN TEACH US ABOUT INVESTING

The "infinite monkey theorem" conjectures that given enough time, a monkey pounding away randomly on a keyboard will eventually type out Hamlet word-for-word. It's a mind-boggling concept to think about, but it's theoretically true. The point of the thought experiment is that, if given enough time, order can arise out of randomness.

A 2013 study from Bayes (formerly Cass) Business School in London calculated the returns ten million (simulated) monkeys picking stocks would produce. For each of the forty-two years covered in the study (1968–2011), a computer-simulated monkey drew a stock randomly from the top one thousand most valuable stocks for that year. After picking the first stock and giving it a 0.001 weight (i.e., 1/1000th), the stock was put back into the pool, and the computer would draw again and again until it selected one thousand times. Because the selected stocks were put back, some stocks were picked multiple times, and others not at all. This was repeated ten million times each year of the study period, providing ten million randomly generated monkey portfolios.

If you took $100 in 1968 and invested it in an index fund that tracked the top one thousand stocks, you'd have about $4,800 at the end of 2011—a nice 9.65 percent return. How did the monkeys do? Well, the ten million random portfolios *crushed* the market: "Half of the monkeys produced a terminal wealth value greater than $8,700; 25 percent produced a terminal wealth value greater than $9,100; while 10 percent produced a terminal wealth value greater than $9,500."[10] Nearly every one of the ten million monkey portfolios beat the market.

Let that sink in for a minute. Active managers struggle mightily to beat the market, yet randomly generated monkey portfolios handily beat it? How can that be? It happened because there's a fundamental flaw in the stock market.

WHY THE MARKET IS FLAWED

The stock market is capitalization weighted. Bigger, more valuable companies have more of an effect on how the market performs than smaller, less valuable companies. So, when you invest in an S&P 500 index fund, for example, you're investing in the five hundred stocks in that index in proportion to each company's relative value. For example, as I write this chapter, the top five companies in the S&P 500 (Apple, Microsoft, Amazon, Tesla, and Google) currently compose 24 percent of the overall index. The bottom five stocks make up a mere 0.04 percent of the index. So, an S&P 500 index fund provides your portfolio an outsized dose of the biggest companies in the index. Thus, investing in a cap-weighted index fund is riskier than other weighting schemes because of the concentrated exposure to the largest companies in the index.

But the cap-weighted structure has worked well for investors (as of late 2021) because the top-weighted stocks such as Apple, Microsoft, and

Amazon have been powerful performers for more than ten years.[11] But this hasn't always been the case. Over more extended periods, the market's capitalization weighting has led to underperformance relative to other methods of weighting stocks.

The reason for this is straightforward. In a cap-weighted index over-valued stocks will be overweighted in the market compared to their intrinsic value and undervalued stocks will be underweighted. Over time, the under- and over-weighted stocks will tend to revert to their fair values, so a greater volume of overweighted capital will decline in value than the amount that appreciates. Hence, over time, the cap-weighted market provides sub-par returns.

What this means is that your portfolio will outperform the market if (a) you are broadly diversified (meaning you own most or all of the stock market), (b) you weight your holdings differently than the market, and (c) you give it enough time. In addition to finding that monkey portfolios outperformed the market, the Bayes Business School authors found that portfolios assembled with alternative weightings—such as dividends paid, cash flow, book value, and sales—handily beat the cap-italization-weighted market portfolio. Numerous other studies have reached the same conclusion.[12]

The conclusion to draw is that the popular cap-weighted market port-folio is fundamentally flawed. A broadly diversified portfolio weighted by using almost any set of rules other than capitalization should outperform the market over (long) periods with a high degree of certainty.

IF THE MARKET IS FLAWED, WHY IS BEATING IT SO HARD?

Investing in a broadly diversified manner differently than the market is a simple concept but not easy to follow because it is behaviorally hard. A perfect example is my own investments in low-volatility weighted index funds.

A well-known rule of investing is that if you seek higher returns, you need to assume more risk. But there's an important anomaly secreted in this accepted wisdom: over time, stocks with low volatility tend to outperform ones with higher volatility (i.e., riskier stocks). Thus, an index that weights stocks according to volatility (with the lower-volatility stocks weighted more heavily than higher-volatility ones) should outperform the riskier portfolio over time.

Based on this research, along with other studies that indicated that investing in noncapitalization weighted indexes provides better returns, years ago I began investing my own money in low-volatility index funds. These funds acted differently than the market. They outperformed some years and underperformed others. But over the ten years prior to 2020, they beat the market. Then in 2020, the low-volatility funds massively underperformed. By massive, I mean it was really bad. How bad? My small-cap low-volatility ETF (exchange traded fund) investment returned a negative 17 percent for the year versus its benchmark's return of a positive 17 percent, making for an underperformance of 34 percent. That's horrible.

This massive underperformance has tested me. I've struggled with not selling my low-volatility ETFs in 2020, and I haven't added any money to them since, even though I know I should. The point is that swimming against the market tide is not easy; investing differently than the rest of the market is a wild ride. Emotionally, it can be tough to stick to the strategy over the short term, even if you're confident that it will outperform over the long.

My experience is borne out in the Bayes Business School study. The researchers found numerous periods during the forty-two years studied in which all ten million of the monkey portfolios (and all the factor-weighted portfolios) underperformed the market, even though the monkeys and every one of the factor-weighted strategies significantly outperformed the market over the long term. Figure 6.6 shows how the monkey portfolios compared to the market over rolling three-year periods. You can see that most of the time, all or none of the monkeys beat the market. As such, sticking with the monkey portfolios would be challenging given the volatility as compared to the market returns.

PROPORTION OF MONKEYS BEATING MARKET-CAP
ON THREE-YEAR ROLLING BASIS

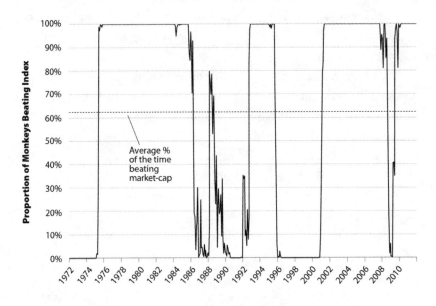

FIGURE 6.6[13]

What's true of simulated monkeys and factor-weighted portfolios is also true of active managers. A study by Vanguard found that of the active managers who beat the market over the fifteen years studied, 97 percent experienced at least five years of underperformance, and more than 60 percent experienced seven or more years of under-performance. Furthermore, two-thirds of these star managers underperformed for three or more consecutive years on their bumpy road to outperformance.[14] Imagine how hard it would be to stick with (or add money to) an investment manager who'd underperformed for three or more years back-to-back-to-back. From my experience working with clients, I can tell you that it's very hard indeed.

It's tough to stay with an investment strategy or investment manager through years of underperformance. The fact that investment managers often can't afford to stick to their strategies when they're out of favor compounds the problem. If a manager's performance falls too far behind his benchmark (which is cap-weighted), many investors will leave, and he might go out of business.

We saw an example of this years ago with an investment manager our firm used—a small-cap growth firm focused on buying growth companies at a reasonable price (known as a "GARP" strategy). The firm had performed well compared to the small-cap growth index for years but experienced some rocky times as returns in small-cap growth began being driven by tech and biotech companies with rapidly rising valuations that didn't make any money. As a GARP manager that looked at earnings, profits, and reasonable valuations, they didn't own these high-flying stocks and their returns suffered. After a few years, their clients began pulling out their money. Then a mutual fund company for whom the firm managed funds fired it. In about a year, the firm dropped from managing over $3 billion to less than $1 billion. Then it went out of business even though its long-term strategy was sound and may have delivered strong performance again.

WHAT SHOULD WE DO WITH THIS KNOWLEDGE?

In 2016, I had dinner with two men: the chief investment officer of a firm that provides both cap-weighted and factor-weighted indexes, and the top investment strategist of one of the largest investment consulting firms in the world. After a few glasses of wine, our discussion turned to how we would invest $100 million if we won Powerball. Both gentlemen said that the vast majority of their investments would be in the cap-weighted index.

"Why wouldn't you use an index weighted to a factor like quality, dividends paid, or low volatility since those strategies should deliver higher performance over the long term?" I asked.

Both gave me the same response: it's too hard behaviorally, and they weren't sure they could stick with a strategy that delivered years of underperformance.

This conversation has stuck with me over the years. If two seasoned and erudite investment experts don't think they can emotionally handle being different than the market, what does that say for the rest of us? It reflects something I think of as the *paradox of the herd*: to get different returns than the market, you must invest differently but that means leaving the herd. That's not easy because the herd provides safety—perhaps not in reality, but emotionally.

Knowing that the market is flawed but hard to beat is a vital mental model in our tool chest. As an investor, you should ask yourself if you can bear experiencing lower returns than the market for long periods. Most people can't, and they should buy index funds that track the cap-weighted market so that the pain of underperforming the market is alleviated by the knowledge that the herd shares their pain. Additionally, cap-weighted index funds are low-cost and tax efficient, which is another reason they may be appropriate for investors.

If you think you have the grit and discipline to stick with a strategy that may look terrible for years, you should consider investing in a fund weighted based on factors other than market capitalization. Major index fund companies such as Vanguard, iShares, S&P (SPDRs), DFA, ProShares, and Invesco all have ETFs that track factor-weighted indexes such as equal-weighted, dividend-weighted, quality-weighted, profitability-weighted, book value-weighted, and momentum strategies.

Investing with active managers who also follow a proven strategy is a fit for some investors. At our firm, we employ a handful of active managers who have provided excellent returns for our clients. Of course, we've used some who have not done well and have even gone out of business, like the GARP manager. The key is that if you use an actively managed fund, you need patience to withstand years of underperformance because even the best active managers underperform for years at a time.

A successful strategy can be to combine core holdings of index funds with active managers or factor-weighted portfolios. This sort of hybrid approach, with index funds providing market returns and the other investments providing potential outperformance, can be easier to stick with from a behavioral perspective than just utilizing one type of investment.

What's most important is (a) to have a strategy and (b) to stick with it. Discipline and patience are two of the most important determinants of successful investing.

A WORD ABOUT PRIVATE INVESTMENTS

This chapter (and most of this book) has focused on publicly traded securities. Investments in private companies (or private real estate) through private equity and venture capital firms are a different animal. While there's luck involved in private investment results, private investment managers can provide differentiated returns for a few reasons.

First, the playing field in private investments, unlike in the public market, is not level. Obtaining an information advantage when investing in publicly traded securities is practically impossible. The 2002 Sarbanes-Oxley Act and the protections the SEC affords to investors in public companies have leveled the information playing field. To comply with these regulations, information about public companies must be distributed evenly and fairly. And the internet provides near-instantaneous access to company news and material information whether you're sitting in an office on Wall Street or in a cabin in Idaho. In this game, no one has an informational edge. Be wary of investment managers who claim one.

Because most private company financial information is tightly guarded, investors in private companies have a corresponding ability to gain an information advantage.

Second, most private investment managers are specialists in the type of companies they invest in. They often gain seats on the boards of companies they own, which allows them to take an active role in shaping the strategy and operations of their investments.

Third, top-performing private investment managers' reputations attract companies seeking capital, giving them a bigger pool of investment opportunities. For example, a biotech firm raising a round of capital visited our offices and highlighted that a well-known Silicon Valley venture capital firm was an investor. Having this well-respected investment firm as an investor was like a Good Housekeeping Seal of Approval and made the idea of our clients' making an investment in their company more attractive. Because of the positive signaling that having the right investor provides, private companies tend to seek out investments from well-known firms with stellar reputations.

For these reasons, top private investment managers can deliver persistent market-beating returns. Evidence is seen in the dispersion of returns between top and median investment managers in publicly traded securities versus private assets.

Figure 6.7 shows the dispersion of investment manager returns in various types of investments. The left side of the chart shows the difference in returns among managers in publicly traded stocks and bonds, and the right side shows return differentials for private managers. The grey bars show the range of returns while the dots indicate the median and top 5 percent performers. Notably, the returns of the top public stock managers compared to the median manager are slight compared to the differential of private managers on the right side of the chart. This indicates that private asset managers have varying skill levels and access to information, whereas the public stock and bond managers are mired in a battle on an even playing field. But note that the dispersion between high-performing private investment managers and low-performing ones is enormous, which means that there is more risk in private investments—to benefit, you must be invested with a top-performing manager.

Of course, investing in private assets requires a lot of money. The minimums for private equity and venture capital funds are at least a few hundred thousand dollars and often over $1 million. If you're fortunate enough to have the financial resources and access to top managers, adding private investment funds to a portfolio provides a decent chance of adding market-beating returns.

AVERAGE ANNUAL MANAGER RETURNS BY ASSET CLASS

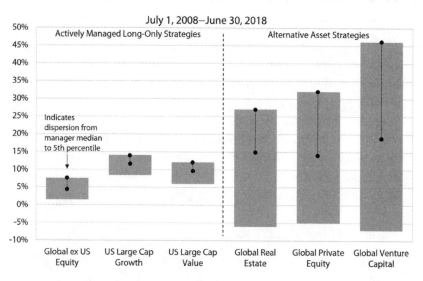

FIGURE 6.7[15]

CREATING VERSUS PRESERVING GREAT WEALTH

You may be wondering how there are so many super wealthy people in the world if it's so hard to pick investments that will deliver outsized returns. How can you generate tens or hundreds of millions of dollars of wealth through investing given the dour view of skill versus luck this chapter has laid out? The answer is that you probably can't. With rare exception, if you want to generate significant wealth, you must be actively involved in a successful business. High-income earners like doctors and lawyers make a nice living, but people who vault into tens of millions of dollars or more of wealth are business owners with remarkably similar strategies. They:

- concentrate their assets, usually in a single company. This increases the chances of winning big if their one big bet pays off.

- tolerate a high level of risk: their success or failure depends on their company. If it takes off, they are rich; if it flounders or fails, they aren't.

- are obsessed: they invest almost all their time and talent in their business. Building the company is their singular focus and takes over much of their lives.

And luck plays a role too. Looking back, successful company owners can identify how everything seemed to come together "just so." If a few things had happened a bit differently, their company wouldn't have been as successful. On the flip side, bad luck kills off many otherwise promising businesses.

Being a business owner is risky. Yes, the payoff can be huge, but there's also a good chance that there will be no gold at the end of the rainbow, as around 70 percent of companies don't make it to their tenth birthday.[16]

On the flip side, investing in a diversified portfolio is more about prudently growing and preserving wealth than making you a zillionaire. In fact, the strategies for preserving wealth are largely the opposite of those for generating it (see Table 6.1):

- Instead of being concentrated, diversify. Spreading wealth among many investments eliminates the chances of losing it all.

- Lower the overall level of risk by reducing leverage and building a margin of safety by allocating to bonds and cash.

- Involvement moves from active to passive. Being an investor means investing in someone else's company. Investors generally don't influence the success of the companies in which they invest (unless they are a private equity manager, which is its own business).

- Mitigate the effects of luck by following a disciplined investment process. Setting portfolio strategy and rebalancing are essential tools for long-term success.

STRATEGIES FOR CREATING AND
PRESERVING GREAT WEALTH

Creating Great Wealth	*Preserving* Great Wealth
Concentrated	Diversified
Higher Risk	Lower Risk
Active Personal Involvement	Passive Involvement
Luck	Process

TABLE 6.1

Preserving and smartly growing wealth requires a mindset and discipline that avoid huge losses. Years ago, I discussed with a client whether to put half of her wealth into a new business venture. If the business failed and she lost that money, it would affect her lifestyle and financial security. On the other hand, if the start-up business took off and doubled or tripled her wealth, very little would change. She already had enough to achieve all her lifestyle, charitable, and financial goals. Accordingly, she invested just 20 percent of her wealth into the new business and found other investors to make up the difference.

Note that preserving wealth doesn't preclude excellent returns; over the past decade, a 70/30 portfolio of globally diversified stocks and bonds more than doubled in value. Compounding returns in a diversified portfolio can turn great wealth into even greater wealth. But if you start with a modest investment, a doubling of value in a decade is a long way short of the outsized returns needed to turn it into tens or hundreds of millions of dollars.

THE MENTAL MODELS AND
HOW TO APPLY THEM

In December of 2008, a client sent me the details of a fund's returns and asked whether I thought he should invest in it. The fund had done well, having returned about 11 percent annually over the prior eighteen years, roughly in line with the S&P 500. What was surprising to me was the consistency of the returns. From 1990 through mid-2008, it had never lost more than 1 percent. The S&P 500, by comparison, had multiple drawdowns of over 10 percent during that period, including a 49 percent loss after the dotcom bubble burst in March 2000.

I smelled a rat. It just didn't seem possible that any investment manager could match the stock market's return for so long with almost no volatility. I told my client I didn't believe in the fund's returns. He told me that I had passed his test; the fund he had sent me was a feeder fund into Bernie Madoff's Ponzi scheme.

Wouldn't it be nice to be able to put our money with an investment manager with the skill to weave deftly in and out of stocks at the just right time and provide us with great returns with minimal heartache? Sadly, such investment managers don't exist. Managers and strategies that provide long-term outperformance always deliver some underperformance along the way. Picking consistently winning investment managers is confounded by the role of luck in investment results. Is the manager touched by genius, or just lucky?

The essential mental models to keep in our heads include:

1. Luck plays a big role in investing, so we shouldn't read too much into good or bad results over short periods. Randomly selected stocks, middle-schoolers, and monkeys can score outstanding returns; grizzled investment veterans can have dismal results. And vice versa.

2. Most active managers underperform after fees. This doesn't mean that you should never use an active manager—just be aware that the odds are against them outperforming.

3. Most stocks underperform the market. Realize when you buy an individual stock that the odds are stacked against you. This also explains why so many active managers struggle to beat the market.

4. Beating the market requires investing differently than the market, which requires great heart and discipline. If you choose to break off from the herd, it's essential to stick with your strategy through the inevitable ups and downs.

5. It is easier to outperform in private investing, primarily due to information asymmetries that don't exist in public markets. If you have the financial resources, adding private investments to a portfolio with skilled investment managers is a sound strategy.

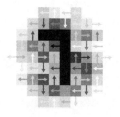

CHAPTER 7

THE TREND IS NOT
YOUR FRIEND

*A trend is a trend is a trend. But the question is, will it bend? Will it alter its
course through some unforeseen force and come to a premature end?*

—ALEXANDER CAIRNCROSS

My friend Rob was an early Bitcoin miner back when one Bitcoin was a
few hundred dollars. "Mining" meant that he earned his coins by running a computer program that verified Bitcoin transactions by solving
complex math problems (it sounds crazy, but that's how it works). After
a year, he'd earned a few thousand dollars' worth and cashed out. He
bought a couch and a good bottle of whiskey, and paid down some credit
card debt. I remember Rob's glee as he told a group of us at a party that
he'd made thousands of dollars with almost no effort; his computer had
mined while he slept.

Unfortunately, Rob sold his Bitcoin way too early. If he'd waited and
sold it in April 2021, he would have netted more than $1 million. Even
though Rob was an early proponent of Bitcoin specifically, and cryptocurrencies in general, he never figured the Bitcoin he mined in 2015

at a few hundred dollars a coin would be worth over $60,000 each six years later.

But Rob isn't alone. A lot of people missed the massive runup in Bitcoin price. Since its inception, Bitcoin has been met with skepticism and even derision. For example, in 2017, J.P. Morgan CEO Jamie Dimon called Bitcoin a fraud, and in 2018, Warren Buffett called cryptocurrencies "rat poison squared." Even now, Bitcoin's future is uncertain. Will cryptocurrencies break into the mainstream and be accepted like dollars, pounds, euros, and yen? If so, will Bitcoin still be a crypto leader? Or will other cryptocurrencies like Ethereum or others that don't yet exist displace it? No one knows.

Investing in trends, like cryptocurrencies, seems like a good way to make out-sized profits: spot one, invest in it, and then find somewhere to stack your Benjamins. But it's not that easy. Trendspotting success is only apparent in retrospect. There are challenges to investing in trends that every investor should know about. Let's hit the big ones: (1) it's difficult to spot a trend early, (2) trends don't always turn out as imagined, and (3) it's difficult to find a successful needle in a haystack of competitors.

IT'S DIFFICULT TO SPOT A TREND EARLY

Founded in 1881, at the dawn of the camera age, Kodak was the twentieth century's dominant film company. By the 1970s, Kodak had a 90 percent share of film and an 85 percent share of camera sales in the United States. Kodak was so synonymous with photography that occasions ripe for memorializing were widely known as "Kodak moments."

Even though Kodak was at its core a film company, in 1975 it was a Kodak engineer named Steve Sasson who invented the digital camera. It was toaster-sized and took twenty-three seconds to capture low-resolution images of just 0.01 megapixels (an iPhone 12 Pro camera is twelve megapixels) saved to a tape drive (see Figure 7.1). It only took black-and-white photos and viewing them required hooking up the camera to a TV.

THE FIRST DIGITAL CAMERA

FIGURE 7.1

Not surprisingly, digital cameras were slow to catch on. I remember getting my first one around the time my first child was born in 1999. The images were grainy, and it could only store six pictures. It was more novelty than camera.

Of course, as the technology advanced, and the advantages of digital mounted, film cameras slowly, then quickly, became obsolete. And now standalone digital cameras are also going the way of the dinosaur. As smartphones became the primary picture-taking device, sales of digital cameras dropped 87 percent from 2010 to 2019.[1]

And how did Kodak do during the rise of the digital camera trend? Even though it invented the digital camera, it never loved it. Kodak executives believed people liked the touch and feel of printed photos too much to go completely digital. Plus, they worried about killing off their cash cow—the film business—and viewed digital cameras as an existential threat. As digital cameras and then camera phones took off, Kodak's revenue plummeted, and its profits turned negative. Kodak went from 80,000 employees in 2000 to less than 20,000 in 2010. In 2012, it declared bankruptcy.

One shouldn't be too hard on Kodak executives though. Predicting how a trend will evolve is tough. As consumers purchased their first digital cameras in the 1990s, it was possible to imagine that they might someday replace film cameras, but who would have thought that cell phones would evolve to include high-quality digital cameras, let alone to foresee picture and video sharing mobile apps like Instagram, Snapchat, and TikTok. Anyone who says they predicted this is lying.

Kodak's inability to recognize and capitalize on a transformative trend is as much the rule as an exception. It's challenging to discern fantasy from reality in the early stages of an emerging trend or technology, and great ideas often seem outlandish near their inception. Examples of this abound as early transformative technologies and trends like travel via train, the telephone, movies, television, catalog shopping, home computers, video games, and even the internet were derided in their early stages:[2]

- "No one will pay good money to get from Berlin to Potsdam [on a train] in one hour when he can ride his horse there in one day for free." —King William I of Prussia, 1864

- "This 'telephone' has too many shortcomings to be seriously considered as a means of communication. The device is inherently of no value to us." —Western Union, 1878

- "The cinema is little more than a fad. It's canned drama. What audiences really want to see is flesh and blood on the stage." —Charlie Chaplin, 1916

- "TV will never be a serious competitor for radio because people must sit and keep their eyes glued on a screen; the average American family hasn't time for it." —the *New York Times*, 1939

- "The world potential market for copying machines is 5,000 at most." —IBM, to the eventual founders of Xerox, 1959

- There is no reason anyone would want a computer in their home." —Ken Olson, president, chairman, and founder of Digital Equipment Corp (a maker of mainframe computers), 1977

I've been as guilty as anyone in not appreciating early trends. I didn't think CDs would replace vinyl or cassettes. Then I didn't think digital downloads would displace owning CDs. I thought Twitter would never take off. The idea of expressing yourself in 140 characters or less seemed ridiculous. I thought the concept behind Venmo—combining a payment system with social media—was one of the dumbest things I'd ever heard of. I was even skeptical of texting; why would I want to text a friend when I could send him an email or call him up?

The inertia of the status quo is a powerful impediment to our ability to spot trends. Humans usually imagine a future that's only slightly different from the present. Even great works of science fiction fail to foresee what the world will be like in the not-too-distant future. For example, the *Foundation Trilogy* by Isaac Asimov is set in a time when humans have spread across the galaxy and inhabit thousands of planets. Book One, published in 1951, focuses on a band of scientists who settle a planet at a far edge of the galaxy to create a great encyclopedia containing humanity's collective knowledge to shorten the coming of a new dark age. They have to do this because while they may have spaceships, they don't have the internet or Google.

All they have are big, fat, heavy encyclopedia volumes. Like the ones you donated to your local library (or threw out) decades ago.

EXPONENTIAL GROWTH MAKES
TRENDSPOTTING PROBLEMATIC

Trends are hard to spot in the early stages because they don't produce significant change at first. They tend to start small and grow incrementally.

But as growth builds on growth, fundamental change breaks through. To understand this, we must recognize how linear growth (how our brains work) and exponential growth (how significant changes happen) differ.

ALLIE AND TABATHA

Allie, a precocious ten-year-old, thinks she should get an allowance. She puts together a presentation for her parents proposing $10 per month in return for walking the dog, cleaning her room, and going to bed on time without complaint. She requests an annual increase of $1 per year so that she'd get $11 per month at age eleven and $12 per month when she's twelve, and so on. Her parents think her proposal is excellent and that an allowance of $10 per month that increases by $1 per year is reasonable, so they agree.

Allie tells her best friend Tabatha about her allowance deal and suggests she talk to her parents about a similar arrangement. Tabatha loves the idea. Just like Allie's parents, Tabatha's agree to $10 per month. But Tabatha tweaks her proposal. She suggests that her monthly allowance should increase by 10 percent each year rather than $1. Her parents realize that means that next year they'll pay her $11 per month and just a wee bit over $12 per month the following year. That seems reasonable, so they agree.

Allie's and Tabatha's allowance arrangements sound similar, but they're not. Allie's allowance will grow linearly; Tabatha's allowance will grow exponentially. Linear growth is where the rate of increase is a constant independent of previous growth, and it results in steady rises. With exponential growth, the rate of increase is proportional to what is being grown—meaning the increase depends not simply on the original base but also on all past growth. This causes growth to increase faster and faster because what is being measured gets larger.

Table 7.1 depicts what the girls' monthly allowance amounts look like up to age eighteen.

**ALLIE'S AND TABATHA'S MONTHLY
ALLOWANCE PROPOSAL**

Age	Allie Allowance (Linear Growth)	Tabatha Allowance (Exponential Growth)
10	$10.00	$10.00
11	$11.00	$11.00
12	$12.00	$12.10
13	$13.00	$13.31
14	$14.00	$14.64
15	$15.00	$16.11
16	$16.00	$17.72
17	$17.00	$19.49
18	$18.00	$21.47

TABLE 7.1

At first, the difference between the two allowances isn't significant; they are the same at eleven and only differ by $0.10 at twelve and $0.31 at thirteen. But by age eighteen, Tabatha's parents are shelling out $3.44 more per month than Allie's parents—or about 19 percent more, a material difference. By twenty-nine, Tabatha's allowance will be double Allie's, and at age seventy (presuming their parents are still alive and for whatever reason still giving their now elderly daughters allowances), Tabatha is raking in over $3,000 per month while Allie is making do with $70. Figure 7.2 illustrates the differences.

Add time, and exponential growth becomes especially potent as growth on top of growth generates significant change. A key feature of exponential growth is that it seems to start gradually and then accelerates over time. Unfortunately, humans generally are linear thinkers and don't easily grasp how exponential growth can create extraordinary change. Conceptually, we have a hard time envisioning the second half of the chessboard—the place where exponential growth begins to change everything.

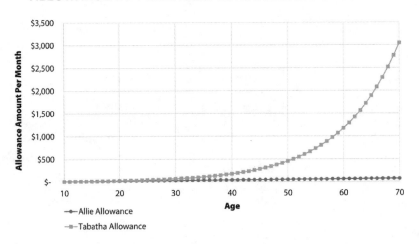

ALLOWANCE DIFFERENCES: LINEAR VS. EXPONENTIAL

FIGURE 7.2

THE SECOND HALF OF THE CHESSBOARD

Futurist Ray Kurzweil coined the phrase the "second half of the chessboard" referencing a fable about the invention of chess.[3] According to the legend, the wise man who invented chess presented the game to his king, who was so enthralled that he asked the man to name his reward. The inventor said that he'd like an amount of wheat equal to the number of grains derived by following a simple rule: one grain on the first square of the chessboard, two on the second, four on the third, and so on until square sixty-four. The king, thinking, *What's a few grains of wheat?*, agrees.

Of course, the king thinks like a human and doesn't understand that continued doubling results in two billion grains of wheat in the chessboard's thirty-second square, and the sixty-fourth square will have 9.2 quintillion grains of wheat (or 9,223,372,036,854,780,000), which is two billion times more than the first thirty-two squares, or the first half of the chessboard. All sixty-four squares taken together add up to more than 18 quintillion grains of wheat, or about 1,700 times more than what the whole world produces now.

FOLDING PAPER

While the king is swearing at his chessboard, ask yourself this: How thick would a sheet of paper be if you could fold it in half fifty times?[4] Thinking about the second half of the chessboard concept, I guessed ten miles, which I thought was super thick, but it turns out that my estimate fell ridiculously short.

A sheet of paper is about 0.1 millimeters thick, so at ten folds it would have 1,024 layers and be four inches thick. Twenty folds give you 1,048,576 layers, which is 344 feet (a little over half the height of Saint Louis's Gateway Arch). Thirty folds are 1,073,741,874 layers, which is about sixty-seven miles thick, which is ten times higher than commercial airliners fly. Forty folds is 1,099,510,000,000 layers, which is almost 70,000 miles, or almost one-third of the way to the moon. See where we're going here? Fifty folds is 1,259,000,000,000,000 layers, nearly seventy million miles, which is almost the distance from Earth to the sun. So, my guess of ten miles fell just a bit short. Repeated doubling, which is a type of exponential growth, is an explosive process and one for which our minds are ill-equipped.

HOW TO THINK ABOUT EXPONENTIAL GROWTH— BELOW-THE-WATERLINE THINKING

If asked to name the tallest mountain on Earth, most people would say Mount Everest. At 29,035 feet above sea level, it is the *highest*. But technically, it isn't the *tallest* (which is the distance from base to peak). That would be Hawaii's Mauna Kea. It's only 13,803 feet above sea level (less than half Everest's height), but the base of the mountain extends almost 20,000 feet below the water. So, in total, Mauna Kea is 33,500 feet tall—nearly a mile taller than Everest.

The idea that a lot can be going on below the waterline is a good analogy for thinking about exponential growth. Growth on growth can happen without attracting attention, and then, suddenly, everything changes massively.

Let's say you run a company called Oak Inc., which makes widgets. Oak Inc. is the market leader and sells about five million widgets a month. As Oak's CEO, you keep abreast of industry trends, trying to spot any up-and-coming widget competitors. However, given your size, and the fact that there are only so many hours in the day, you'll only pay attention to a potential competitor when it produces 10 percent of the widgets you do, or 500,000 widgets. That's your waterline.

Now Acorn Inc. (see what I did here?) is a new company making widgets using a new technology that results in better widgets for less money. At first, they only produce a few prototypes. Then after some successful trade shows, they sell one widget the first month, two the second, four the third, and continue to double their sales each month. In month twenty, a bit over a year and a half after their first sale, the repeated doubling results in Acorn selling 524,288 widgets. At this point, you and the other Oak executives are wondering where they came from. You're concerned, but figure they sell only about 10 percent of what you do, so you're not too concerned. But, unfortunately for Oak, Acorn has built a better mousetrap, and its sales continue to double monthly:

Month 21:	1,048,576
Month 22:	2,097,152
Month 23:	4,194,304
Month 24:	8,388,608
Month 25:	16,777,216

Now Acorn has moved from selling 10 percent of what you do to tripling your monthly sales in just five months. It's as if Acorn came from nowhere. But Acorn didn't come from nowhere. It's been growing for two years. You didn't notice until Acorn broke the waterline of 500,000 units, at which point it's too late for your mighty Oak.

Figure 7.3 shows Acorn's growth for the first twenty months—up to the waterline of 500,000 widget sales. Note how flat it looks up to month sixteen.

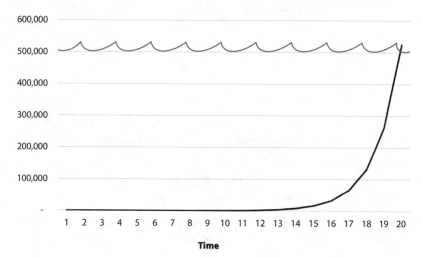

ACORN INC.'S EXPONENTIAL GROWTH: FIRST 20 MONTHS

FIGURE 7.3

Figure 7.4 projects the growth out five more months and shows Acorn's sales blowing way past the waterline. Again, due to the scale of increase of the last few doublings, prior exponential growth looks flat until about month twenty.

ACORN INC.'S EXPONENTIAL GROWTH: FIRST 25 MONTHS

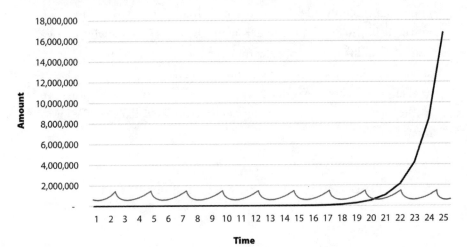

FIGURE 7.4

The previous example of the chessboard, folding paper, and Acorn's growth all assumed the growth rate as doubling. But the effects of exponential growth don't require doubling. Exponential growth at 50 percent, 20 percent—or as we saw in the example of Allie's and Tabatha's allowances—even 10 percent, can be potent.

The key concept of below-the-waterline thinking is that things that grow exponentially don't move the needle early on but then seemingly produce huge effects as they crest the waterline.

Even industry experts who follow trends closely miss how quickly change occurs when underlying growth is exponential. For example, on March 1, 2020, the US had sixty-nine confirmed cases of COVID-19. By March 15th the number of cases had jumped to 2,951, a huge increase that demonstrated that infections were growing exponentially. Over the following two days—March 16 and 17—infectious disease experts were surveyed about the number of reported cases the US would have as of March 29, not quite two weeks in the future. The average prediction was 20,000 cases, a massive 6.7 times increase.

But the reality was much more dire. On March 29, the US had nearly 125,000 cases or an increase of forty-two times. Exponential growth is hard for everyone.

ALL SORTS OF THINGS GROW EXPONENTIALLY

Not all growth is exponential, but new business models, technologies, and ideas that deliver significant change do grow exponentially and do so at high rates of increase. Take Netflix.

You might remember that Netflix began as a DVD-by-mail service. In their 2004 annual report, Netflix described its business as follows:

> We are the largest online movie rental subscription service providing more than 2,600,000 subscribers access to a comprehensive library of more than 35,000 movie, television and other filmed entertainment titles. Our standard subscription plan allows subscribers to have up to three titles out at the same time with no due dates, late fees or shipping charges for $17.99 per month. In addition to our standard plan, we offer other service plans with different price points that allow subscribers to keep either fewer or more titles at the same time. Subscribers select titles at our Web site aided by our proprietary recommendation service, receive them on DVD by U.S. mail and return them to us at their convenience using our prepaid mailers. After a title has been returned, we mail the next available title in a subscriber's queue.

That was in 2004, which was the same year my wife and I went to Mexico for our tenth wedding anniversary. On our way back I ended up in a long customs line next to some store managers from Blockbuster Video returning from a corporate retreat. I was a Netflix subscriber and was curious about how they saw the video rental landscape.

I asked, "Are you concerned about the rise of Netflix and its DVD-by-mail service?"

They were not.

"People like to come into our stores and browse titles and get advice from our employees," one said. "You can't recreate that experience by mail. Plus, people don't want to wait a few days to get their movies by mail. They want to watch what they want the same day."

That made sense to me. I liked going to Blockbuster, browsing movies, and getting suggestions from them or even other customers. And it was nice to watch it immediately, not a few days later when the DVD came in the mail. Yet, I wondered if they didn't have a blind spot because I also liked using the Netflix service with its massive catalog of movies and the algorithmic recommendations of what I might like based on my past rentals. Not to mention no late fees.

We now know Netflix as a streaming service and content creator, but it wasn't until 2007, when it was ten years old, that it launched its streaming service. In its 2007 annual report, Netflix revealed that building their DVD rental subscriber base was a means to an end: "We believe . . . that by growing a large DVD subscription business, we will be well-positioned to transition our subscribers and our business to internet-based delivery of content." Netflix became the leading subscription video streaming platform in the world.

Blockbuster and other brick-and-mortar video rental companies didn't see it coming. The number of Netflix subscribers was tiny compared to in-store video customers in the early 2000s. Just 2.6 million subscribers in 2004? That was nothing to Blockbuster. But by 2012, Netflix and other on-demand services drove Blockbuster into bankruptcy. From 2000 to 2010, Netflix enjoyed nearly 50 percent annualized subscriber growth and has sustained massive growth up through the end of 2021. (In 2022, it seems as if the growth trajectory may be heading in a different direction, which sometimes happens with trends—as discussed in the next section.)

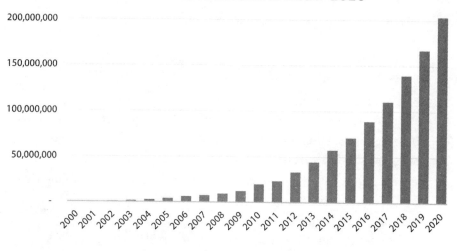

FIGURE 7.5

Does this hockey stick curve look familiar? Remember Tabatha's allowance and Acorn's widget sales growth.

■ VENMO

Venmo and other electronic payment services such as PayPal, Square, and Apple Pay are transforming both person-to-person and business-to-consumer payment transactions. Founded in 2009, Venmo is one of the leading platforms individuals use to send payments to each other. I use Venmo to pay my landscaping company and the woman who cuts my hair, give my children money, and to split the costs of dinners with friends. I use Apple Pay when I buy groceries, grab a coffee at my local shop, and buy lunch at my favorite deli. Not only do I seldom write checks, I find I'm pulling a credit or debit card out of my wallet less and less.

As of 2021, over fifty million people in the United States use Venmo. During the first few years of its life, Venmo saw its total payment volume increase an astounding *30 percent per month*. Talk about growth on growth! Its more recent growth is still strong, growing at an 83 percent compound clip from 2014 through 2020. Venmo's astonishing growth left major banks flat-footed and playing catch up.

■ SOLAR POWER

Sometimes it's an exponential decline and not growth that spurs change. Consider solar power. In 1977, the price of solar averaged $76 per watt. By 2020, the cost had declined to less than $0.10 per watt, and solar is now a cheaper power source than fossil fuels. Given the affordable nature of solar power, the forces of capitalism will undoubtedly lead to a material shift in how our energy is produced.[5]

Exponential change is so hard to wrap our heads around that even industry experts underestimate the pace of transformation that we've seen in the renewable energy space. For example, energy experts surveyed in 2014 expected that the cost of solar would drop by about 10 percent by 2020, an estimate that was way below the actual decline of 50 percent.[6]

■ OTHER EXAMPLES OF EXPONENTIAL GROWTH

Other examples of exponential growth abound:

- Adoption of the internet and ownership of mobile phones both followed exponential growth patterns.
- Facebook grew its monthly users from 1 million to 845 million between 2004 and 2011—a 162 percent annual growth rate, and which put MySpace and Friendster out of business.
- The first Uber ride was taken on July 5, 2012. Three and a half years later, Uber hit the one billion ride milestone, five billion rides just eighteen months later, and ten billion a year after that.[7]
- We're in the early stages of an exponentially growing trend: electric vehicles. EVs only made up about 5 percent of new vehicle sales

in the US and 10 percent in Europe as of late 2021. But sales are growing exponentially, so overnight, it may soon seem like EVs are everywhere if the exponential growth continues.

US ELECTRIC VEHICLE SALES

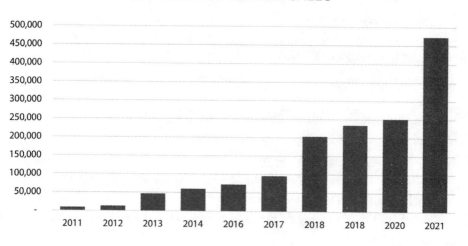

FIGURE 7.6⁸

TRENDS DON'T ALWAYS TURN OUT AS IMAGINED

Well-established trends seem like they'll go on forever, but they don't; innovation, new ideas, and technology alter the path of established trends and create new ones.

THE MALTHUSIAN CATASTROPHE

Thomas Malthus was an eighteenth-century philosopher and economist. In 1798, he published his famous work, "An Essay on the Principle of Population." He observed that population growth increased exponentially while food production grew linearly. Based on these trends, he predicted

that population would outgrow food supply in the not-too-distant future
and lead to famine, disease, war, and catastrophe. He dourly noted that
"the power of population is so superior to the power of the earth to produce subsistence for man, that premature death must in some shape or
other visit the human race."[9]

At the time of Malthus's prediction, agricultural technology hadn't progressed much for centuries. Farming required considerable human labor
with hoes, scythes, and sickles. Oxen and horses pulled wooden plows.

When Malthus made his prediction, he didn't foresee Industrial
Revolution innovations like the iron plow, canning, the development
of commercial fertilizers, Mendelian advances in crop and livestock
breeding, steam and later gas-powered tractors, and so on. These technologies increased crop and livestock yields while reducing the human
labor required. Figure 7.7 shows GDP growth in the UK from 1270 to
2016 and illustrates how economic growth was stagnant until the Industrial Revolution. Thus, it's hard to blame Malthus for taking established
trends and extrapolating them into the future to make his predictions.

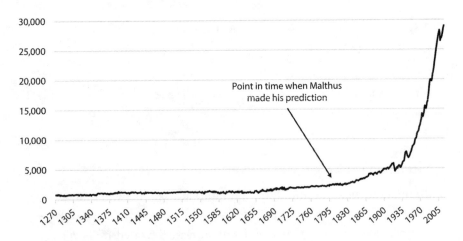

REAL GDP PER CAPITA IN THE UK 1270–2016

FIGURE 7.7[10]

Malthus's catastrophe has yet to materialize, but feeding a world headed to a population of nine billion (while adding a climate crisis) will be—to put it mildly—a challenge, and population growth could very well outstrip food supply in the future. Malthus may ultimately be proven correct, albeit hundreds of years later. Time will tell.

But the fundamental lesson of the failure of Malthus's predictions up to now is that firmly established trends, even longstanding and seemingly durable ones, can and do change.

THE RISING (AND SETTING) SUN

The 1988 movie *Die Hard* starring Bruce Willis depicts a gang of thieves, who, posing as terrorists, seize a skyscraper in Los Angeles and take its occupants hostage. The building is the headquarters to the Nakatomi Corporation, a fictional Japanese conglomerate. The terrorists' goal is to steal $640 million in untraceable bearer bonds. In 1988, it made perfect sense that the movie would depict a company with a massive stash of cash as Japanese. At that time, Japanese cars were better made than American cars and Japanese companies like Sony, Sharp, and Panasonic dominated consumer electronics. Floundering US businesses made pilgrimages to Japan to learn the secrets of Japanese quality assurance and "just-in-time manufacturing" techniques.

Japan's stock market reflected its economic might, as illustrated in Figure 7.8 (which looks like Acorn's exponential growth).

Japanese companies and billionaires used their cash to purchase American companies and real estate. In the late 1980s, Japanese money bought the Pebble Beach golf resort, the Mobil Building in Manhattan, the Biltmore Hotel in Los Angeles, and Rockefeller Center.[11] Japanese enterprises also snapped up iconic American companies like Firestone and Columbia Pictures. All this made it seem as if Japan was taking over the entire US economy, and it appeared to be on course to become the world's predominant economic power.

JAPAN'S NIKKEI 225 STOCK MARKET INDEX 1950–1989

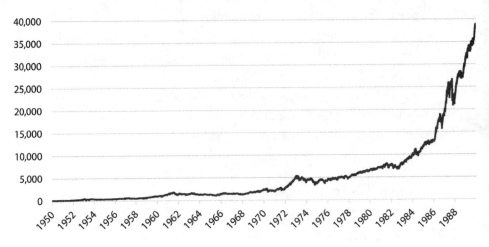

FIGURE 7.8[12]

Then in the early 1990s, the trend of Japan's rising dominance sharply reversed. Its economy overheated and sparked inflation. In response, the Japanese Central Bank raised interest rates and kept raising them. High rates tanked their economy and the stock market. Between its 1989 peak and early 2009, Japan's stock market lost 80 percent of its value and has yet to regain its high-water mark.

Japan's importance to the world economy has taken a back seat to China's, which is now America's primary economic rival. Some look at China's growth and follow the trend line to predict when it will surpass that of the United States.

But before you go long on China, remember that a rising sun also sets.

THE FRACKING REVOLUTION

Until the mid-2000s, the US had been one of the world's biggest importers of natural gas. In 2003, 15 percent of the US demand for natural gas was met by net imports of over three trillion cubic feet of natural gas, nearly all from Canada. In that same year, Houston-based Cheniere Energy Partners began constructing a massive liquefied natural gas (LNG) terminal in Sabine Pass, Louisiana. This terminal, the first of its kind in the US, would receive natural gas imports from overseas from specialized LNG transport ships. Around the time of the terminal's completion in 2008, Cheniere stated in its annual report that the business rationale of the import terminal was based "on the belief that LNG [imports] can be produced and delivered at a lower cost than the cost to produce some domestic supplies of natural gas or other alternative energy sources." Given the 50+ year history of the US as a substantial net importer of natural gas, constructing an import terminal made total sense.

In 2002, about the time Cheniere was raising capital for its Sabine Pass import terminal, Oklahoma-based Devon Energy acquired a small oil company called Mitchell Energy for $3.5 billion. For decades, Mitchell Energy, led by its founder and CEO George Mitchell, sought an economical method of fracturing porous rock to access oil and gas held within it. While it had been known for 150 years that oil and gas could be extracted from shale, existing methods were uneconomical. In 1998, Mitchell cracked the code (as well as the shale rock) by using a technique known as hydraulic fracturing (or "fracking"), which used large amounts of water, sand, and chemicals, delivered at high pressure to extract the oil and gas. The CEO of Devon Energy later said, "At that time, absolutely no one believed that shale drilling worked, other than Mitchell and us."[13]

This new method of extracting oil and gas from shale rock, combined with new horizontal drilling methods, upended oil and gas production. In 2017, the US went from a net importer of natural gas to a net exporter.

Within a few years after completing the Sabine Pass import terminal, demand for LNG imports crumbled due to substantial new domestic supply from shale fields in North Dakota, Pennsylvania, Oklahoma, and Texas. In 2012, Cheniere changed course to profit from the US being an exporter of gas and began constructing natural gas export terminals at Sabine Pass at the cost of $5 billion.

Fracking and horizontal drilling have had the same effect on oil production as it has on natural gas. Like natural gas, oil production in the US had been on a downward trend for decades before the fracking revolution. Then in the mid-2000s, fracking and horizontal drilling reversed the downward trend (see Figure 7.9).

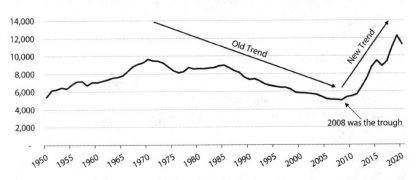

**US FIELD PRODUCTION OF CRUDE OIL
(THOUSAND BARRELS PER DAY) 1950–2020**

FIGURE 7.9: OIL PRODUCTION CHANGING TREND

THE GREAT HORSE MANURE CRISIS

The Industrial Revolution spurred an urbanization movement as new factories created jobs and economic growth that drew workers from rural areas and other countries. For instance, in 1850, New York City had 590,000 residents, and by 1900 there were 3.8 million New Yorkers.[14] Likewise, London's population grew from 2.6 million to 6.5 million during that same period.[15]

The booming growth of cities generated many issues including air pollution, lack of trash disposal and sanitation, plus rampant disease from having so many people packed together. Factory laborers, many of them immigrants, commonly lived in horrible conditions in slum tenements that were crowded and dark. (I highly recommend visiting New York's Tenement Museum for insight into those harsh living conditions.)

Horses primarily powered the transportation of people and freight until the early 1900s. People traveled in carriages, buses, and streetcars on rails, all drawn by horses. Goods and materials moved around cities by horse-drawn wagons. So as a city's human population boomed, so did its horse population. Around the turn of the century, an estimated 170,000 to 200,000 horses lived in New York City.[16]

All those horses generated a lot of waste—a single horse produces between twenty to thirty pounds of manure and about two liters of urine a day. That translated into New York's 200,000 horses generating about five million pounds of manure a day along with about 100,000 gallons of urine. And feeding all those horses was problematic because an average horse eats about ten to twenty pounds of hay per day. Large swaths of farmland around major cities were devoted to producing hay and oats to feed horses. As the number of horses needed for transportation increased, so did the number of the horses required to transport horse feed into the cities and move manure out of the cities, creating a circular problem.

Disposal efforts couldn't keep up with the generation of manure. Manure caked streets in major cities, and "when it rained, the streets turned to muck. And when it was dry, wind whipped up the manure dust and choked the citizenry."[17] In 1894, the *Times* of London predicted, "In 50 years, every street in London will be buried under nine feet of manure." Similarly, one New York commentator "estimated that unabated, horse droppings would rise to the level of third-story Manhattan windows by 1930."[18]

The smell and overall grossness weren't even the most significant problems; the massive amounts of manure and urine attracted insects that spread disease, creating a health crisis.

The manure problem seemed intractable. "When the world's first international urban-planning conference was held in 1898, it was dominated by discussion of the manure situation. Unable to agree upon any solutions— or to imagine cities without horses—the delegates broke up the meeting, which had been scheduled to last a week and a half, after just three days."[19] The horse manure crisis was the biggest threat to continued urban growth and had no obvious solution.

But then, in the early 1900s, the manure problem was solved not by discovering better methods of cleaning up after horses but by replacing horses as a means of transportation. By 1912, there were more automobiles in New York than horses; in 1917, the last horse-drawn streetcar was retired, and by 1930—the year that three stories of manure were predicted—horses had been wholly replaced.

The phrase "The Great Horse Manure Crisis" is now used as a shorthand reference to how seemingly insurmountable problems can be rendered moot by technological advancements, even if the primary purpose of the technology wasn't to solve that particular problem.

STEIN'S LAW

Ben Stein may be best known as the tedious teacher in *Ferris Bueller's Day Off* and as host of the game show "Win Ben Stein's Money." What's less known about Stein is that his father, Herbert Stein, was a prominent and respected economist who chaired President Nixon's economic council of advisors.

Herbert Stein coined what has come to be known as Stein's law, which simply states: "If something cannot go on forever, it will stop." Stein's law may appear reductive, but it tells us that when we see a trend that isn't sustainable, it isn't. Trends that seem as though they will continue forever just won't. They never do. So, the Roman Empire fell; Moore's law, proposed in 1965, predicted that computer processor speeds would double every eighteen months but has begun to fail,[20] and the US won't always be the world's dominant power.

And because trends end, health-care costs—which, if they continue to rise, will soon account for over half the US economy—will decline.

Stein's law doesn't tell you when a trend will stop; it states that if it can't go on forever, it will stop at some point. This is incredibly useful to keep in mind, especially when a trend that confronts us seems to keep going and going and going. That trends don't go on forever isn't necessarily a bad thing because their demise is often the result of new ideas, innovation, and technology.

Notably, Stein's law has two corollaries concerning things that can't go on forever:

- It will go on longer than we think (known as Davies' Corollary).
- It will stop even if nobody does anything to stop it.

IT'S DIFFICULT TO FIND A SUCCESSFUL NEEDLE IN A HAYSTACK OF COMPETITORS

A challenge of trends is that even when you spot one early and it persists, it's difficult to make money investing in the trend due to the competitive nature of early industries and technologies.

PICKING WINNERS: THE AUTO INDUSTRY

In retrospect, the triumph of the automobile appears inevitable, but in 1900, the future of the car was anything but certain. It was a novelty at the turn of the twentieth century; there were only 0.11 cars per thousand people compared with about fifty non–farm horses per thousand people.[21] There were few paved roads and no gas pump infrastructure. Cars were prone to break down. And they were expensive; in the early 1900s, cars cost about $850 while a horse and buggy could be had for $50.[22] Most people believed that automobiles would never amount to more than an indulgence for the wealthy.

Let's say you were alive in 1900 and an early version of a venture capitalist. You decide that the horseless carriage is an exciting trend and has legs (pun intended). Even though there are myriad challenges, you decide to invest in automobiles (see Figure 7.10).

Of course, you're right. The inflection point was 1914. That year, the number of horses peaked and began to decline, while the number of cars started increasing rapidly. By 1925, the number of vehicles had grown by 1,200 percent, and they surpassed the number of horses.

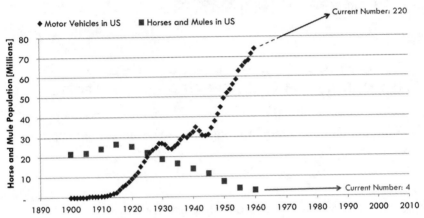

MOTOR VEHICLE REGISTRATION AND NUMBER OF HORSES AND MULES IN THE US

Source: ARK Investment Management LLC, Bureau of Transportation Statistics, Bloomberg Intelligence, EVvolumes.com, IDC

FIGURE 7.10[23]

The question remains, however, which car company would you invest in during the early 1900s? The top US automobile manufacturers in 1902 were:

- Locomobile
- Oldsmobile
- Rambler
- White
- Knox
- Packard
- Stanley Automobile
- Union

In hindsight, we know that Oldsmobile survived and became part of General Motors, so that would have been a good company to invest in. But Locomobile? Stanley? Union? All long-term busts.

A further confounding variable to investing in the early automobile industry was choosing which technology platform would power cars. In 1900, most car engines weren't gasoline-powered internal combustion engines; the leading technologies were steam and electricity. (It's fun to see electric vehicles making a comeback more than one hundred years later. Will steam also make a comeback? LOL.)

It would have been tough to pick a winner in the early 1900s. Between 1899 and 1919, 775 car companies entered the industry, and during that same twenty-year period, 600 went out of business. Only seven companies or brands that still exist today were formed before 1920: Buick, Cadillac, Chevrolet, GMC, Dodge, Ford, and Lincoln.[24]

The automobile industry isn't unique. It's common for an industry to consolidate as it matures. Over the years, there have been over five hundred companies that made televisions. Today, just ten manufacturers produce 75 percent of all TV sets globally.[25] And there have been over a hundred manufacturers of mobile phones, yet as of 2021, just two mobile phone manufacturers, Apple and Samsung, have 78 percent of the US mobile phone market.[26] In 1992, Motorola had a nearly 50 percent share in the United States. By March of 2021, it had 4 percent.

THE EARLY INTERNET ERA

In 1995, I visited my brother, who was attending law school at the University of Virginia. As he showed me around the school, he said, "Let's go to the computer lab. I have something to show you that will blow your mind."

He logged into a computer, pulled up a program called Netscape, and showed me the internet for the first time. Yes, mind blown. Of course, I'd heard of the internet or the "World Wide Web," but using it for the first time still shocked me.

Was I living under a rock? No. In 1995 there were only thirty-five million internet users worldwide—just 0.6 percent of the world population. And even seeing it, it was impossible for me to imagine what it would grow into and how it would change all our lives. (Shopping for dog food! Ability to look up ages and heights of celebrities! Cat videos!)

Let's play a mental game. Suppose you could travel back to 1995 for a day with $10,000 and the opportunity to buy stock in internet companies. Off the top of your head, which ones would you buy? You can't buy Google because it didn't exist. Neither did Facebook, nor Netflix. Microsoft and Apple would have been good bets, but both would have provided a very wild ride, and you could say they aren't really internet companies.

According to venture capital firm Kleiner Perkins, the top ten most valuable internet companies in 1995 were:

1. Netscape
2. Apple
3. AxelSpringer
4. RentPath
5. Web.com
6. PSINet
7. Netcom On-line
8. IAC/Interactive
9. Copart
10. Wavo Corporation[27]

Apple obviously sticks out, but between 1995 and 1997 it lost two-thirds of its value and seemed headed for the large trash heap of 1990s tech companies.

Remember searching the internet in the 1990s? You'd open your web browser and then decide which search engine to use. Maybe you'd pick Lycos, MSN, or Alta Vista. Or perhaps it would be Yahoo!, Dogpile, Inktomi, or

Ask Jeeves. And when you ran a query using one search engine, you'd rerun it on another one because it would produce different results. Then along came Larry Page and Sergey Brin, two friends who met at Stanford. Their insight was that the number of links to and from a website was a marker of the site's quality and relevance. So, they created algorithms that focused on the quality of search results. Their search engine company, Google, was formed in 1998 and was the twenty-first search engine. Its IPO wasn't until 2004. Investments in earlier search engines were not profitable investments over the long-term. That Google was the twenty-first search engine is important to keep in mind when considering investing in early industry leaders.

EARLY MOVERS AND FAST FOLLOWERS

The early movers in a new industry usually don't end up the winners. Before Facebook and Twitter, social media meant MySpace and Friendster. Apple's iPod wasn't the first mp3 player, and the iPhone wasn't the first smartphone, yet Apple came to dominate both markets. Netscape, the first browser, had 90 percent of the market, was flattened by Microsoft's Internet Explorer, which peaked at 95 percent market share in 2004, which, in turn, was surpassed by Google Chrome, now the browser of choice for 70 percent of people.[28]

Companies that are fast followers tend to end up with the greatest market share. Research out of the University of Southern California found that market pioneers fail about half the time, and as a group, they only average 7 percent of the long-term market share. On average, the companies that end up dominating young industries enter the market thirteen years after the pioneers.[29] Why do followers often beat the early movers? Some experts believe it's because followers don't have to invest in R&D (the product has already been developed and tested by the early movers) and assume less risk because the product has already proved itself in the market.

The creative destruction that tore through the automobile and internet industries is typical in the evolution of new technologies. The phrase *creative destruction* refers to the "incessant product and process innovation by which new production units replace outdated ones."[30] It leads to the rise and fall of companies, both in young and mature industries, but with a greater rate in developing industries as innovation rules the day.

Creative destruction is a corollary to the idea that trends are difficult to spot early. Once a trend is established, it becomes widely known; once it's widely known, there are many companies and investors competing to take advantage of the trend. At that point, the competition results in higher company valuations and reduces the likelihood of investors making money off the trend. Several promising technology-driven trends that have emerged recently illustrate this: the sharing economy, artificial intelligence, genetic engineering (CRISPR), blockchain, and autonomous transportation, to name a few. As their promise becomes accepted, more and more companies compete for dominance. For example, Google has been a significant player in developing an autonomous car, but now Uber, Apple, Tesla, GM, Ford, and others have entered the ranks. Who will be the winner(s) of the autonomous car war? At this point, it's difficult to predict.

THE MENTAL MODELS AND HOW TO APPLY THEM

Profitably investing in trends is challenging:

- It's hard to spot trends early, partially due to the challenges of comprehending the nature of exponential growth.

- Established trends can change course rapidly as new competitors and technologies upend trends. Remember the Malthus catastrophe.

- It's hard to pick winners. As new technologies create new industries, many companies enter, and most fail. Early pioneers usually aren't the long-term winners. Instead, fast followers often are the most successful.

This doesn't mean that you should never invest in trends. Instead, approach them with your eyes wide open. Here's how you can take advantage of trends that makes sense:

1. Be skeptical. That will help you resist the urge to jump on the new thing.

2. Diversify. As tempting as it is to go all in on one promising company, remember that it's hard to pick winners early. If you want to invest in a trend, using a thematic ETF tracking an index, a commodity, or a bunch of funds is an excellent way to hop on a trend in a diversified manner, such as ETFs that focus on genomics, healthcare innovation, fintech, robotics, cybersecurity, clean energy, or blockchain, to name a few.

3. Use venture capital or specialty funds. Unless you have information or knowledge that gives you an advantage in an early industry or trend, it's wise to use venture capital funds or specialty managers to identify trends and pick the potential winning companies. Venture capitalists develop expertise and information networks to invest in trends and early industry profitably. Investing through a diversified fund may not seem as fun as picking individual winners but will significantly increase your chance of turning a profit. The sad truth is that it's unlikely that your trendspotting will be profitable (unless you get awfully lucky). That's because if you know about a burgeoning trend, so do other investors.

Finally, don't fret about missing out on a new trend. You probably have exposure to whatever trend you want to invest in already. A diversified portfolio of public stocks includes companies that are taking advantage of trends. For example, many of the oil and energy companies that are common in diversified portfolios are investing heavily in alternative energy. If you own Amazon, you also own its investments in cloud infrastructure. Similarly, if you own Google or Apple, you're invested in the promise of autonomous vehicles. Samsung and Panasonic provide investments in emerging battery technology. Most established public companies are constantly scanning the horizons looking for trends that may affect their industries.

CHAPTER 8

THE TRIVIAL MANY
VERSUS THE VITAL FEW

Our world is dominated by the extreme, the unknown, and the very improbable
(improbable according to our current knowledge)—and all the while we spend our time
engaged in small talk, focusing on the known, and the repeated.

—NASSIM TALEB, *THE BLACK SWAN*

Years ago, I interviewed a young analyst to fill an investment position at our firm. His resume said that he'd played college basketball at a power-house basketball school, so I expected him to be tall. But as he got out of his seat to shake hands, I realized that *tall* didn't adequately describe this guy—adjectives like *towering* and *colossal* popped into my mind. He was 7'2", and I'd never met anybody so tall. I knew a few people who were around 6'8"—which is very tall—but 7'2" is six inches taller than that. Wow.

Later that evening, I went to a concert with about 1,000 people (the band was Modest Mouse). As I waited for the show to start, I noted that nobody in the audience was anywhere near seven feet tall. Most everyone seemed to be around average height, with the tallest person about 6'5".

If the man I'd interviewed earlier had walked into the concert, everyone would have gawked at him, but the *average* height of the crowd would have been raised only a smidge, a mere 0.01"—unnoticeable.

As I looked around at the other concertgoers, I recognized a twenty-something young woman from a family who had billions of dollars of wealth. It struck me that by walking into the concert venue, she massively changed the average wealth of the concertgoers. If the heiress was worth $1 billion, and the other people at the show had a total net worth of about $100,000 each (a generous estimate for the young hipsters in atten-dance), she would raise the average wealth in the room by ten times—from $100,000 to $1 million—a huge difference that is certainly noticeable.

Both the analyst and heiress were outliers; one extremely tall, the other extremely rich. However, the nature of their extremeness couldn't have been more different. The analyst, while tall, was only 25 percent taller than the average American adult male. But the heiress's wealth was orders of magnitude greater than the norm. The median house-hold in the United States has about $125,000 of wealth, 8,000 times less than the heiress's $1 billion. To put it in perspective, if height were distributed like wealth, an outlier of the heiress's proportion would be 46,000 feet tall.

This is the difference between data following *a bell curve*, like height, and data following a *power law distribution*, such as wealth. Understanding the difference between the two is crucial to being an educated consumer of investment advice. (Buckle up now because we're about to get into statis-tics. It's unavoidable and, as you'll see, critical. And more interesting than you might expect.)

BELL CURVES EVERYWHERE

The first science requiring precise measurement was astronomy. After the invention of the telescope in the early seventeenth century, astron-omers began charting the movement of planets and stars to unravel the mysteries of the Universe. However, accurate measurements were hard to do, as imperfections in telescope lenses, uneven mounting, varying atmospheric conditions, and user error all interfered. Galileo was the first to observe that the distribution of these telescope observation errors followed a pattern: (1) errors were distributed symmetrically around the actual value, and (2) there were many more small errors than large ones.

What Galileo had described is now known variously as the *bell curve distribution* or *normal distribution.*

Fast forward to the mid-1800s when a Belgian astronomer and mathematician named Adolphe Quetelet came across a seemingly mundane data set published in a medical journal: the chest circumferences of 5,738 Scottish soldiers. While the data was unremarkable, what Quetelet did with it was not. He added all the chest sizes together and divided that sum by the number of soldiers (a time-consuming exercise without a calculator). This gave him an average chest size of thirty-nine and three-quarter inches—the first known average of a human feature.

Sifting through the data, Quetelet noted that most chest sizes were pretty close to average, and variations from the average become rarer the greater the deviation. For instance, a chest size of forty-one inches (1.25" bigger than average) was common among the Scottish soldiers—934 out of 5,738—while a chest size of forty-eight inches (about eight inches larger) was rare—only one soldier had such a massive chest. Plotting the chest sizes in a histogram (similar to a bar graph) produced the now-familiar bell curve shape (see Figure 8.1).

Calculating the average chest size led Quetelet to conclude that it would be possible to construct an average-man prototype. He loved this idea, so he sought out data on human attributes and calculated average heights, weights, complexions, education, and age of death to determine what he imagined to be the whole of the average man.

Quetelet's work opened the floodgates, and scientists started looking for bell curves everywhere. And they found them. In the distributions of human height, weight, blood pressure, shoe size, limb length, and intelligence, as well as in distribution of size of animals of the same species.

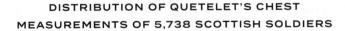

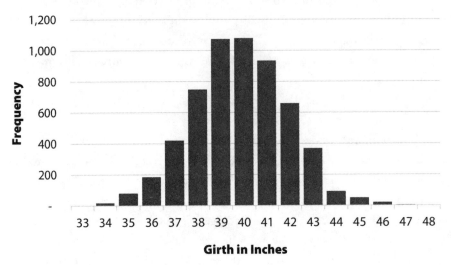

FIGURE 8.1

When data fits a bell curve distribution, mathematics defines the extent to which we can expect differences from the average through a concept called *standard deviation*. With a normally shaped bell curve, 68 percent of observations will fall within one standard deviation above and below the average, 95 percent will fall within two standard deviations, and 99.73 percent will be within three standard deviations. As you move out to higher and higher standard deviations, expected occurrences become infinitesimally rare; for instance, a five standard deviation observation is recorded once in about 3.5 million.

It's helpful to see what this looks like graphically. In Figure 8.2, the average IQ is 100, and the standard deviation is fifteen points, which means that 68 percent of the population's IQ is between 85 and 115, and 95 percent of the population falls between 70 and 130. A tiny sliver of humanity will have an IQ above 130 or below 70.

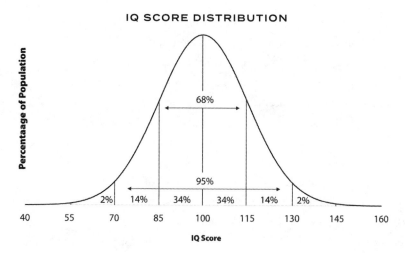

FIGURE 8.2

Now let's look at height in a similar chart (see Figure 8.3).

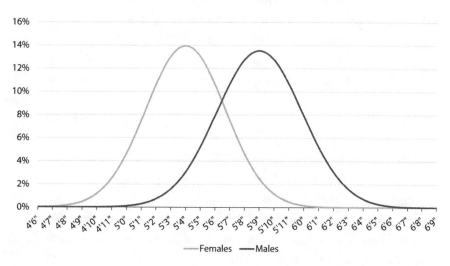

FIGURE 8.3

The average height for American men is a bit over sixty-nine inches (5'9"), and for women, it's just a smidge under sixty-four inches (5'4"). The standard deviation for height is 2.9 inches for males and 2.7 inches for females. That means 68 percent of American men are between 5'6" and 6'0", and 68 percent of American women are between 5'1" and 5'7"; 95 percent of all males are between 5'3" and 6'3", and 95 percent of all females are between 4'11" and 5'9". Only about 1 percent of women are six feet or taller, and about 1 percent of men are 6'4" or taller.

Therefore, Joe being 5'10" is pretty common, but Frank is somewhat unusual at 6'3", and NBA teams are interested in signing Steve, who's a vanishingly rare seven-footer. The bell curve allows us to estimate that out of the more than 150 million adult males in the US, there are only about one hundred who are seven feet tall or taller.

Things that follow a bell curve distribution fit our expectations. I'm pretty sure I'll never meet anyone who is 7'6", let alone 10 feet tall. I'm even less likely to make the acquaintance of anyone with an IQ of two hundred or more. Trees aren't thousands of feet high; no animals weigh one thousand tons, and humans can't run fifty miles per hour. The bell curve says so. In that way, consciously or not, it shapes our expectations and allows us to make certain predictions confidently.

But bell curve distributions aren't universal, and using them to shape expectations where they don't apply is a big mistake that can have serious consequences.

HOW THE BELL CURVE BETRAYED ME

In late 1998, I transitioned from practicing estate planning and tax law to being a wealth advisor at Arthur Andersen, then a global Big Five accounting and consulting firm. I had majored in finance in college and loved my investment classes, so I was excited to enter the investment world. During my first year at Andersen, I focused on building my investment chops by attending training sessions, reading stacks of books and papers about investing, and becoming a certified financial planner and registered investment advisor.

In investment classes in college, and again during my first year at Andersen, I learned that stock market returns follow a bell curve distribution. That meant that we could model a portfolio's expected returns and volatility using statistics and could advise our clients about what to expect from the stock market and their portfolios. As such, the bell curve provided a sense of certainty about the future.

In 1999, near the peak of the dotcom bubble, I confidently explained to my clients that the stock market historically averaged about a 10 percent return over long periods and that returns followed a bell curve with a standard deviation of about 16 percent. Based on the expected average return and standard deviation, I told clients we could expect the stock market to:

- Return between positive 26 percent and negative 6 percent, 68 percent of the time

- Return between positive 42 percent and negative 22 percent, 95 percent of the time

- Experience a significant drop of more than three standard deviations—38 percent or more—only once in one hundred years.

What I told my clients about stock market returns and volatility was financial orthodoxy; I wasn't telling them anything special. But over the next few years during the dotcom bust the S&P 500 dropped 49 percent, and the tech-heavy Nasdaq fell 77 percent and didn't recover for fifteen years.

These drops represented greater than two and three standard deviations. The good old reliable bell curve dissolved before our eyes, and our clients rightfully panicked. Our faith in the bell curve meant that we hadn't prepared clients for the sort of calamitous losses they were enduring. Some of them couldn't stand it and sold out of the market as it dropped.

The dotcom bust opened my eyes to the flaws of the bell curve when applied to investing. I never trusted it again.

RANDOMNESS MILD AND WILD

Benoit Mandelbrot, the father of fractal geometry, and Nassim Taleb, author of *The Black Swan* (among other great books), referred in a coauthored paper to things that follow a bell curve distribution as providing "mild randomness." There is variability, but most of the events we observe conform to our expectations.[1] Mild randomness is the world we live in with respect to height, intelligence, birth weight, and other things that follow a bell curve distribution.

If the stock market followed a bell curve, on most days there would be small price movements around the average, more significant price movements would be rarer as we moved away from the norm, and massive price changes would almost never happen. But that's not the stock market we know and love. There are more small price movements *and* wild price swings than what the bell curve predicts. If human height was like the stock market, we'd usually encounter people right around average height, and every once in a while, we'd run into people hundreds or thousands of feet tall.

Examples of the stock market violating bell curve expectations abound. Here are two:

- Between 1900 and the end of 2006, ten days notched a return of 9.19 percent or more. A 9.19 percent return is 8.6 standard deviations from the average daily return of 0.75 percent. According to Javier Estrada of IESE Business School in Barcelona, Spain, "A return of that magnitude should be observed every 250,890,349,457,896,000 trading days, or one every 1,003,561,397,831,590 years." Yet, "ten such returns were observed in 107 years."[2] And since 2006, there have been four additional days with returns greater than 9.19 percent. So, nearly impossible daily price movements have occurred fourteen times since the beginning of the twentieth century!

- The most extreme example of why the bell curve doesn't describe stock market returns is its nearly 23 percent drop on October 19, 1987. Writing about the drop in his 2000 book *When Genius Failed*, reporter Roger Lowenstein of the *Wall Street Journal* noted,

"Economists later figured that, on the basis of the market's historical volatility, had the market been open every day since the creation
of the Universe, the odds would still have been against it falling
that much in a single day. In fact, had the life of the Universe been
repeated one billion times, such a crash would still have been theoretically 'unlikely.'" [3]

We get lulled into thinking that the stock market delivers mild randomness because, most of the time, it does. Days, months, and even years
go by with the market bouncing around within an expected range. But
then, every so often, wild randomness erupts as huge price swings occur
with little or no warning. Figure 8.4 depicts the daily price movements
of the S&P 500 since 1978. You can see how the market moves close to
the average for years and then unexpectedly goes crazy. Note that a three
standard deviation event should occur less than once every hundred years.

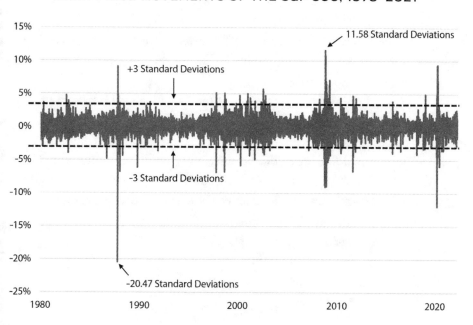

DAILY PRICE MOVEMENTS OF THE S&P 500, 1978–2021

FIGURE 8.4

Extreme price movements happen often enough that the only thing surprising about them is that we are surprised when they happen. According to Mandelbrot and Taleb, using bell curve–based statistics in investing is like "focusing on the grass and missing out on the (gigantic) trees."[4]

To understand what lies beneath those wild market swings, we need to dive into a world in which bell curves do not apply.

FRACTALS AND POWER LAWS: BETTER MODELS OF THE FINANCIAL MARKETS

THE COASTLINE PARADOX

Lewis Fry Richardson was an English mathematician, a Quaker, and a pacifist. He wanted to discover a way to minimize the incidence and severity of wars and developed a hypothesis that proposed that the likelihood of two neighboring countries going to war was proportional to the length of their shared border. In collecting data about the length of the border between Spain and Portugal, he noticed that a Spanish encyclopedia listed the border as 987 kilometers while a Portuguese encyclopedia claimed it was 1,214 kilometers—a considerable difference. He found similar reported discrepancies when looking at borders shared by other countries.

Why? The answer lay in the scale of the resolution of the measuring. Because a border is often defined by a geographic feature—a river, a mountain range, a coastline—it's often irregular. Thus, the exact length measured will depend on how detailed the measurement of every turn, squiggle, and jut of the natural features that define the border.

For example, using measuring units of 100 kilometers, Great Britain's coastline is about 2,800 kilometers long; with 50 km units, it's 3,400 kms, and with a 100-meter measuring stick, it's 17,820 kms.

So, oddly, the length of a border or coastline is not fixed, and you can't know what it is except in reference to the scale of the resolution of the device being used to measure it.

GREAT BRITAIN'S COASTLINE PARADOX

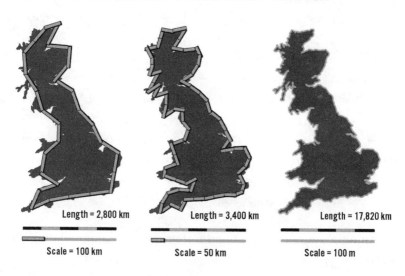

| Length = 2,800 km | Length = 3,400 km | Length = 17,820 km |
| Scale = 100 km | Scale = 50 km | Scale = 100 m |

FIGURE 8.5[5]

FRACTALS

An entire branch of mathematics arose out of the coastline paradox: fractal geometry. In 1967, mathematician Benoit Mandelbrot published the groundbreaking paper "How Long Is the Coast of Britain? Statistical Self-Similarity and Fractional Dimension." In the article, he noted that "seacoast shapes are examples of highly involved curves such that each of their portion can—in a statistical sense—be considered a reduced-scale image of the whole."[6] In other words, as you zoom in and zoom out on a coastline, it has the same approximate rough shape. This attribute—looking similar at both more precise and less precise resolutions—is called *self-similarity*. Go outside and look at a fern. Each of the fern's fronds looks like a smaller fern, and a piece of a frond looks like a whole fern.

Mandelbrot's insight was that most shapes in nature follow a self-similar pattern as coastlines and ferns. The smooth shapes of Euclidean geometry that we learn in school—squares, rectangles, triangles, circles— don't serve us when describing the natural world. Mandelbrot noted that:

> [Euclidean shapes] are concepts in men's minds and works, not in the irregularity and complexity of nature. How many natural objects around you really fit these old Greek patterns? Maybe the surface of a pond, when there is absolutely no wind or wave, appears truly flat like a plane. Maybe the irises of your children's eyes, if you gaze deeply at them, appear close enough to circular. But how many other smooth, natural things can you name? Clouds are not spheres, mountains are not cones, coastlines are not circles, and bark is not smooth, nor does lightning travel in a straight line.[7]

Think of a tree. What you observe from a distance—a trunk that splits out into branches, which split into smaller branches, and so on—is similar to what you see when you zoom in on specific portions of the tree. Figure 8.6 shows the contrast between the complex, rough, and self-similar nature of a tree and the smooth Euclidian shape of the church building and steeple. The difference is striking.

FIGURE 8.6: A TREE AND A STEEPLE AT MCKENDREE UNIVERSITY

Likewise, examine Figure 8.7, which is a picture I took on the road to El Calafate in Argentina with Mount Fitz Roy and the Cerro Torre in the background. Again, the man-made road is straight and regular, and the road sign is a Euclidian rectangle, while the mountains create jagged, non-Euclidean, self-similar shapes.

FIGURE 8.7: THE ROAD TO EL CALAFATE

Mandelbrot dubbed the complexity and roughness of shapes found in nature as *fractal*, which comes from the Latin word for broken. Thus, a fractal is a geometric shape that can be broken into smaller parts, with each little part being a smaller-scale facsimile of the larger. "As you zoom in on any portion of it as if with a microscope, the pattern does not get simpler as you would normally expect. 'Proper fractals' remain equally complicated at every level of magnification."[8]

So how does fractal geometry relate to investing? The roughness, wild randomness, and self-similar pattern of fractals better describe price changes in the financial markets than the bell curve. Investment price movements are self-similar, whether you view them over a day, a month, a year, or a decade. If you removed the time scale, and zoomed in and out on the returns, you couldn't distinguish between daily, monthly, or yearly price movements.

Figures 8.8, 8.9, and 8.10 of an S&P 500 tracking stock [SPY] over different periods illustrate this point. One of the charts is twenty-seven days of price changes, one is twenty-seven months, and one is twenty-seven years. Can you tell which is which?

S&P 500 PRICE CHANGES

FIGURE 8.8: TWENTY-SEVEN DAYS, MONTHS, OR YEARS?

S&P 500 PRICE CHANGES

FIGURE 8.9:TWENTY-SEVEN DAYS, MONTHS, OR YEARS?

S&P 500 PRICE CHANGES

FIGURE 8.10: TWENTY-SEVEN DAYS, MONTHS, OR YEARS?

Each of the preceding charts has a different pattern but displays similar characteristics in terms of ups and downs. Without the dates and the scale, it's impossible to tell which is the daily, monthly, or annual price return. Figure 8.8 is annual data (1994–2020), Figure 8.9 is monthly data (January 1, 2004–March 1, 2006), and Figure 8.10 is daily data (December 31, 1994–February 7, 1995).

In his book *The (Mis)behavior of Markets: A Fractal View of Risk, Ruin, and Reward*, Mandelbrot shows the chart with four sets of graphed data reproduced in the following figures. Two of the data figures show actual daily price movements of securities, and two are fake. One fake was generated using the mathematics of the bell curve, and the other uses fractal mathematics. Can you tell which of the two are real and which ones are fake?

> THE ROUGHNESS, WILD RANDOMNESS, AND SELF-SIMILAR PATTERN OF FRACTALS BETTER DESCRIBE PRICE CHANGES IN THE FINANCIAL MARKETS THAN THE BELL CURVE.

TWO REAL AND TWO FAKE SETS OF STOCK PRICE CHANGE DATA

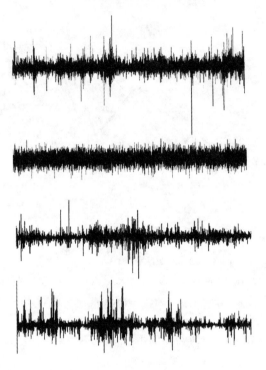

FIGURE 8.11

The second example sticks out as obviously fake. The returns are too smooth. There isn't enough variability. That's an example of mild randomness, and it uses bell curve math. Examples one and three represent actual daily price movements of stocks. The fourth example is a simulation using fractal mathematics. The fractal simulation looks just like the real data: most price movements are very close to the average, but there are also periods of significant volatility with large price swings. Thus, viewing the markets through a fractal lens gives us the proper perspective about what sort of market volatility we should expect.

Data that is fractal produces a *power law distribution* rather than a *bell curve distribution*. Therefore, thinking in terms of power laws rather than bell curves is essential for developing proper expectations for invest-ment returns.

POWER LAWS—THE TRIVIAL MANY VERSUS THE VITAL FEW

The American linguist George Zipf discovered something significant about language in 1949: a small number of words are frequently used, and most words are used rarely. He ranked words by their frequency and found that the top word in any language is used about twice as often as the second word, three times as often as the third used word, and so on. This is Zipf's law and is a type of power law.

Zipf's law also describes income distributions in a country: the person who makes the most money makes about two times more than the number two income earner and so on. It applies to the income distributions of companies, network effects on the internet, gene expression, and city size (the most populous American city—New York—in 2021 had a pop-ulation of about eight million, twice that of the next largest, Los Angeles, with just under four million, and so on).

Hearing about Zipf's law may remind you of the 80/20 rule, and if so, it's because that's another type of power law. The 80/20 rule is called the *Pareto principle*, named after Italian economist Vilfredo Pareto, who noted that 20 percent of the pea pods in his garden provided 80 percent of his peas. He was studying income and wealth at the time, and the discovery in his garden led him to note that 20 percent of the people owned 80 percent of the land in Italy. Similarly, he found that 20 percent of people earn 80 percent of Italy's total income. The Pareto principle is not a hard and fast rule, but rather an observation that indicates that a small number of inputs (like 20 percent) often can be responsible for most of the output (80 percent).

This 80/20 concept has applicability in many areas of business and life. For example:

- In many companies, 20 percent of the clients/customers generate 80 percent of the revenues.

- Often, 20 percent of salespeople are responsible for 80 percent of sales.

- In health care, 20 percent of patients use about 80 percent of the health-care system's resources.

- People typically wear 20 percent of their clothes 80 percent of the time.

- In a home or office, 20 percent of the carpet/flooring gets 80 percent of the traffic.

The 80/20 aspect of the Pareto principle only tells part of the story. (Perhaps 80 percent.) In *The Black Swan*, Nassim Taleb writes that the 80/20 rule could "easily be called the 50/01 rule; that is, 50 percent of the work comes from 1 percent of the workers. This formulation makes the world look even more unfair, yet the two formulae are exactly the same. How? Well, if there is inequality, then those who constitute the 20 percent in the 80/20 rule also contribute unequally—only a few of them deliver the lion's share of the results."[9]

For instance, suppose you have a business in which 20 percent of your clients generate 80 percent of your revenue. You might decide to get rid of the 80 percent of your clients and focus on the lovely 20 percent that are your biggest revenue generators. But Taleb's point is that you will still have an 80/20 ratio (remember your fractals), with 20 percent of your remaining clients generating 80 percent of your remaining revenues. And so on.

Zipf's law and the Pareto principle are examples of power law distributions, meaning that relatively few inputs generate the most significant effects, with the rest tapering off quickly. With power law distributions, it's the "trivial many versus the vital few"—which is what happens to the average wealth at a concert venue when a billionaire strolls in.

A good way to think about power law distributions is to picture a seesaw (see Figure 8.12). On one side are the trivial many and on the other are the vital few who offset the greater number of observations to provide the resulting average.

THE TRIVIAL MANY VS. THE VITAL FEW

FIGURE 8.12

Many things follow a power law distribution. Take the distribution of page views on my blog, *The Interesting Fact of the Day* (www.theifod.com). As of July 2021, I've posted 498 blogs that have received a total of 426,382 views, which is an average of 856 views of each post. But because those views follow a power law distribution, few posts have received a great number of clicks, with the highest one getting over 60,000. But 86 percent have gotten less than the average of 856. Figure 8.13 shows the distribution of my blog's page views.

DISTRIBUTION OF IFOD BLOG POST CLICKS

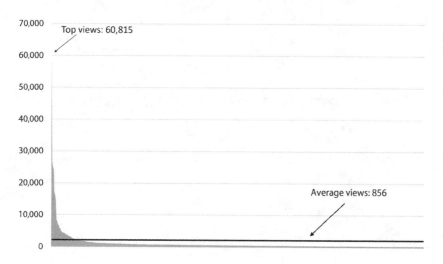

FIGURE 8.13

Looking at absolute daily percentage changes in the S&P 500 from 1978 to 2020 (when sorted by biggest to smallest) provides a power law distribution nearly identical to my page views (see Figure 8.14).

This power law distribution of returns means that there are a vital few days that drive stock market returns. As a consequence, missing those few days produces outsized effects on investment returns. For example, Table 8.1 illustrates that if you could avoid the twenty worst days in the market over twenty years, your return would increase by 490 percent. That would be good. Missing the market's twenty best days would reduce your return by 84 percent. Bummer.

S&P 500 DAILY PERCENTAGE CHANGES 1978–2020

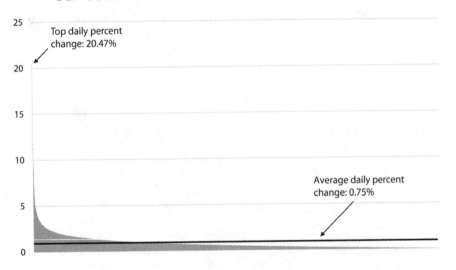

FIGURE 8.14

HOW MISSING THE BEST AND
WORST DAYS AFFECTS RETURNS

$1 Million Invested in 1997			
	Ending Value	Total Return	Annualized Return
Missing 20 Worst Days	$29,063,283.80	2806%	13.8%
Missing 15 Worst Days	$22,097,830.96	2110%	12.6%
Missing 10 Worst Days	$16,113,615.30	1511%	11.1%
Missing 5 Worst Days	$11,138,229.44	1014%	9.4%
Portfolio Value	$6,702,979.82	570%	7.0%
Missing 5 Best Days	$4,236,193.03	324%	4.7%
Missing 10 Best Days	$3,074,103.20	207%	2.9%
Missing 15 Best Days	$2,323,462.96	132%	1.1%
Missing 20 Best Days	$1,815,123.88	82%	−0.8%

TABLE 8.1

Similarly, a relatively small number of months effectively have generated all the returns in the stock market. According to the previously mentioned Professor Javier Estrada, just sixty months (out of 1,272, or 7 percent) from 1900 to 2006 averaged an 11 percent return; the rest of the months (or 93 percent) averaged a miniscule 0.01 percent.[10]

Plotting individual stock returns also produces a power law distribution. Figure 8.15 shows the distribution of the returns of individual stocks in the S&P 500 over twenty years, from 2000 to 2019. Again, most stocks provide poor to middling performance, and a relative few account for most of the return.

CUMULATIVE RETURNS OF S&P 500 CONSTITUENT STOCKS 2000–2019

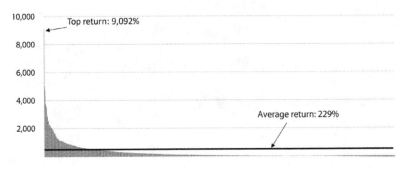

FIGURE 8.15

Venture capital, which invests in early-stage private companies, follows a power law distribution. A successful VC investment results in an exit—a private sale, a merger with another company, or an IPO. Figure 8.16 shows the distribution of the valuations of the one hundred biggest exits of venture capital funds over a period of 13⅓ years, from 2009–2022.

VCs make a lot of investments to realize very few big hits.

TOP 100 US VC-BACKED TECH EXITS 1/1/09–4/30/22 (BY VALUATION AT TIME OF EXIT)

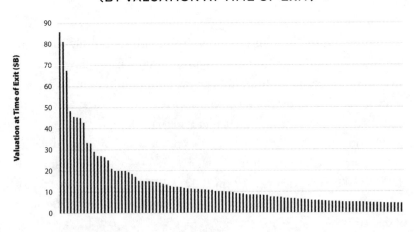

FIGURE 8.16[11]

SO, WHY DO BELL CURVE STATISTICS CONTINUE TO BE USED?

Bell curve–based projections of market returns and volatility provide a comforting sense of certainty because they estimate that randomness will be mild and outliers will be rare. But this provides a false sense of certainty once we know that's not how the markets behave. Mandelbrot and Taleb believe the bell curve paradigm persists because it caters to our "psychological biases and our tendency to understate uncertainty in order to provide an illusion of understanding the world."[12]

Plus, a fractal view of the market doesn't predict what future returns will be, like the bell curve does. Instead, accepting the fractal/power law view of financial markets means accepting inherent uncertainty and wild randomness. As noted in the prelude of Mandelbrot's book *The (Mis)behavior of Markets*, "reading this volume will not make you rich . . . but it will make you wiser—and may thereby save you from getting poorer."[13]

Most investment professionals know that the bell curve doesn't capture the pattern of stock market returns accurately. It's common knowledge that distributions of returns have *fat tails*, which means that extreme events occur much more often than bell curve statistics say they will, and the probability is that returns will move beyond three standard deviations either way, plus or minus. But instead of chucking the flawed model, the investment management industry pays lip service to the bell curve's inapplicability and just plows ahead with projections of returns and volatility based on it. The tragedy is that setting investor expectations using the mild randomness of the bell curve (as I did in 1999 at Arthur Andersen) doesn't prepare them for the wild randomness that's bound to occur.

THE MENTAL MODELS AND HOW TO APPLY THEM

The bell curve is a useful statistical tool in many areas of life, but it's misapplied in the investment arena. It wrongly sets the expectation of mild randomness, when we should be prepared for wild randomness. Nobody likes uncertainty, and our need for certainty is often what shapes our actions. We'd rather use a flawed model that provides a sense of certainty than a more accurate model that tells us that extreme events are bound to happen unexpectedly.

Instead of relying on what we now know to be fanciful projections of movements and returns, you will be better served if you:

- Embrace the uncertainty inherent in the markets; prepare for gigantic swings that could (and will) be just around the corner.

- Stress test your portfolios by modeling what would happen if we experienced another 1929 crash, a 2000 dotcom bust, or a 2008–2009 financial crisis (or an even bigger event). Will your portfolio still meet your cash flow needs?

- Stress test yourself. Can you emotionally handle that much volatility?

- Maintain an adequate margin of safety to ride out extreme downside events. Using the bell curve to approximate investment returns is like heading out to sea thinking that the waters will generally be calm with a few moderate storms when, in reality, the seas will mostly be calm, but there will be tempests of historic proportions that blow up randomly. If you knew such violent storms were likely to occur, would you set out in a boat designed for moderate storms?

- Avoid excessive debt.

- After designing your portfolio to weather wild storms, sail on. Moving in and out of investments may result in missing the best days in the market, thereby devastating portfolio returns.

CHAPTER 9

NAVIGATING OUR
BEHAVIORAL BIASES

The foundation of political economy and, in general,
of every social science, is evidently psychology.

—VILFREDO PARETO (1906)

A few years ago, I traded in my car for a new one. My old car, a 2006 BMW 5-Series, looked great. It was great. It was fast, had cool wheels, a stick shift, and a great stereo. I took good care of it. I kept it clean, even waxed it regularly, and I had all the recommended maintenance done on time. I loved that car, and I was sure I'd get a lot of money for it.

My dealership didn't share my enthusiasm. Their offer was a bit below the car's Kelly Blue Book value. I was perturbed and lobbied my sales guy for why it was worth more.

Me: "It's a stick. That's super rare."

Sales Guy: "There's a reason it's rare. Most people don't want one. Not having an automatic transmission hurts the value."

Me: "Real drivers like stick shifts."

Sales Guy: "That may be true, but a manual transmission makes it harder for me to sell."

Me: "It has low mileage."

Sales guy: "Yup. We considered that in setting the price. But it's twelve years old. Low miles doesn't make it newer."

Me: "The saddle color leather is massively cool."

Sales guy: "If you like it. Some people don't. A unique interior color doesn't help me. It makes your car harder to sell."

And so around and around we went. I thought about selling the car myself, but I didn't want the hassle, so I begrudgingly accepted the dealer's insulting trade-in offer. I was far from happy about it.

Maybe you've experienced something similar; you want to sell something and find out you've overvalued it. A realtor friend told me that prospective sellers almost always overvalue their homes, and that's a problem because listing houses for more than their market value makes them harder to sell. So, they sit on the market, weeks and months go by, the house gets a bad reputation, the owners get increasingly frustrated with the broker, and so it goes.

THE ENDOWMENT EFFECT

We all overvalue what we have. This is a behavioral bias called the *endowment effect.*

The seminal study of the endowment effect was conducted at Cornell University by Richard Thaler, the 2017 winner of the Nobel Prize in Economics. He divided a class of Cornell students into two groups. One group got Cornell coffee mugs; the other didn't. Then students from each group were told to negotiate to buy and sell the mugs. The result? The average mug owner demanded about two times what the buyers were willing to pay. Consequently, only a few changed hands.

Another experiment performed by Thaler involved pens and chocolate. He gave some students pens and then asked if they were willing to trade their new pens for chocolate. Fifty-six percent voted to keep the pens, turning up their noses at the proffered chocolate. When other students without pens were given a choice between a pen or chocolate, 76 percent chose chocolate. Both groups, when surveyed later, indicated a strong preference for chocolate (which is tasty) over pens (which are dull). And yet, even though they preferred chocolate, the students endowed with pens didn't want to give them up.[1]

Examples of the endowment effect outside the classroom abound:

- Traders and investors are biased toward stocks they own and tend to overvalue them.

- A study by Duke psychologist Dan Ariely found that study subjects given NCAA Final Four tickets were only willing to sell them for about fourteen times more than the price that other participants were willing to pay for them.

- The Boston Red Sox and Chicago White Sox traded players in 2015. When fans were asked about the transaction, 80 percent of White Sox fans were against it, and 100 percent of Red Sox fans surveyed were against the trade.

- Chimps have shown that they experience the endowment effect. Even though chimps prefer peanut butter over juice (60 percent versus 40 percent), if they are given juice, they're very reluctant to trade for peanut butter.

The endowment effect may seem irrational, but there are evolutionary reasons why we cling to and overvalue what we possess. Property rights, contracts, money, banks, insurance, and warranties—all those protections designed to encourage and safeguard trade—are relatively modern innovations. Without them, the risk of giving up the known (what we possess) for the unknown is very high, or so our brains tell us, so we are saddled with the endowment effect.

In addition to the endowment effect, there are hundreds of built-in biases that color our thinking and decision making. These biases persist because they aided our survival in an ancient world of scarcity and mortal risk that rewarded what our brains told us was the safer course. Other biases evolved because of our need to be part of a social group and seek status because belonging and status improved an individual's chances of survival and reproductive success. Thus, we can think of ourselves as having ancient brains while living in a modern world.

Behavioral biases don't just distort the perceived value of our possessions; they lead us to make poor decisions in every aspect of our lives, including investments. Knowing them, understanding them, and recognizing them when they pop up will allow you to resist them and make better decisions. We're going to examine four of the most important ones to know about to be a better investor: the storytelling bias, hindsight bias, loss aversion, and overconfidence.

STORYTELLING BIAS

In their groundbreaking paper, "Judgment Under Uncertainty: Heuristics and Biases," Amos Tversky and Daniel Kahneman, pioneers in the field of behavioral biases, described an American named Steve:

> Steve is very shy and withdrawn, invariably helpful but with little interest in people or in the world of reality. A meek and tidy soul, he has a need for order and structure, and a passion for detail.[2]

Tversky and Kahneman then ask whether Steve was more likely to be a librarian or a farmer. I guessed librarian. I also imagined that Steve still lived with his parents, liked to wear sweater vests, and owned a cat. I doubted he had a girlfriend and figured he drove a nondescript compact sedan (nothing like my undervalued BMW). Maybe, like me, you made up a story about Steve based on Tversky and Kahneman's brief sketch.

But the odds greatly favor Steve being a farmer. Why? It's just math. In the United States, there are about 2.2 million male farmers and just 25,000 male librarians. That means there are eighty-eight times as many male farmers as male librarians. So, it's possible but highly unlikely that Steve's a librarian.

Don't feel bad if you jumped to the same conclusion as I did. We rarely stop to consider base rate probabilities. Instead, it's human nature to view the world through stories and ignore, as Kahneman put it, "the statistics of the class to which the case belongs."[3]

STORIES ARE MORE POWERFUL THAN FACTS

From a physical standpoint, you wouldn't bet on *Homo sapiens* becoming the Earth's dominant species. We don't have sharp teeth and big jaws, we lack fur to keep us warm, and we're slower and weaker than lions and tigers and bears. (Oh my!) Ants can carry twenty times their body weight. Our senses—sight, hearing, smell, etc.—are vastly inferior to felines, canines, the great apes, birds, and others. We *Homo sapiens* rule the globe (more or less) because of our ability to work together in large groups toward shared goals.

In his book *Sapiens*, historian Yuval Noah Harari suggests three major revolutions in our species' history: a cognitive revolution about seventy thousand years ago, an agricultural revolution ten thousand years ago, and a scientific revolution five hundred years ago. These three developments allowed humans to leap to the top of the food chain very quickly (on an evolutionary timescale). Of the three, the cognitive revolution was the biggest driver of our species' survival and success. That happened when we developed language and, with it, the ability to communicate abstract ideas.

Storytelling allowed us to create and share complicated ideas efficiently, and stories enable large groups of strangers to identify and work together. According to Harari:

> Any large-scale human cooperation—whether a modern state, a medieval church, an ancient city or an archaic tribe—is rooted in common myths that exist only in people's collective imagination. States are rooted in

common national myths. Two Serbs who have never met might risk their lives to save one another because both believe in the existence of the Serbian nation, the Serbian homeland, and the Serbian flag. Judicial systems are rooted in common legal myths. Two lawyers who have never met can nevertheless combine efforts to defend a complete stranger because they both believe in the existence of laws, justice, human rights—and the money paid out in fees.[4]

Everything that Harari mentions (nations, laws, money) is conceptual; none of it has a physical reality; they're agreed-upon fictions. Stories have the almost magical ability to make events and things that don't tangibly exist inculcate values, like the story of underdogs fighting for freedom as in the *Star Wars* movies or stories of a hero's journey like in *The Odyssey*. The difference between the real and the imaginary, finally, is not that important.

Without stories, we couldn't pool our resources as we do, becoming greater than the sum of our parts, or maintain our complex social structures. Stories lead people to believe in shared goals and purposes.

Much of our interactions with other people consists of telling stories. I tell you a story about something that happened to me; you respond with your own story, and this lets me know that you understand the story I told you. And so it goes, back and forth.

We identify other people as members of our group or tribe if they tell similar stories. For example, in September 2021, I attended my first face-to-face conference since the start of the COVID-19 pandemic. The conference started off with lunch. I was randomly seated with seven other people. After brief introductions, we started sharing stories about when, if, and how our offices opened back up; the challenges of working from home; and what share of our respective workforces were vaccinated. We quickly realized that we all had similar experiences and challenges. We bonded and made it a point to stop and chat with each other throughout the conference. Exchanging stories around a lunch table created a mini tribe for the duration of the conference.

Because we've evolved to be storytellers and story exchangers, we pay special attention to stories; they greatly influence our worldview and our decisions. A single story can exert more sway over our decisions than reams of data, analysis, and statistics.

BASE RATE IGNORANCE

A study published in 2004 illustrates how much power stories have over us.[5] Volunteers acted as patients. The researchers told them they had a fictitious disease called Schistomanliasis, an infection caused by a parasitic worm that, if left untreated, would result in death within a year or two. Two drugs (also imaginary) were presented as treatment options: Fluortrexate and Tamoxol.

Fluortrexate, the patients were told, cured Schistomanliasis 50 percent of the time; Tamoxol's effectiveness was presented as variably as 30 percent, 50 percent, 70 percent, or 90 percent effective. So, the patients had to choose between Fluortrexate, at 50 percent effective, or Tamoxol, at one of the various effectiveness rates.

If the study had stopped there, it would be unremarkable because the participants would have surely picked the treatment with the highest rate of efficacy, whichever that happened to be. The twist was that the researchers told the participants about the outcomes for two patients before asking them to pick their drug. For Fluortrexate (the control drug) at 50 percent efficacy, the story was neutral:

> Chris was unsure if the decision was right or wrong (i.e., was ambiguous). Doctors were not certain whether the worm was destroyed. Doctors were unable to determine whether the disease would resume its course. At one-month post-treatment, Chris is having good days and bad.

For Tamoxol, the participants were told one of two different stories: (1) a positive outcome history, or (2) a negative outcome.[6] The positive story:

Pat's decision to undergo Tamoxol resulted in a positive outcome. The entire worm was destroyed. Doctors were confident the disease would not resume its course. At one-month post-treatment, Pat's recovery was certain.

The negative story:

Pat's decision to undergo Tamoxol resulted in a poor outcome. The worm was not completely destroyed. The disease resumed its course. At one-month post-treatment Pat was blind and had lost the ability to walk.

The story of a single patient's outcome, told different ways to different groups, turned out to have a massive impact on the drug chosen. The treatment decisions are summarized in Figure 9.1.

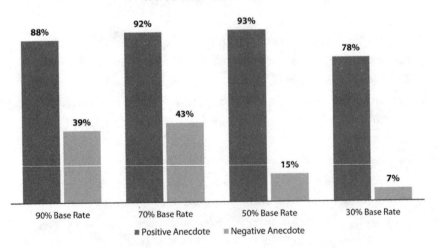

PERCENTAGE OF PATIENTS CHOOSING TAMOXOL TREATMENT

FIGURE 9.1: SUMMARY OF MEDICAL DECISION STUDY

If stories didn't sway the decision making, the participants would have chosen Tamoxol 100 percent of the time when it had 90 percent or 70 percent effectiveness because Fluortrexate had a lower base rate of success of 50 percent. And no one would have (or should have) chosen Tamoxol when it was just 30 percent effective. But that's not what happened. As shown in Figure 9.1, when Tamoxol was presented as being 90 percent effective paired with a negative story, only 39 percent chose it.

This is an astounding outcome. Stories about a single patient's experience made the study participants throw the base rate out the window and make a bad decision.

BAD BLOOD

A compelling story can lead to a bad investment, and anybody who invested in a company named Theranos found this out the hard way.

Theranos was a medical device company founded by Elizabeth Holmes, a confident and charismatic Stanford dropout. She liked to tell a story about how as a child, she was terrified of needles and hated having her blood drawn. This fear drove her to develop a technology that would allow blood tests to be performed with a single drop of blood from a finger prick. The development of this new technology, if successful, would be a game changer as, rather than having to go to a doctor's office or a lab, people could get cheap, convenient, and fast blood tests at pharmacies. These blood tests could spot disease early and conveniently provide much-needed inexpensive and quick blood testing in developing countries.

It was a great idea. The problem was that it didn't work. It may not even have ever been real. In January 2022, Holmes was convicted of fraud, and as I write this chapter is facing sentencing.

In 2018, journalist John Carreyrou published a book titled *Bad Blood*, describing the Theranos scam in depth.[7] When you read about all the red flags that indicated that the company was fraudulent, it seems ridiculous that it could have suckered anyone. But Theranos's list of investors reads like *Who's Who* of the 0.1 percent: media mogul Rupert Murdoch, Oracle founder Larry Ellison, former Secretary of Education

Betsy DeVos, Walmart's Waltons, as well as numerous venture capital firms. Moreover, Theranos's board included such luminaries as former Secretaries of State George Schultz and Henry Kissinger, and former Defense Secretary Jim Mattis. How did these wealthy investors and respected board members get hoodwinked? A primary reason was that Holmes's story was compelling, inspirational, relatable (who likes having blood drawn?), and she told it well. The power of her story blinded investors and board members.

STORY LESSONS

The world of investing is full of stories. Investment managers tell stories about their past successes and about what opportunities the future holds. Our friends and acquaintances tell us stories about their successful investments at cocktail parties and social gatherings. The financial media tells stories about threats and opportunities in the economy and the market. We're bombarded with stories. And we're swayed by them because that's how we're wired.

Developing a mental model about stories is essential to successful investing. That starts with understanding that a story will have an outsized effect on your decision making. Train yourself to seek out the base rate (as with farmers and librarians or drug treatment options) and add that to the mix. For example, when considering an individual stock, set aside the stories related to the stock and realize, as discussed in Chapter 6, that most stocks underperform the market, so the odds are against your single stock pick being a good idea. Or, when considering a start-up company with a compelling story, think about the base rate statistics for start-ups: less than 50 percent make it to their fifth year, and 70 percent fail within ten. And when considering an actively managed fund, remind yourself that the vast majority of active managers underperform the market after fees. This will help counterbalance the stories they tell about their successes.

Learn to recognize when you're being told a story and realize that the story will have an outsized effect on your decision making.

HINDSIGHT BIAS

I didn't see the 2008 financial crisis coming, but when I looked back on it a few years later, it seemed obvious that a witch's cauldron had been long brewing. The causal chain of cheap credit that led to a housing bubble that burst, coupled with imperiled banks that were undercapitalized because of financial deregulation, was clear when viewed with the benefit of hindsight.

Hindsight bias is the idea that because the past can be easily explained from our perch in the present, the future should be predictable. For example, I considered buying shares of Tesla a couple of years ago when it was about $50 per share, but I didn't. Now, as I write this, the stock is trading at over $1,000 per share. Looking back, I feel dumb for not buying at $50 because *now* it seems evident that Tesla stock was about to take off.

Of course, what I knew at the time told a different story. Tesla was struggling with production and quality issues on its Model 3; the company wasn't profitable; there was talk about it going bankrupt or being sold cheaply to a tech company or another car manufacturer. The possibility that Tesla stock would increase more than twenty-fold over a few years was fanciful—and only one of many different possible outcomes.

In Figure 9.2, we see how the past seems linear when viewed from the present.

HOW THINGS LOOK IN RETROSPECT

FIGURE 9.2: HOW EVENTS LOOK IN RETROSPECT FROM POINT D

When you're sitting at event or time D, causation appears clear: A caused B, which led to C and resulted in D. Of course, when we're living at point A, points B, C, and D don't yet exist. At point A, there is a multitude of possible Bs, Cs, and Ds. The linear progression from A to B to C to D exists only in retrospect, with causation an often-spurious add-on. Figure 9.3 more accurately represents what reality looks like when you are sitting at point A.

WHAT THINGS LOOK LIKE

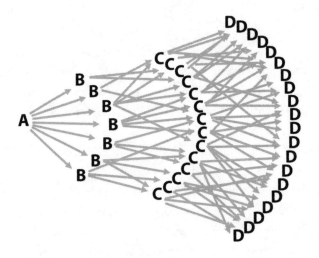

FIGURE 9.3: WHAT EVENTS LOOK LIKE FROM POINT A

When we're sitting in the present (which is the only place we can be), countless B, C, and D events are possible. If you could see all the potential paths that *didn't* occur when you look back from point D, it looks like Figure 9.4, in which the black arrows are what actually happened.

WHAT THINGS WERE REALLY LIKE

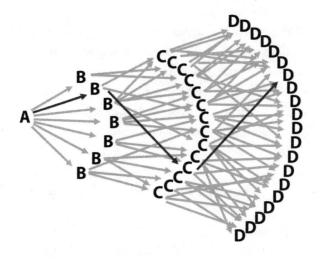

FIGURE 9.4: WHAT EVENTS WERE REALLY LIKE FROM POINT D

INVISIBLE HISTORIES

Figure 9.4 presents a mental model I call *invisible histories*—things that could have happened but didn't.

Here's a story that illustrates this concept. Heading into 2008, both of my friends Jeff's and Susan's investment portfolios mainly consisted of stocks. As the financial crisis blossomed into a panic during early 2009 and the stock market was dropping like a rock, each worried that the world's financial system would collapse, and they were afraid that the stock market would follow. They both sold sizeable chunks of their portfolios at a significant loss to have the cash to ride out the volatility.

The market bottomed soon after Jeff and Susan sold their stocks, and by the time they each reinvested, they'd missed out on a lot of gains. However, each viewed their decision to exit the market quite differently.

Jeff looked back with regret. Whenever he thought about the gains he missed, it made him ill. When he looked at his portfolio, he saw the ghost of the money he would have made if he hadn't sold those stocks when he did. His decision haunted him.

Susan came at it from a different angle, one that embraced the concept of invisible histories. She believed that she had made the best decision she could at the time with the information at hand. She recognized that things could have turned out much differently than they did. The financial crisis could have deepened. The economy could have slid into a depression. The stock market could have declined a lot more than it did. In other words, she recognized that when she decided to sell her stocks, there were many possible future outcomes, but only one happened. Susan says that if she had to do it over again, she would make the same decision.

Viewing the past through the lens of invisible histories is an essential mental model for fighting hindsight bias and regret. Whenever we make decisions, we should understand that we can't see around the corner of time into the future. Thus, it's best to not pat yourself on the back too much whenever things work out the way you expect and acknowledge that things could have turned out very differently. On the flip side, if events don't result in what you imagined, realize that your expected outcome followed an invisible history; it could have happened, but for better or worse, it didn't.

THE RESULTING FALLACY

Super Bowl XLIX (49) between the Seattle Seahawks and the New England Patriots featured one of the most controversial play calls in the history of the NFL. Late in the fourth quarter, the Seahawks were down by four points, so they had to score a touchdown to win. After a miraculous circus-like catch by wide receiver Jermaine Kearse, the Seahawks were at the Patriots' five-yard line. After a four-yard run on a first down, the Seahawks found themselves second and goal at the one-yard line with twenty-six seconds remaining in the game. Given that Seattle had one of the best running backs in the league in Marshawn Lynch, pretty much everyone expected Seattle to run the ball. But Seattle head coach Pete Carroll called a pass play instead, which didn't end well for the Seahawks as Patriots defensive back Malcolm Butler edged out the intended receiver and intercepted the pass in the endzone. The Patriots ran out the clock, and the Seahawks lost the Super Bowl 28–24.

With the benefit of knowing the result—that the pass was intercepted—the decision to pass on the one-yard line appears to be a horrible decision. Football pundits and fans all agreed that it was an awful call. Why wouldn't you hand the ball off to Marshawn Lynch in a short-yardage situation on the goal line?

It was a bad result, and it cost Seattle the game. But does that bad result mean that calling a pass play was a wrong decision?

University of Michigan economist Justin Wolfers thinks game theory justifies Pete Carroll's decision to pass. What second-guessers miss is that when two evenly matched teams compete, doing what is expected all the time is not a winning strategy. Writing in the *New York Times*, Wolfers explained that play calling is similar to playing rock-paper-scissors: "If Carroll will definitely play scissors, Belichick will respond with rock. The only way to make Belichick's job hard is for Carroll to make it impossible for him to guess what he will play next. And the only way to do that is for his strategy to appear random."[8]

It just so happened that the Patriots were ready for the pass play and executed their defense perfectly. But it was close. Had the play worked, everyone would have hailed Carroll as a genius play-caller who outmaneuvered Patriots coach Bill Belichick.

We tend to judge the quality of decisions by the results they produce. But good decisions sometimes produce bad results, and bad decisions can produce good ones. This tendency to judge decisions primarily by results is a form of hindsight bias known as the *resulting fallacy*, a phrase coined by former professional poker player Annie Duke.

Annie Duke gained deep insight into human behavior by playing poker because the thousands of games she played over her career were like little laboratories of human decision making in the face of uncertainty. A combination of skill and luck created the results in most situations. According to

Duke, the resulting fallacy occurs when we create "too tight a relationship between the quality of the outcome and the quality of the decision." She says, "knowing the outcome infects us" and causes us to judge a decision or process based mainly on that.

Duke explains, "In chess, if I lose a game, it's pretty certain that I made a bad decision somewhere, and I can go look for it. That's a totally reasonable strategy. But it is a very unreasonable strategy in poker. If I lose a hand, I may have played the hand literally perfectly and still lost because there's this luck element to it. The problem is that we're all 'resulters' at heart."[9]

> WE TEND TO JUDGE THE QUALITY OF DECISIONS BY THE RESULTS THEY PRODUCE. BUT GOOD DECISIONS SOMETIMES PRODUCE BAD RESULTS, AND BAD DECISIONS CAN PRODUCE GOOD RESULTS.

Recognizing the resulting fallacy mental model is essential to fighting hindsight bias. The world is filled with randomness, and many outcomes are the result of luck, which means sometimes good decisions don't work out.

SUNK COSTS AND THE LOSS AVERSION BIAS

Imagine you and your significant other go to a movie. Ten minutes in, you realize the movie is horrible. Like *Waterworld*, *Battlefield Earth*, or *Cats* (the movie) bad. What do you do? You've paid $30 for the tickets, so it feels like leaving now will cost you $30.

This is a classic example of the sunk cost fallacy, in which we allow unrecoverable expenses (time, money, or effort) to inform current decisions.

Sitting in the theater, you now have two choices:

1. Suffer through the movie and have a rotten time, having already invested $30, or

2. Leave the movie and do something else with your time, having already spent $30.

In either case, you've spent $30. It's a sunk cost. With that realization, it's best to set it aside and make your decision without reference to it. Ruminating over sunk costs is human nature and pops up in all sorts of situations in our lives.

For example, it's common in relationships: "I don't want to break up with my girlfriend—even though she treats me terribly and is no fun—because it will mean I've wasted the past two years of my life."

. . . with employees: "We've invested so much time, effort, and money training Kieffer, so we aren't going to get rid of him even though he's a low performer."

. . . in business: "I'm going to add more money to my failing company because I don't want to lose all the money and effort I've already invested in it."

. . . with experiences: "My rental ski boots are killing me, and it's too cold, but I'm going to keep skiing instead of calling it a day and having a beer because I already spent $150 on my lift ticket."

Setting aside sunk costs when making decisions is challenging because we hate to lock in a loss. To battle the sunk cost fallacy, try to adopt the mental framework in Figure 9.5 by comparing your two possible paths.

MENTAL FRAMEWORK FOR SETTING ASIDE SUNK COSTS

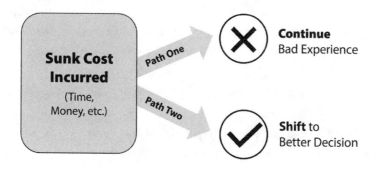

FIGURE 9.5

Here's a coincidence. As I was typing this section, I got a call from my daughter, Claire, who's in grad school. She told me that over the past few weeks, she's spent hours and hours working on a paper. Last night when reading through her draft, she concluded that her topic wasn't very good, so she decided to write an entirely different paper on a wholly different topic. This morning she met with her professor and proposed the new subject. The professor agreed that her new topic was much better and that the old one wouldn't have earned her a very good grade.

My daughter said to me, "Dad, it was soooooooo hard to start over. I spent so much time on the prior topic, and I didn't want to waste all the time I'd spent, but I realized that to do well in my class I needed a better topic."

I'm so proud of her. She set aside her sunk costs and picked a better path. It's a simple concept but rarely easy to apply.

Adopting the mindset of "I've already spent the money (or time or effort), but I'm going to set that aside and move in a different direction" is difficult because we view gains and losses asymmetrically. Losses are more painful than gains are pleasurable. This asymmetry is known as *loss aversion.*

PROSPECT THEORY

Like the other biases in this chapter, there's an evolutionary reason for loss aversion. From a survival perspective, more bad things can happen to us than good ones. This was especially true in pre-modern times. Rolf Dobelli, in his book *The Art of Thinking Clearly*, notes the following:

> One stupid mistake, and you were dead. Everything could lead to your rapid departure from the game of life—carelessness on the hunt, an inflamed tendon, exclusion from the group, and so on. People who were reckless or gung-ho died before they could pass their genes on to the next generation. Those who remained, the cautious, survived. We are their descendants.[10]

Thus, historically, we enhanced our survival and reproductive chances when we prioritized threats over opportunities. This concept that we weigh gains and losses differently was introduced to the economics community by Daniel Kahneman and Amos Tversky in a 1979 research paper. They called their theory about how humans view gains and losses differently *prospect theory*.[11]

Prospect theory is full of nuances and interesting takeaways about our different views of gains and losses. Its significant findings are:

1. Losses are about 1.5 to 2 times more painful than gains are pleasurable. As I write this chapter, the S&P 500 is up about 20 percent year-to-date. That feels great. But I would feel worse to a much greater degree than I feel great now if the market were down 20 percent.

2. Evaluation of gains and losses is relative to a reference point. Our reference points reset over time and turn into high-water marks. If the $500k you've invested in your portfolio hits $1 million and then it drops to $800k, you feel like you've lost $200k, even though you only invested $500k. Few of us think that we're still up $300k.

3. There is varying sensitivity to gains and losses. A $100 loss is the same dollar amount whether your $1,000 goes down to $900 or your $200 goes to $100. However, the second one is more painful.

4. People engage in risk-seeking behavior to avoid taking a loss. When we're faced with the possibility of both a gain and a loss, we tend to be risk averse. But when we are faced with locking in a loss, we tend to double-down and take more risk to avoid incurring it. Kahneman provides this example:

   - *Problem 1: Which do you choose? Get $900 for sure or a 90 percent chance to get $1,000?*

- *Problem 2: Which do you choose? Lose $900 for sure or a 90 percent chance to lose $1,000?*[12]

Even though the two problems provide mathematically equivalent outcomes, most people pick getting the $900 for sure in Problem 1, forgoing the 90 percent probability of earning $1,000 but avoiding the 10 percent chance of getting nothing. In Problem 2, most people choose the 90 percent chance of losing $1,000, holding on to that 10 percent chance of losing nothing. Why so? Kahneman explains, "In the mixed case, the possible loss looms twice as large as the possible gain. In the bad case . . . the pain of losing $900 is more than 90 percent of the pain of losing $1,000. These insights are the essence of prospect theory."[13]

APPLYING THE LOSS AVERSION MENTAL MODEL

Loss aversion in all its flavors negatively impacts our investment behavior. It causes us to misjudge risk by ascribing outsized pain to losses and skewing our evaluation of risk and reward. Here are two helpful behavior hacks that fight loss aversion:

First, avoid looking at your portfolio. Even though the market goes up over long periods, it fluctuates significantly over short ones. Over months and years, the market records gains on 52 percent of trading days, provides a positive annual return 69 percent of the time, and delivers a positive ten-year return 89 percent of the time. If losses are twice as painful as gains are pleasurable, frequently checking your portfolio will cause you mental distress. Taking a look at your portfolio every day will provide approximately two units of pain half the time, compared to only one unit of pleasure the other days, rewarding you with more pain than pleasure by a two-to-one margin.

Second, make yourself take losses. About five years ago, I met with a client who owned millions of dollars in a struggling company. The stock was way down from where he bought it. We'd been advising him to reduce his ownership of this stock for years, but he was reticent to lock in his loss. At each meeting, he said he wanted to wait to sell when it returned to positive territory. After he again refused to sell, I proposed the following: "Given your strong belief that this company's stock will rebound, would you like to buy more of it?"

"No," he said quickly. "I don't think that's a good idea. This stock has been dropping for years, and the outlook for the company is poor. There's no way I'm buying more if it."

I said, "But in effect, you are rebuying this stock each day you don't sell it."

That finally got through to him. He realized this wasn't a good stock to own if he had such a strong aversion to buying more. The next day we made the trade, and within two years, the company had declared bankruptcy.

The story's point isn't that you should sell every investment when it's down; inactivity and patience are generally better investment practices than tinkering and trading. The lesson is that you should be mindful of your loss aversion when making investment decisions. Asking yourself, "Would I buy more?" can help you make a more rational decision.

OVERCONFIDENCE: THE MOTHER OF ALL BIASES

My colleague, Carl, is a horrible driver. Every time I ride with him, I feel like I'm putting my life at risk. He drifts out of his lane, tailgates, rarely uses his signals, and drives too fast. But when we travel together to see clients, he insists on driving our rental car. After a particularly harrowing trip back to the airport, I asked him how he'd rate his driving.

"I'm a great driver," he said emphatically, a bit put out that I'd asked. Carl truly believed it. He had no doubts.

Carl isn't alone in this. Studies have consistently found that the vast majority of drivers rank themselves very highly. A 1981 survey of American drivers found that 93 percent put themselves in the top 50 percent of driving ability.[14] My favorite study is from 1965. Researchers surveyed one hundred drivers, fifty of whom were in the hospital with injuries from car crashes. The other fifty had spotless driving records. You know what comes next. Based on their self-ratings, the two groups were indistinguishable. On a continuum of skill, both groups judged themselves closer to expert drivers than poor drivers. Police reports on the hospitalized drivers found that thirty-four of these driving experts were responsible for their accidents.[15]

It's ludicrous that injured drivers who caused their own accidents would be as confident in their driving ability as those with spotless records, but that's how humans are wired: we're all overconfident. We see ourselves through rose-colored glasses. For example:

- We tend to think that we're better than we are: that we're smarter, better looking, and more fun and likable than is true.

- We think we're better than others. In competitive situations, we tend to think of ourselves, our company, our team, etc., as relatively better than other people, companies, and teams.

- We think our futures are brighter than other people's futures.

- We think we know more than we really do. As a result, we make predictions of the future and think they're more accurate than they turn out be.

- We think we have more control over our lives than we really do.

Daniel Kahneman says that overconfidence is the bias he'd most like to change if he had a magic wand.[16] In their textbook on decision making, Max Bazerman of Harvard and Don Moore of the University of California, Berkeley call overconfidence the "mother of all biases" and blame overconfidence for "wars, stock market bubbles, strikes, unnecessary lawsuits, high rates of entrepreneurial bankruptcy, and the failures of corporate mergers and acquisitions."[17] Arguably, Russia's invasion of Ukraine in early 2022 was due to overconfidence—Putin and his generals reportedly thought the war would last days, overestimating their own military prowess while simultaneously underestimating Ukraine's resolve.

Additionally, Chernobyl, the Challenger explosion, the invasion of Iraq, and the sub-prime mortgage crisis can all be traced to overconfidence.

THE ILLUSION OF EXPLANATORY DEPTH

How confident are you that you can explain how a simple toaster works—the type where you put bread in a slot and push down a lever? Think about it for a bit, and then rate your perception of your toaster knowledge on a scale of zero (you have no idea) to one hundred (you can explain precisely how it works). If you're like most people, you've rated yourself highly (especially if you're a guy; guys believe it's manly to be mechanically inclined).

I gave myself a ninety.

Now ponder this: How does the toaster lever stay down while the bread is toasting? Have you ever noticed that it won't stay down if the toaster is unplugged? Why not?

Finished pondering? It's because the lever is held down by an electromagnet that needs electricity to work. I had no idea—mind blown. When I learned that fact, it occurred to me that the ninety I gave myself in toaster knowledge might be a little high.

We tend to think we understand the world around us and how things work much better than we actually do. This flaw in our reasoning is called *The Illusion of Explanatory Depth* and is one of many flavors of overconfidence bias.

Researchers at Yale conducted a groundbreaking study about the illusion of explanatory depth.[18] Study participants were asked to rank how well they could explain how forty-eight different items work: among them zippers, flush toilets, helicopters, ballpoint pens, and sewing machines. At each step of the process, they were asked to evaluate their knowledge of the items. After their initial rating, they wrote detailed explanations of how a handful of selected items worked. After they wrote their descriptions, the researchers asked a specific question about each item. For example, for a helicopter, they might be asked to explain, step-by-step, how a helicopter changes from hovering to flying forward. Or for a toaster, they'd be asked how the lever stays down. Finally, an expert explanation about how the item worked was given to the participants, so they could compare their explanation to the experts.

How did the test work out? Initially, just as I did with toasters, the participants rated their knowledge highly. But once they had to explain in depth how an item worked, they realized they didn't know as much as they thought, and they lowered their scores. After being asked a tough question, they realized they knew even less and lowered them more. Finally, after reading an expert explanation and comparing it to what they wrote, they learned how little they knew and concluded that their initial self-evaluations were ridiculously high.

Thinking we know more about how the world works than we do affects our opinions and beliefs, and how we make investment decisions.

A recent *New York Times* article, "Nobody Really Knows How the Economy Works," explained that economics orthodoxy holds that expectations of inflation are a key driver of inflation.[19] So, if people expect higher prices, they'll behave in a manner that drives prices higher. But the article noted that a recent Federal Reserve research paper found that there was no evidence for this. The first sentence of the Fed paper states: "Mainstream economics is replete with ideas that 'everyone knows' to be true, but that is actually arrant nonsense."[20]

This is the illusion of knowledge in a nutshell.

WHY WE'RE OVERCONFIDENT

Overconfidence leads to overinflated self-perceptions, unrealistic expectations, and bad decisions, including Carl's insistence on taking the wheel when we rent cars. Given all the problems overconfidence creates, you'd think that evolution would select for humility. But there are reasons it doesn't.

First, overconfidence confers psychological benefits, such as self-esteem, mental health, and greater motivation.[21] When we think we're better than we are or compare ourselves favorably to others, we feel good.

Second, there are social and status benefits conferred by appearing confident. Confidence makes people more persuasive and influential, which is why it is elevated in people in positions of rank or authority. Interestingly, research shows that overconfidence and status often form a self-perpetuating feedback loop: elevated status leads to overconfidence, and overconfidence is an attribute of those who attain higher status.[22] And, higher status generally leads to greater reproductive success.

We can see the advantages of overconfidence in how people who display it appear more compelling and believable. We tend to correlate a person's confidence with their level of knowledge and competence.[23] No one wants to hear their dermatologist say, "Ew, gross, I have no idea what that rash is."

Finally, research from the University of Edinburgh and the University of California, San Diego suggests that confidence, even when baseless, can lead to greater success when competing with others. The study authors note that, "Overconfidence . . . encourages individuals to claim resources they could not otherwise win if it came to a conflict (stronger but cautious rivals will sometimes fail to make a claim), and it keeps them from walking away from resources they would surely win."[24] Thus, being confident scares away competitors and adversaries, which increases one's chances of survival and reproduction.

WHAT TO DO ABOUT OVERCONFIDENCE

What should we do about this mother of all biases? First, it is imperative to recognize that we're all overconfident (yes, I'm talking to you). None of us knows as much as we think we do. Whenever we make decisions, we need to step back and be less sure of what we know. In essence, we need to have more humility about how much we know.

Second, recognize that we are drawn to overconfident people, and an expert's confidence level and ability to make accurate predictions are negatively correlated. Yet, it is (over)confident experts who we're most likely to hear from in the media. Thus, whenever you're on the receiving end of advice from a confident advisor, practice skepticism.

BEHAVIORAL BIASES MENTAL MODELS AND HOW TO APPLY THEM

We all tend to ascribe behavioral biases to *other* people (an example of our overconfidence bias), and we think that we'll be able to avoid those biases if we just learn about them. Unfortunately, that's not the case. These deeply ingrained biases have developed over hundreds of thousands of years of evolution, and we can't easily set them aside.

I've read scores of books on behavioral biases, as well as whitepapers and articles. Plus, I have a professional certificate from Harvard University in "Investment Decisions and Behavioral Finance." Yet I still fall victim to behavioral biases, and I kick myself every time I realize it. But I'm getting better. I'm on the lookout for them and try to resist them when I see them.

Battling our biases is an uphill battle, but we can make progress. Chapter 10 is about what good investment behavior looks like and how to practice it. There are processes and strategies that we all can put in place that will help us make better decisions without being overly influenced by biases.

CHAPTER 10

BEHAVIOR—THE MOST IMPORTANT INGREDIENT

Investing isn't about beating others at their game.
It's about controlling yourself at your own game.

—JASON ZWEIG

Years ago, I was preparing for upcoming client meetings and noticed the difference in returns between two client portfolios—let's call them Client A and Client B (not their real names). Client A's portfolio had beaten Client B's returns by about 3 percent per year over the prior ten years. That's a huge difference. If both clients started with the same amount, at the end of ten years, Client A's portfolio would be 30 percent larger than Client B's.

But they didn't start with the same amounts. Client A was a housekeeper for one of our clients, and her portfolio was worth $40,000. Client B was a retired investment banker with an MBA from a top business school, and his portfolio was north of $100 million.

How did the housekeeper outperform the investment banker? She practiced better investment behavior. While the percentage difference in their returns was glaring, I wasn't particularly surprised because it's consistent with patterns we've observed at our firm in portfolio returns.

We call one pattern *the paradox of the unsophisticated sibling*. Teachers, social workers, and stay-at-home parents who spend zero time reading about investments or the economy frequently beat their siblings who went to business school, read the *Wall Street Journal*, or even work in finance. How does this happen? Unsophisticated investors often have better investment behaviors than more sophisticated ones.

We call a second pattern we've observed *the paradox of the small portfolio*. Because they can meet the higher minimums required to access star investment managers and alternative investments, large portfolios have an advantage over small ones. But we've found that small portfolios typically outperform larger ones. Why? Our clients tend to pay less attention to their smaller portfolios, and that's a good investment behavior.

When I talk about clients who don't do as well as I (or they) expect, I do so with empathy and without judgment because I've been there. My 401(k) account, which is invested in just four index funds, has outperformed my "outright" portfolio, where I can buy and sell whatever I want. Why has my 401(k) done better than my outright account? Because I practice better investment behavior with my 401(k).

What does it mean to have good investment behavior? Let's dig in.

IN PRAISE OF INACTIVITY (AND FEMALE INVESTORS)

My younger daughter is on her college field hockey team. When she was home for summer break last year, she asked me to help her practice what field hockey players call "stick stops" at a nearby field.

Audrey: "Dad, I need you to hit the ball at me very hard from over there (about fifteen yards away). You think you can do it?"

Me: "Of course I can do it."

Audrey: "It's not so easy. What makes you so sure?"

Me: "Because I've played sports all my life, and I've got excellent hand-eye coordination. I can totally do this. No sweat. You just grab your stick and get ready."

It didn't go well. From fifteen yards, I could hit the ball either (a) hard or (b) straight. Not both. So, I moved closer, about ten yards away. Again, I struggled. I was pretty good from five yards, which wasn't much help to her. We switched to a different drill in which I just fetched balls. I was a star at that.

As we left the field, my daughter said, "You know what? Even though you're my dad and all, you're still just a boy. You thought you could do it even though you'd never done it before, pretty much like every boy I've ever known."

Ouch.

So why am I sharing this paternal humiliation with you? My daughter's insight that males have a problem with overconfidence is backed by research, especially in the finance arena.[1] We know that overconfidence is the "mother of all biases," which would lead one to believe that men are worse investors than women. Well, one would believe right.

The seminal study on this topic, "Boys Will Be Boys: Gender, Overconfidence, and Common Stock Investment," examined account data from over 35,000 investment accounts at a large discount brokerage over seven years and found that male investors trailed females by about 1 percent per year.[2] Analysis of the data showed that both genders were equally bad at picking stocks; on average, stocks bought by both genders did worse than stocks they sold. So, why did women fare better? Because they traded 45 percent less often. This makes sense. If more trading leads to lower returns, then trading less should mean better returns, which is precisely what the study found.

Why do men trade more? The researchers concluded that men traded more than women because they were more overconfident. For example, single women reported having less investment experience than single men, yet the demographic data showed that single women had the best returns, followed by married women, then married men, with single men bringing up the rear. As a guy, I find this sobering. I guess I should be thankful that I'm married!

A recent study by Fidelity supports the "Boys Will Be Boys" findings. Their examination of five million customer accounts over ten years found that women investors outperformed men, even though only 19 percent of the women surveyed said they felt confident about selecting investments.[3]

Even though female investors tend to outperform males, they shouldn't be too smug about their investment results because they *underperform* dead people. Yes, dead people. An internal review by Fidelity of their client accounts that posted the best returns between 2003 and 2013 found that "the best investors were either dead or inactive—the people who switched jobs and 'forgot' about an old 401(k), or the people who died and the assets were frozen while the estate handled the assets."[4]

The lesson is clear: More activity leads to lower returns. And it's not just retail investors. A study of pension plans and their decisions to hire and fire investment managers found that they would have been better off sticking with their existing managers than making a change.[5] Figure 10.1 shows that after pension plans fired managers who performed poorly and hired those who had performed well, the fired managers tended to outperform the hired ones.

CUMULATIVE EXCESS RETURNS OF INVESTMENT MANAGERS BEFORE AND AFTER HIRING OR FIRING, 1994–2003

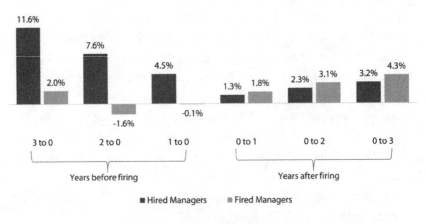

FIGURE 10.1[6]

It's worth noting the level of expertise of those making the hiring and firing decisions. Pension plans have expert professional staff overseeing their investments and usually use investment consulting firms. They have resources, information, and analytical tools way beyond those most individual investors can access. Yet, these professional investors made what turned out to be terrible hiring and firing decisions and, in aggregate, would have been better off if they had done nothing.

That inactivity is more profitable than activity is an essential mental model to have in our toolbox. Of course, sometimes action is necessary. You can't do nothing when there are portfolio additions and withdrawals or where market returns of different asset classes tilt the portfolio out of balance. So, what's the best way to apply the benefits of inactivity to practical portfolio realities?

Follow simple algorithms.

> THAT INACTIVITY IS MORE PROFITABLE THAN ACTIVITY IS AN ESSENTIAL MENTAL MODEL TO HAVE IN OUR TOOLBOX.

THE BEAUTY OF SIMPLE ALGORITHMS

A baby isn't immediately handed over to its parents when it's born. Medical personnel score the infant in five areas: appearance, pulse, grimace, activity, and respiration. Known as the Apgar score, this evaluation method is a quick and standard way for doctors to evaluate the newborn's health. Doctors grade the newborn from zero to two in each of the five categories and then use interventions like warming or oxygen to improve low scores.

Before the development of the Apgar score in 1952 (by anesthesiologist Dr. Virginia Apgar), doctors used their judgment in an unstructured way based on whatever factors they deemed relevant to determine whether a newborn was in distress. According to Dr. Richard Smiley, chief of obstetric anesthesia at New York-Presbyterian/Columbia University Medical Center, the impact of the "ridiculously simple" Apgar score has been tremendous. "The score gave physicians and nurses a requirement to look at the newborn in an organized way, and it's helped prevent the death of countless babies."[7] Before the Apgar score, babies born small and blue with breathing troubles were often judged too sick to be saved. Application of the Apgar criteria gives medical professionals specific interventions to improve low scores.

The Apgar score is just one example where a simple algorithm serves as a valuable complement to expert judgment. Our brains can only store about seven items of information in our working memory, so when there is lots of information, we quickly become overloaded. Plus, we often focus on the wrong things. Simple algorithms like the Apgar score provide a way to cut through the multitude of factors that may or may not be relevant to a decision and focus us on the most important ones.

SIMPLE ALGORITHMS IMPROVE EXPERT JUDGMENT

Examples where simple algorithms lead to better outcomes than human judgment alone abound.

- Heart attacks. A 1995 study found that emergency room doctors performed no better than a coin flip when deciding whether a patient presenting with chest pains needed to be admitted to the ICU. The study found that "Physicians' admission decisions appeared to be more heavily influenced by pseudo-diagnostic information than by information of objective predictive power."[8] The doctors tended to over-weight factors related to heart disease risk—like age, smoking habits, hypertension, and cholesterol levels—and failed to appropriately weigh criteria that would indicate whether the patient was having a heart attack right then. The researchers tested the use of laminated cards with a decision tree that walked ER docs through steps for determining whether to admit a patient to the ICU. The simple cards significantly improved the doctors' decision making.

- Job interviews. Studies have found that interviews provide little to no benefit in selecting qualified candidates. In fact, they're nearly useless, certainly in the unstructured way they're usually conducted. Interviewers tend to be affected by factors that aren't relevant to job performance, such as attractiveness (we're biased toward good-looking people), height (taller people are perceived as having greater leadership capabilities), extroversion (extroverts may be warmer or more personable in an interview setting), which college they went to, what they're wearing, and so on. What works better? Using standardized scoring to evaluate candidates based on criteria relevant to the job. A meta-analysis of more than 150 studies of interview effectiveness found that using a mechanical formula to guide hiring decisions produced better results than unstructured judgments.[9]

- Marital happiness. Robin Dawes was a psychologist and a pioneer in human judgment best known for championing the idea that linear models with simple algorithms better inform assessments than experience-based factors. In 1976, he published a study that showed a simple formula can predict whether a marriage will be successful: the rate of sexual intercourse minus the rate of arguments.[10] In other words, if a couple registered more acts of lovemaking than quarrels, then their marriage was solid, while the opposite—having more arguments than intimacy—was a warning sign. Subsequent studies have found that this formula is more accurate than the clinical judgments of marriage counselors with decades of experience.

- Baseball. In his best-selling book *Moneyball* (which was turned into a movie starring Brad Pitt), Michael Lewis chronicles how Billy Beane, the general manager of the Oakland A's, put together playoff-caliber teams with one of the lowest budgets in Major League Baseball. Beane's insight was to use statistics-based criteria for evaluating players instead of just relying on his scouts' judgment. Instead of focusing on a player's physical characteristics and all the hundreds of statistics available about the player, Beane used just two criteria: (1) slugging percentage (total bases divided by at-bats) and (2) on-base percentage (the rate at which a batter gets on base for any reason). If the player excelled in these two areas, they were likely to be strong contributors to the team's success. Other teams copied the A's success using these simple rules and have revolutionized the scouting of baseball players.

Other areas where simple algorithms have been shown to be superior to unstructured human judgment include psychological diagnoses, brain damage assessments, determining whether an injured ankle should be x-rayed, parole decisions, and university admissions. Predefined and relevant criteria focus decision making and cut through the noise.

SIMPLE ALGORITHMS IN INVESTING

Investing is fraught with noise and behavioral pitfalls. As we've learned:

- Our pattern-seeking brains see causal relationships where none exist.
- We hate uncertainty, so we seek expert predictions of the future even though stock market forecasts are generally wrong. Or we overload ourselves with information as we look for patterns that will tell us what the future holds.
- We have ingrained biases—such as loss aversion and hindsight bias—that negatively affect our ability to make rational decisions.
- Stories we hear of great-sounding investments cause us to ignore base rates of success and failure.
- We make emotional decisions based on fear and greed.

For all these reasons and more, good investment behavior is challenging. We need simple rules to save us from ourselves.

Investment algorithms are simple rules that are adopted in advance of making any investment decisions and are typically housed in a document called an *investment policy statement* (or IPS). An IPS (at a bare minimum) will determine:

- An asset allocation strategy. That is, the proper mix of stocks, bonds, cash, real assets, private equity, and venture capital for different types of portfolios. An asset allocation for a simple portfolio might be 5 percent cash, 20 percent municipal bonds, 50 percent US stocks, and 25 percent international stocks.

- A rebalancing policy. This is the set of rules for when some investments are sold, and others purchased. While there are various rebalancing strategies, the most common is to rebalance when the values of the different asset classes deviate more than a set amount from the strategic allocation. For example, a rebalancing strategy might call for US stocks to be bought if they decline to 45 percent of the total portfolio or sold if they rise past 55 percent. The portfolio is then periodically rebalanced so that US stocks are at a 50 percent level.

- Guidelines about selecting and firing investment managers.

Rules like these take emotion out of investing and focus decision making on math. For example: Assume the strategic asset allocation detailed in the first bullet point of the preceding list. Due to stock market increases, the percentages have shifted to 15 percent cash and bonds, 57 percent US stocks, and 28 percent international stocks. Your portfolio is worth $1 million, and you need to withdraw $100,000. The simple rules of the asset allocation say that you should withdraw $70,000 from US stocks and $30,000 from international stocks because they are above the strategic allocation. Funding your cash needs from those investments will bring your asset allocation back in line. You'll do this even if you're caught up in the euphoria of a rising stock market and don't like the idea of selling your high-flying equities.

Now, again assume the strategic asset allocation detailed in the first bullet point and imagine that a bear market is ravaging the stock market. While your cash and bonds have held their value, your stocks have declined, and your portfolio has dropped from $1 million to $775,000. Ouch. Your portfolio is now 35 percent cash and bonds, 43 percent US stocks, and 22 percent international stocks. If your rebalancing policy is triggered by the increase in the cash and bond percentage of your portfolio and the decline in your equities, you'll sell $77,500 of your bonds and buy stocks to bring your allocation back in line. You'll do this even if you fear (and the pundits say) the stock market will keep falling.

The simple rules of asset allocation and rebalancing force you to buy low and sell high—the very definition of successful investing. Plus, selling what has gone up and buying what has gone down takes advantage of regression to the mean.

From an investment perspective, this isn't sexy. It's much more fun to try to pick stocks, sectors, trends, and investment managers that you think will be big winners. But as our housekeeper and investment banker illustrated, sophisticated and sexy don't necessarily win. To be a successful investor, boring and unsexy is usually the way to go. (And with all the time you'll save not reading and researching the markets you can work on adding sexiness to other areas of your life.)

CHOOSE SIMPLICITY OVER COMPLEXITY

INVESTMENT INDUSTRY ENTROPY

In physics, entropy refers to a closed system's general progression from order to disorder. It's one of the universe's fundamental laws and is summarized as "things fall apart." Or, "rust never sleeps." For example, when thrown to the wind, an ordered deck of cards scatters in a disordered fashion, while an unordered deck thrown to the wind does not reorder itself. Also, when you drop an egg, it breaks; a broken egg won't pull itself back together (*vide* Humpty Dumpty) no matter how hard you try or how long you wait. Entropy gives time its arrow; the past flows into the future, not vice versa.

The financial system has its own version of entropy: it progresses from simplicity to complexity. Over the past fifty years, we've seen the rise of mutual funds, ETFs, hedge funds and the alternatives industry, derivatives, structured products, collateralized loan obligations, credit default swaps, the securitization of debt instruments, liquid alternative funds, and so on. Have these innovations and the accompanying rise in complexity been beneficial to investors? The answer, on the whole, appears to be no. Greater size and complexity generate fees and taxes that eat into returns and make practicing good investment behavior more challenging. Vanguard founder John Bogle put it this way: "Financial institutions operate by a kind of reverse Occam's razor. They have a large incentive to favor the complex and costly over the simple and cheap, quite the opposite of what most investors need and ought to want."[11]

Even when a financial innovation initially offers greater simplicity, it evolves toward greater complexity. For example, the index mutual fund industry, which offered a simple way to gain low-cost, diversified equity exposure, gave rise to single stocks that track indexes in the form of ETFs. That seems straightforward and nice. But what began as a single ETF that tracked the S&P 500 has since spawned over 7,600 ETF products. Looking to expand the investable universe of ETFs, the investment industry has created more indexes than stocks (5,000 US indexes versus about 4,000 US public companies).

Access to thousands of ETFs tracking thousands of indexes provides an easy mechanism for investors to focus on specific industries or trends that interest them. For instance, if you want to invest in companies related to electric vehicles, you can buy an ETF that tracks an electric vehicle index. But should you really buy ETFs that focus on specific themes or sectors? Do you know something other investors (including the pros) don't know about EV stocks? As we learned in Chapter 7, investing in trends is challenging.

SHOULD YOU INVEST LIKE A UNIVERSITY ENDOWMENT?

University endowments are known for their complex asset allocations across alternative investments (which are basically anything other than bonds and publicly traded stocks). Because endowments publish their asset allocations and investment returns, we can get a good read on whether complex portfolios perform better than simple ones.

Investing like endowments is called the *endowment model* (also called the Yale model). It was developed by David Swenson, Yale's longtime chief investment officer, and popularized in his 2000 book, *Pioneering Portfolio Management*. The primary characteristics of the endowment model are:

- Broad diversification across asset classes
- Low allocations to assets with low expected returns, such as fixed income and commodities
- High allocations to illiquid assets such as hedge funds, private equity, private real estate, and venture capital

Beginning in the mid-1980s, Swenson (who died in 2021) led Yale's endowment to an 11.3 percent annualized return over the twenty years ending June 30, 2021. That made it the top-performing endowment for that period.

Since its popularization in the 2000s, the endowment model has attracted fans throughout the investment industry. Tax-exempt investors such as pension plans and foundations, as well as taxable high net worth individuals, have sought to emulate Yale's and Swenson's model.

But Yale's returns weren't just about its philosophy. Yale employs roomfuls of investment and legal professionals; it has numerous strategic partnerships and a name that gives them access to top investment managers. While other endowments have delivered stellar, Yale-like returns (such as Washington University in St. Louis, which notched the top endowment return of 65 percent for fiscal year 2021 and was the second-highest performer in fiscal year 2020), most endowments have struggled to keep up.

The National Association of College and University Business Officers (NACUBO) and TIAA annually release their "Study of Endowments," which provides a report of university endowment investment allocations and returns. The NACUBO-TIAA study provides data on 720 university endowments, ranging from the 29 with less than $25 million to 136 with more than $1 billion. The data shows that the larger endowments have made more significant allocations to alternative asset classes like hedge funds, private equity, venture capital, and real assets. The smaller endowments have made relatively larger allocations to public stocks and bonds. All 720 endowments roll up to the allocation on the right side of Figure 10.2; as a comparison, a simple 70/30 index fund model—70 percent equity, 30 percent bonds and cash—is on the left.

ALLOCATIONS OF 70/30 INDEX
PORTFOLIO AND ALL ENDOWMENTS

70/30 Indexed   **All Endowments Average**

FIGURE 10.2

In terms of passive versus active, endowments use active managers for 70 percent of their domestic public stocks and 90 percent of their international equities. Of course, all their private equity, venture capital, and real asset investments are active.

Are the illiquidity, complexity, and fees inherent in the endowment model worth it for universities? Let's compare endowment returns to the simple indexed portfolio of 70 percent publicly traded stocks and 30 percent bonds and cash shown in Figure 10.2.[12] The data shows that endowments and a 70/30 index portfolio have generated returns that are indistinguishable. The median endowment in the NACUBO-TIAA study is slightly higher than the 70/30 index portfolio over the past one and five years but marginally less over ten and fifteen years, as shown in Figure 10.3.

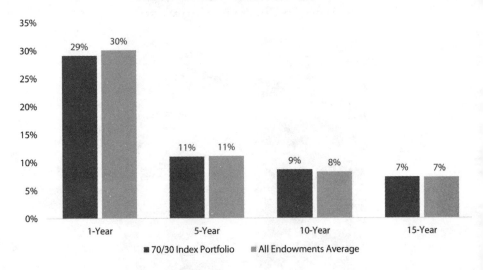

ANNUALIZED RETURNS OF
70/30 INDEX VS. ALL ENDOWMENTS

FIGURE 10.3

Digging more deeply into the data:

- In general, larger endowments performed better than smaller ones over all periods. While the study offers no reason for that, the higher returns of large endowments are likely due to their more aggressive allocations to private equity and venture capital (and better access to top funds in those asset classes) combined with a lower allocation to bonds.

- Overall, the endowments' active public stock investment managers underperformed the market.

- Speaking of the market, the S&P 500 has had a fantastic fifteen-year run, returning just under 11 percent per year. Investments in almost any other asset class failed to keep up, resulting in the endowments underperforming the S&P 500 over the fifteen-year period.

Yale, Washington University, and other top endowments demonstrate that the endowment model can deliver exceptional returns. However, the NACUBO-TIAA study indicates that many universities are spending a lot of time, resources, and expense trying to emulate the top-performing endowments without much to show for it. For individual investors, this should be a red flag. If endowments, with all their resources, aren't doing any better as a group than a simple index portfolio, then the odds are against individual investors matching the returns of the top endowments by using the Yale model.

Then there are taxes. Endowments, unlike individual portfolios (except for retirement accounts), are tax-exempt. If endowments had to pay taxes, they would invest in a more tax-efficient manner. In their paper, "What Would Yale Do If It Were Taxable?,"[13] authors Patrick Geddes, Lisa R. Goldberg, and Stephen W. Bianchi of investment firm Aperio Group conclude that if Yale paid taxes, it would alter its investment allocations by:

- eliminating active equity managers and hedge funds,
- reducing allocations to private equity and real assets, and
- increasing the percentage in index funds and municipal bonds.

In other words, Yale would move closer to a 70/30 index portfolio than the endowment model if it had to pay taxes, as you do.

And David Swenson agreed. In 2005, he published a second book, *Unconventional Success: A Fundamental Approach to Personal Investment*, directed at the individual investor in which he advised broad diversification using index funds, disciplined rebalancing, and a long-term focus.[14] Furthermore, in 2009, Swenson updated *Pioneering Portfolio Management* and warned against most investors following Yale's approach. Specifically, he noted that "Few institutions, and even fewer individuals, exhibit the ability and commit the resources to produce risk-adjusted excess returns."[15]

THE ALLURE OF INVESTMENT COMPLEXITY

About ten years ago, I attended an investment conference for family offices. Everyone (except me) was from a large (mainly $1 billion-plus) single-family office. On day two of the conference, we were split into six mock investment committees and given the task of designing an investment portfolio for a fictitious family that had just netted $1 billion from the sale of their business. After hours of work and deliberation, each committee presented their proposed portfolios to the entire group. The first five committees recommended portfolios reminiscent of the Endowment Model. Figure 10.4 shows the proposed allocation of Committee Five, which was typical of what the committees presented.

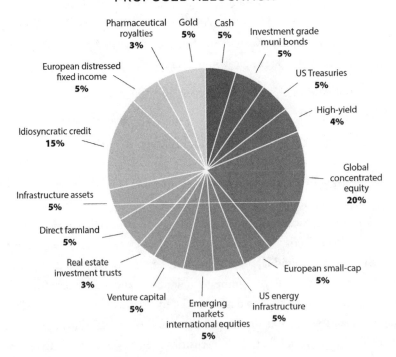

INVESTMENT COMMITTEE FIVE'S PROPOSED ALLOCATION

FIGURE 10.4: A TYPICAL INVESTMENT COMMITTEE PROPOSAL

My investment committee, number six, presented last. Our proposed allocation was straightforward: just two investment funds—a municipal bond fund and an index fund that tracks the global stock market (see Figure 10.5).

INVESTMENT COMMITTEE SIX'S PROPOSED ALLOCATION

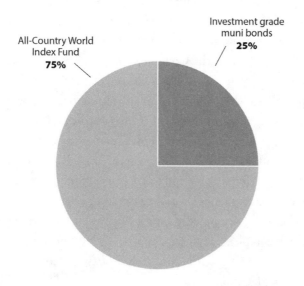

All-Country World Index Fund **75%**

Investment grade muni bonds **25%**

FIGURE 10.5: THE SIMPLE PROPOSAL FOR INVESTING $1 BILLION

When our committee presented our allocation, people chuckled. One audience member said, "Just two funds for $1 billion? Are you serious?" We were. Our portfolio would be cheap—less than 0.1 percent in fees—and extremely tax efficient. Administering the portfolio would be a breeze and promote good investment behavior because investment decisions would be limited to buying or selling just two funds. We asked the other thirty-five or so investment professionals in the audience to raise their hand if they were more than 75 percent confident they could beat our simple portfolio over the next ten years. Nobody did.

That night, over cocktails, I was approached by a man who worked at a $10 billion single-family office. He said that our committee's presentation was troubling. He admitted that his complex portfolio had lagged a simple portfolio like the one we proposed. Plus, his portfolio generated a ton of tax drag. But moving to a simple portfolio would mean he'd have to fire all fourteen of his investment staff and maybe himself. Also, he didn't think the family that employed him would be happy with such a simple portfolio. They wanted sophisticated investments they could talk about with their friends.

Our simple portfolio has done well over the ten years since I attended the conference, posting an 9.5 percent annual return. How did the complex portfolio of Investment Committee Five do? Since we don't know which investment managers would have been employed, or how the committee would have shifted allocations among asset classes over time, we can't say for sure. But an analyst at my firm constructed Investment Committee Five's portfolio using mainly index funds and representative active funds and found that it returned 8.2 percent annually, materially lagging our two-fund portfolio (at the end of ten years the simple portfolio would have about 14 percent more assets than the complex one).

Over the years, I've noted there's a correlation between a portfolio's size and how complex people expect it to be. No one at the conference would have batted an eye if I'd proposed just two funds for a $100,000 portfolio. But $1 billion invested in just two funds? Heresy! The bigger the portfolio, the stronger the siren song of complexity.

I've seen thousands of investment portfolios over my career: those of friends, clients transferring from other firms, and the dozens that our firm oversees as a family office that other investment advisors (such as Merrill Lynch, Morgan Stanley, J.P. Morgan, and Bank of America) manage. With rare exceptions, most portfolios are needlessly complex and packed with funds. One recent new client who came from the wealth management arm of a large bank had more than twenty different funds in his portfolio, each with its own strategy. Over the years, all these funds and their inherent complexity had resulted in an expensive, tax-inefficient portfolio that underperformed the market by a few percentage points a year. A simpler portfolio would have served him better.

But recommending a simple portfolio is hard. A few years ago, I had lunch with a financial advisor from a large brokerage firm. Our conversation turned to how we'd each invest a $100 million portfolio. (Among advisors, that's like talking sports.) I said that we'd mainly invest it in municipal bonds and one or two tax-managed index funds to reduce tax burdens. We'd also allocate a portion to private equity and real estate. He replied, "I wish we could recommend such a simple portfolio, but we can't because there's no way clients would pay us. You can be so simple because you're a family office and provide so many other services that your clients value."

Portfolios often end up stuffed with complexity because advisors need to justify their existence.

WHEN ADDING COMPLEXITY IS JUSTIFIED

Simplicity is an essential mental model when making investment decisions. That doesn't mean that every investor should have only two or three index funds. But we should start with simplicity as our default and view complexity with skepticism. We should only add complexity to portfolios when doing so outweighs the benefits of simplicity.

For example, our firm commonly recommends a *tax-managed index separate account.* In this type of account, an investment manager buys individual stocks to create an index for the client and trades stocks to generate tax benefits, so that the fund's after-tax performance beats the index. We believe the near-certain after-tax outperformance of the separate account compared to the overall market is worth the added complexity over just buying an index-tracking ETF.

> PORTFOLIOS OFTEN END UP STUFFED WITH COMPLEXITY BECAUSE ADVISORS NEED TO JUSTIFY THEIR EXISTENCE.

Investing in private equity, venture capital, and private real estate also can be worth the added complexity. The information playing field is not level in private investing, and leading private investment managers provide outsized returns. If you can access top private investment managers, the potential returns warrant the complexity.

WHAT GOOD INVESTMENT
BEHAVIOR LOOKS LIKE

Let's revisit the examples at the beginning of this chapter to recap what good behavior looks like.

THE HOUSEKEEPER AND THE INVESTMENT BANKER

Remember how the housekeeper's portfolio handily outperformed the portfolio of an investment banker? What were the differences in their behavior that made this happen?

The housekeeper didn't read the *Wall Street Journal*, watch CNBC, or follow investment gurus on Twitter. She didn't discuss hot investments with her friends, pay attention to the stock market, or tinker with her portfolio of four index mutual funds. The only thing she did with her portfolio was simple rebalancing when it got out of whack.

In contrast, the investment banker's portfolio was jam-packed with all sorts of funds, strategies, and individual stocks he had selected himself. It looked a lot like Committee Five's complex portfolio from the family office conference (Figure 10.4.) He constantly tinkered, adding and subtracting according to what he saw in the economy and the world. He hired and fired investment managers. He didn't follow an investment discipline of simple algorithms. He usually rejected our advice that promoted inactivity and simplicity. His returns suffered.

UNSOPHISTICATED SIBLINGS

Why do unsophisticated siblings often outperform their more investment-savvy brothers and sisters? As with the housekeeper, unsophisticated siblings tend to be more receptive to simple portfolios. Typically, they are better than their sophisticated brothers and sisters in holding fire in the face of the market's inherent uncertainty and unending turmoil. Unsophisticated siblings are better at following the simple rules of asset allocation and rebalancing and resisting the urge to tinker.

SMALL PORTFOLIOS

Most of our clients have multiple portfolios of different values, and the large portfolios attract more attention than the small ones. This makes sense. You pay more attention to your $50 million portfolio than the $100,000 one you set up for your grandchildren. But more attention often means more activity, more tinkering. More attention makes it harder to follow the simple rebalancing algorithm with larger dollar amounts. In March 2020, when the S&P 500 was down more than 30 percent, selling bonds and buying stocks in the face of bad news was more challenging for a large portfolio than a smaller one. Rebalancing is harder with bigger dollar amounts because more is at stake.

MY 401(K) VERSUS MY OUTRIGHT ACCOUNT

My 401(k) has outperformed my outright account over the past ten years. The 401(k) is invested in four Vanguard index funds: a bond fund, a large-cap fund, a small-cap fund, and an international fund. I go months without looking at it. Money gets added each pay period and invested according to my allocation. Twice a year, it's automatically rebalanced. I don't have to do anything. It's performed great.

I'm not as disciplined with my outright account. My primary investments are in index funds that are factor-tilted (e.g., quality, low volatility). But I also own a few individual stocks, two actively managed funds, and a smattering of thematic investments like ETFs that invest in industrial real estate, cannabis companies, and genomics-focused biotech firms. Thus, I have more than just four index funds, making it harder to practice good behavior. I'm not as disciplined as I should be about rebalancing or adding to investments in my portfolio that are under-weighted. I know I'd be better off just having a handful of index funds in my outright account. It would be simpler and would promote better investing behavior. But I like to buy individual stocks and thematic ETFs now and then. For me, it's fun. Fortunately, my tinkering stays on the fringes, and I practice good behavior with the core of my portfolio. But I could (and should) do better.

EIGHT INVESTMENT BEHAVIOR BEST PRACTICES

Practicing good investment behavior is simple but not easy. It's not easy because we're human. We seek (and often kid ourselves that we find) certainty in an uncertain world. We are at the mercy of fear and greed. But a fantastic thing about being human (in addition to our opposable thumbs) is that we can decide to override our emotions and baser instincts. Here are eight best practices that will help you exercise optimal investment behavior:

1. **Choose inactivity over activity.** Don't tinker with your portfolio. Don't try to time the markets. When fear or greed makes you want to change things up, take a deep breath. Then take another. If you're a man, tell yourself to invest like a woman. If you're a woman, try to invest like a dead person.

2. **Prefer simplicity over complexity.** Start with simplicity as your default. Only add complexity if there is a good reason to do so. Complexity makes good behavior harder, adds fees, and generates more taxes.

3. **Create an investment policy statement.** This will set up your investing algorithms. Follow them. The simple rules of asset allocation and rebalancing will provide guardrails for your behavior and improve your returns.

4. **Build a margin of safety into your portfolio.** Have enough cash that you won't be forced to sell assets when they're down (you want to buy low and sell high, not the reverse). What's a reasonable margin of safety? Our firm advises one to three years of portfolio withdrawals to be held in cash. Plus, having a portion in high-quality bonds provides an additional safety margin. Having sufficient cash and bonds also makes it emotionally easier to ride out stormy markets.

5. **Focus on the long term.** When the market drops, remind yourself that you don't need to cash out today, next week, next month, or

even next year. So don't focus on those periods. Over the short term, the market might be down. Over the long term, history teaches us that the market will be up. Since 1871, the stock market has delivered a positive return 100 percent of the time over twenty-year periods and 89 percent of the time over ten-year periods. But, over shorter time frames, the stock market is much less consistent, delivering positive quarters 63 percent of the time and positive daily returns just 52 percent of the time.

6. **Don't look at your portfolio.** When the market is up, frustration with lagging investments might lead you to sell them. When the market is down, seeing your losses (which, remember, are only on paper) will cause stress, leading you to tinker. Don't.

7. **Have a "play" account.** Some people are fine with simplicity and inactivity; others enjoy researching and investing in individual companies. If you fall into this latter category, having a play account that's relatively small where you buy individual stocks, thematic ETFs, and tinker can provide a nice outlet for your "bad" investing behavior. Having this release will help you to practice good behavior in your larger, more serious accounts.

8. **Find the right advisor.** Following the seven behavior best practices listed above is easier with the guidance of a humble and wise investment advisor. Vanguard champions a concept called "advisor's alpha," which outlines "how advisors [can] add value, or alpha, through relationship-oriented services such as providing cogent wealth management through financial planning, discipline, and guidance, rather than by trying to outperform the market."[16] That's the type of advisor you should look for—one who will help guide your behavior rather than someone who constantly strives to prove their value by suggesting hot investments and loading your portfolio with complexity.

THERE'S GRANDEUR IN THIS VIEW OF INVESTING

In 1859, Charles Darwin published one of the most famous books in history: *On the Origin of Species by Means of Natural Selection, or the Preservation of Favoured Races in the Struggle for Life*, more commonly known as *The Origin of Species*.

What Darwin proposed in the book, of course, was that life-forms evolve. Specifically, organisms change due to the combination of three factors: (1) mutation, (2) selection for or against those mutations, and (3) time—lots and lots of it.

Darwin was aware that his theory would be controversial. It ran contrary to the religious belief that a supreme being created all species in their current form and pronounced them good. Darwin also knew that compared to the creation story, his theory would seem chaotic and inelegant. Evolution relies on randomness and chance; it is unpredictable. Nothing about that is comforting.

Darwin closes his book with an argument that the concept of evolution is beautiful in its own right, more elegant even than the notion of a supreme creator:

There is grandeur in this view of life, with its several powers, having been originally breathed into a few forms or into one; and that, whilst this planet has gone cycling on according to the fixed law of gravity, from so simple a beginning endless forms most beautiful and wonderful have been, and are being, evolved.[1]

Darwin asks us to see that the idea of complex organisms evolving from simple, single-celled life forms over millions of years through randomness and chance is fantastic and beautiful.

Similarly, I ask you to see the grandeur in the view of investing laid out in this book. Initially, it's tough to accept that predictions are useless, and no investment guru can consistently provide you with market-beating returns. Or that successful investing requires focusing on our own behaviors and fighting against our hard-wired biases. I get it. As I mentioned in the introduction, my editor said that learning about the mental models in this book was like being told there's no Santa Claus.

SIMILARLY, I ASK YOU TO SEE THE GRANDEUR IN THE VIEW OF INVESTING LAID OUT IN THIS BOOK.

But another way to look at it—the way I look at it—is that the uncertainty, randomness, and complexity of the economy and the financial markets are fantastic and beautiful. Billions of people in economies across the globe make individual decisions that roll up to create booms and busts, winners and losers. It's me watching you, you watching me, me watching you watching me, and so on, multiplied by the billions. The nature of the economy and stock market—complex and adaptive—creates huge, disruptive swings, punctuated by periods of calm. There are disruptions. There are opportunities. New technologies give birth to new industries with new winners and losers; companies rise and fall.

As we live our lives, we ride this wave of uncertainty. We all face an unpredictable future. Ignoring this reality will not make you a better investor. That's "the uncertainty solution"—accepting the world as it is. Instead of searching in vain for certainty in a world and a market that does not and will never contain it, we're better off accepting things as they are and paying attention to what we can control: our own behavior. We can best do this by focusing on creating a latticework of mental models that will help us make better decisions.

I can't be sure, but it's my hope that this book has helped you along that path.

ACKNOWLEDGMENTS

Writing and publishing this book was a fun-filled journey full of ups and downs. There's no way I could have crossed the finish line without the support and help of many others—it definitely takes a village to produce a book.

First and foremost, a huge thank you to my book coach and editor Nancy Erickson (www.thebookprofessor.com). I would have been completely lost without her—she taught me how to write a book and was my primary editor. David Rosenbaum of RhetorIQ tightened, cut, and sprinkled fairy dust with his edits and overall improved the readability of the book.

Numerous coworkers provided invaluable assistance. Caroline Moore acted as "chief of staff" of the book by taking on whatever needed to be done along the way, including creating many of the images in the book, making editing suggestions, and spearheading marketing and social media. Jenni De Jong worked tirelessly on images and procuring permission for quotes and images. Sam Gogel and Andrew Stange provided essential analysis, research, and charts.

A big thank you to my partners at St. Louis Trust & Family Office, Julie Lilly, Cece Strand, and Michael Small, who were all-in on the idea of me writing a book and generously supported the use of firm resources to make it happen.

Early readers who provided helpful guidance and comments include

Matt Hall, Patrick Geddes, Spencer Burke, Greg Stokke, my brother Drew, daughter Claire, and mother Pam.

Without Dr. Michael Brog's counseling and encouragement I would have never embarked on the journey of writing a book; I found the idea of writing a book terrifying, and Dr. Brog helped me take the plunge. A huge shout-out to my wife Tammy who tirelessly indulges my obsessions, including this book.

A big thank you to friend and author Matt Hall who was a great sounding board about writing a book and then introduced me to Justin Branch at Greenleaf Book Group. I had no idea how much work went into publishing a book. My team at Greenleaf was amazing in shepherding the book (and me) through all the twists and turns.

THE MENTAL MODELS

CHAPTER	MENTAL MODEL	DESCRIPTION
Introduction	The Wisdom Hierarchy	Think of information in four categories: data, information, knowledge, and wisdom. Turn off the noise of data and information. Focus on knowledge or, better yet, wisdom.
1. The Quest for Certainty	Uncertainty	We dislike uncertainty. It makes us stressed and triggers our fight-or-flight response. When we resolve uncertainty, we feel pleasure. So we seek certainty. Recognize when you feel the discomfort of uncertainty. Resist seeking closure, becoming an information junkie, listening to expert predictions, or associating with groups who think just like you do. Instead, sit in your discomfort and focus on what you can control.

CHAPTER	MENTAL MODEL	DESCRIPTION
2. Looking for Causes in All the Wrong Places	Causation Is Tough to Determine	It's risky to think that one thing has caused another. Coincidence can lead us to assume causation. Multiple factors often combine to create outcomes, so it's usually impossible to pinpoint a single cause.
	Correlation Does Not Imply Causation	Just because two things are strongly correlated doesn't mean that one causes the other. Remember that unrelated variables—like Bangladeshi butter production and the stock market—can be highly correlated.
	Regression to the Mean	Regression to the mean describes the phenomenon whereby extreme events are usually followed by ones closer to the average. Regression occurs whenever two variables are less than perfectly correlated, like child and parent heights. Regression to the mean explains why it may make sense to invest in underperforming funds and why outstanding performance is often followed by stumbles.
	The Law of Large Numbers	Beware of drawing conclusions based on small sample sizes. As sample sizes get smaller, variation from the mean increases exponentially. Ignorance of this statistical law has led to a lot of wasted time and money. Asking "what's the sample size?" is critical whenever causation is asserted.

CHAPTER	MENTAL MODEL	DESCRIPTION
	The Highly Improbable Happens All the Time	The highly improbable happens all the time. Coincidences are not supernatural miracles; they're just math. Being surprised by unlikely occurrences can leave us unprepared both in our portfolios and in our lives.
3. The Stock Market Is Not the Economy, (or What Toilet Paper Can Teach Us About Investing)	The Stock Market Is Not the Economy	Economic growth and stock market performance are not correlated. The stock market often rebounds when economic news is bad and declines when it is good.
	The Stock Market Is a Complex Adaptive System	Millions of intelligent agents are all watching each other, learning, drawing their own conclusions, and creating feedback loops, which makes predicting the stock market movements nearly impossible.
	Economic Indicators Don't Predict the Stock Market	Because the stock market is a complex adaptive system, economic indicators and market signals don't predict market performance. The market changes and evolves, and investors learn. Indicators that might be predictive of market returns will be destroyed once they are widely known by those millions of agents.
4. Market Cycles and the Two Axioms of Investing	Markets Move in Cycles but Defy Prediction	Boom followed by bust followed by boom. Cycles vary in duration as well as the height of their peaks and the depth of their valleys, but there are no permanent plateaus. Knowing where you are in the market cycle can help you practice good investment behavior by not getting caught up in the greed of market tops or the panic that accompanies market bottoms.

CHAPTER	MENTAL MODEL	DESCRIPTION
	Economic Stability Creates Instability	Minsky's financial instability hypothesis holds that it is stability that creates the behavior that leads to bubbles and crashes. Thus, times of apparent stability are the riskiest; the best opportunities often occur when everyone else is going cuckoo.
	Market Timing Doesn't Work	Trying to time the markets doesn't work. A primary reason is because the market is a complex adaptive system. Plus, in order for market timing to work you have to be right twice—once at the top and then again at the bottom.
	It's Okay to Invest in Advance of a Bear Market	Waiting to invest until the coast is clear is not a sound strategy. Even if you invest just a few years in advance of a bear market, your portfolio will do fine if you don't panic and follow a disciplined strategy.
	The Limits of Arbitrage	Being right doesn't mean you win because the market can stay wrong for a long time ("the market can stay irrational longer than you can stay solvent"). You must be right at the right time, which is challenging.
5. Beware Experts Bearing Predictions	Economic and Stock Market Predictions Are Worthless	Investment predictions are hopelessly wrong, especially when we need them most. The biggest misconception in investing is that you need to know the future to invest well. Having a crystal ball would be great, but nobody has one. It is better to invest as if you don't know the future (which is the case).

CHAPTER	MENTAL MODEL	DESCRIPTION
6. Skill and Luck in Investing	The Skill-Luck Continuum	Luck plays a big role in investing, so we shouldn't read too much into good or bad results over short periods. Randomly selected stocks, middle-schoolers, and monkeys can score outstanding returns; grizzled investment veterans have dismal results. And vice versa.
	Most Investment Managers Underperform the Market	Most active managers underperform after fees. And sticking with those who outperform can be a bumpy ride. This doesn't mean you should never invest with an active manager—but you should consider the odds before you do so.
	Most Stocks Underperform the Market	Buying an individual stock is like flipping a weighted coin where you lose the majority of the time. It's essential to understand the odds before you decide to pick an individual stock.
	Monkey Portfolios Outperform	Beating the market requires investing differently than the market, which requires great heart and discipline. If you choose to break off from the herd, it's essential to stick with your strategy through the inevitable ups and downs.
	Private Investments	It is easier to outperform in private investing, primarily due to information asymmetries that don't exist in public markets. If you have the financial resources, adding private investments to a portfolio with skilled investment managers is the way to go.

CHAPTER	MENTAL MODEL	DESCRIPTION
	Creating vs. Preserving Great Wealth	Great wealth is generated by owning a concentrated position in a single company in which you invest your own blood, sweat, and tears. Investing in the stock market isn't likely to lead to great wealth but can nicely grow wealth generated elsewhere.
7. The Trend Is Not Your Friend	It Is Difficult to Spot a Trend Early	It's hard to spot trends early, partially due to the challenges of comprehending the nature of exponential growth. Remember Oak versus Acorn.
	Trends Don't Always Turn Out as Imagined	Established trends can change course rapidly as new competitors and technologies upend trends. Remember the "Malthusean catastrophe."
	It's Difficult to Find a Successful Needle in a Haystack of Competitors	It's hard to pick winners. As new technologies create new industries, many companies enter, and most fail. Early pioneers usually aren't the long-term winners. Instead, fast followers often are the most successful. Remember that Google was the twenty-first search engine.
8. The Trivial Many versus the Vital Few	The Danger of Using the Bell Curve in Investing	The use of bell curve statistics is commonplace in the investment industry even though it doesn't capture the true nature of how the stock market behaves. Be skeptical of advice based on bell curve statistics.

CHAPTER	MENTAL MODEL	DESCRIPTION
	The Stock Market Is Better Described by Power Law Distributions	Instead of relying on the fanciful projections of movements and returns in the stock market that come from the bell curve, it's better to embrace the uncertainty provided by power law distributions. Expect the unexpected. Wild randomness will erupt. It always does. Prepare your portfolio and your emotions for the volatility of wild randomness.
9. Navigating Our Behavioral Biases	The Endowment Effect	We overvalue things that we own, including our investments.
	The Storytelling Bias	We've evolved to pay attention to and communicate through stories. As such, stories make an outsized impact in our decision making. When we invest, we evaluate stories. Realize that stories will sway your investment decisions, and step back and ask, "what's the base rate?"
	Hindsight Bias	We look back at the past and think we should have known the future. We tend to judge the quality of decisions by how they turned out. Realize that at each moment there are an infinite number of possible future states, only one of which will happen. Adopt the concept of "invisible histories" when looking at past decisions—things could have easily turned out differently and changed the result.
	Loss Aversion	Losses are about two times as painful as gains are pleasurable. This asymmetry leads us to be risk adverse in order to protect gains and risk seeking instead of taking losses.

CHAPTER	MENTAL MODEL	DESCRIPTION
	Overconfidence	We think we know more than we do. This is the mother of all biases and an ingrained human trait. Overconfidence is a primary ingredient in bad decisions. Recognizing our (and others') overconfidence is an essential mental model. Also, realize that we are drawn to overconfident experts, yet confidence and predictive ability are negatively correlated.
10. Behavior— The Most Important Ingredient	Choose Inactivity Over Activity	Don't tinker with your portfolio. Don't try to time the markets. When fear or greed makes you want to change things up, take a deep breath. Then take another. If you're a man, tell yourself to invest like a woman. If you're a woman, try to invest like a dead person.
	Prefer Simplicity Over Complexity	Start with simplicity as your default. Only add complexity if there is a good reason to do so. Complexity makes good behavior harder, adds fees, and generates more taxes.
	Establish Simple Investment Algorithms	Create an investment policy statement. This will set up your investing algorithms. Follow them. The simple rules of asset allocation and rebalancing will provide guardrails for your behavior and improve your returns.

NOTES

INTRODUCTION

1. Peter D. Kaufman, ed., *Poor Charlie's Almanack—The Wit and Wisdom of Charles T. Munger*, 3rd ed. (Virginia Beach: VAPCA Publications, 2015), 166.

2. Berkshire Hathaway, Inc., Chairman's Letter, 1986.

CHAPTER 1

1. Archy O. de Berker, Robb B. Rutledge, Christoph Mathys, Louise Marshall, Gemma F. Cross, Raymond J. Dolan, and Sven Bestmann, "Computations of Uncertainty Mediate Acute Stress Responses in Humans," *Nature Communications* (2016): 7, https://www.nature.com/articles/ncomms10996.

2. Fadel K. Matta, Brent A. Scott, Jason A. Colquitt, Joel Koopman, and Liana G. Passantino, "Is Consistently Unfair Better than Sporadically Fair? An Investigation of Justice Variability and Stress," *Academy of Management Journal* 60, no. 2 (2016): 743–770.

3. S. Epstein and A. Roupenian, "Heart Rate and Skin Conductance During Experimentally Induced Anxiety: The Effect of Uncertainty about Receiving a Noxious Stimulus," *Journal of Personality and Social Psychology* 16, no. 1 (1970): 20–28, https://doi.org/10.1037/h0029786.

4. Sandra G. Zakowski, "The Effects of Stressor Predictability on Lymphocyte Proliferation in Humans," *Psychology & Health* 10, no. 5 (1995): 409–425, https://www.tandfonline.com/doi/abs/10.1080/08870449508401960.

5. Jerome Kagan, "Motives and Development," *Journal of Personality and Social Psychology* 22, no. 1 (1972): 51–66.

6. Arie Kruglanski, "3 Ways the Coronavirus Pandemic is Changing Who We Are," *The Conversation*, March 20, 2020, https://theconversation. com/3-ways-the-coronavirus-pandemic-is-changing-who-we-are-133876.

7. Richard J. Zeckhauser, "Investing in the Unknown and Unknowable," *Capitalism and Society* 1, issue 2, article 5 (2006), https://ssrn.com/abstract=2205821.

8. A.W. Kruglanski, PhD and E. Orehek, PhD, "The Need for Certainty as a Psychological Nexus for Individuals and Society," *Extremism and the Psychology of Uncertainty* (2011), https://doi.org/10.1002/9781444344073.ch1.

9. Joseph E. Uscinski and Joseph M. Parent, *American Conspiracy Theories* (Oxford: Oxford University Press, 2014), 11.

10. Thom Nulty, "If You Have a Fear of Flying, You're Not Alone," *Denver Business Journal*, March 4, 2001, https://www.bizjournals.com/denver/stories/2001/03/05/ smallb5.html.

CHAPTER 2

1. Eric Oliver and Thomas Wood, "Conspiracy Theories and the Paranoid Style(s) of Mass Opinion," *American Journal of Political Science* 58, no. 4 (October 2014): 952–966.

2. Oliver and Wood, "Conspiracy Theories," 89–90.

3. J.-W. van Prooijen, A. P. M. Krouwel, and T.V. Pollet, "Political Extremism Predicts Belief in Conspiracy Theories," *Social Psychological and Personality Science* 6, no. 5 (2015): 570–578, https://doi.org/10.1177/1948550614567356.

4. Michael Shermer, "Paranoia Strikes Deep," *Scientific American*, September 1, 2009, https://www.scientificamerican.com/article/paranoia-strikes-deep/.

5. Stephen Mumford and Rani Anjum, *Causation: A Very Short Introduction* (Oxford: Oxford University Press, 2013), chap. 1, Kindle.

6. Credit Suisse Research Institute, "The CS Gender 3000: Women in Senior Management," September 2016, https://www.insurance.ca.gov/diversity/41-ISDGBD/GBDExternal/upload/CSRICSGender3000-2016.pdf.

7. "STUDY: Women CEOs Outperform Male CEOs 3 to 1," *Female Entrepreneurs* (blog), May 11, 2015, https://femaleentrepreneurs.institute/ study-women-ceos-outperform-male-ceos-3-to-1/.

8. Rocío Lorenzo, Nicole Voigt, Matt Krentz, and Katie Abouzahr, "How Diverse Leadership Teams Boost Innovation," *BCG* (blog), January 23, 2018, https://www.bcg. com/en-us/publications/2018/how-diverse-leadership-teams-boost-innovation.

9. Alice Eagly, "Women as Leaders: Leadership Style Versus Leaders' Values and Attitudes," Paper presented at Harvard Business School's Research Symposium *Gender*

and Work: Challenging Conventional Wisdom, 2013, https://www.hbs.edu/faculty/conferences/2013-w50-research-symposium/Documents/eagly.pdf.

10. James Thompson, "Corporate Women," *The Unz Review*, August 22, 2017, https://www.unz.com/jthompson/corporate-women/.

11. Example adapted from *Causation: A Very Short Introduction* by Stephen Mumford and Rani Lill Anjum.

12. David J. Leinweber, *Nerds on Wall Street: Math, Machines and Wired Markets* (Hoboken, NJ: John Wiley & Sons, Inc., 2009), chap. 6, Kindle.

13. Ivan O. Kitov and Oleg Kitov, "Exact Prediction of S&P 500 Returns," December 2, 2007, http://dx.doi.org/10.2139/ssrn.1045281.

14. Tyler Vigen, "Spurious Correlations," *Tylervigen.com*, n.d., http://www.tylervigen.com/spurious-correlations.

15. Robin Wigglesworth, "Spurious Correlations Are Kryptonite of Wall St's AI Rush," *Financial Times*, March 24, 2018, https://www.ft.com/content/f14db820-26cd-11e8-b27e-cc62a39d57a0.

16. M. D. R. Evans, Jonathan Kelley, Joanna Sikora, and Donald J. Treiman, "Family Scholarly Culture and Educational Success: Books and Schooling in 27 Nations," *Research in Social Stratification and Mobility* 28, no. 2 (2010): 171–197. https://doi.org/10.1016/j.rssm.2010.01.002.

17. Steven D. Levitt and Stephen J. Dubner, *Freakonomics: A Rogue Economist Explores the Hidden Side of Everything*, revised and expanded edition (New York: William Morrow, 2020), chap. 5, Kindle.

18. C.M. Wright and T.D. Cheetham, "The Strengths and Limitations of Parental Heights as a Predictor of Attained Height," *Archives of Disease in Childhood* 81 (1999): 257–260.

19. Daniel Kahneman, *Thinking, Fast and Slow* (New York: Farrar, Straus and Giroux, 2011), 182.

20. Kahneman, *Thinking, Fast and Slow*, 182.

21. Jordan Ellenberg, *How Not to Be Wrong: The Power of Mathematical Thinking* (New York, NY: Penguin Books, 2014), chap. 6, Kindle.

22. Jyoti Madhusoodanan, "Does a Mutual Fund's Past Performance Predict Its Future?" *Yale Insights*, July 7, 2020, https://insights.som.yale.edu/insights/does-mutual-fund-s-past-performance-predict-its-future.

23. Kirsten Grind, Tom McGinty, and Sarah Krouse, "The Morningstar Mirage," *Wall Street Journal*, October 25, 2017, https://www.wsj.com/articles/the-morningstar-mirage-1508946687.

24. Roman Kraeussl and Ralph Sandelowsky, "The Predictive Performance of Morningstar's Mutual Fund Ratings," *SSRN Electronic Journal* 10.2139/ssrn.963489, August 2007, https://www.researchgate.net/publication/251393863_The_Predictive_Performance_of_Morningstar%27s_Mutual_Fund_Ratings.

25. Michael J. Orlich, Pramil N Singh, and Joan Sabaté et al., "Vegetarian Dietary Patterns and Mortality in Adventist Health Study 2," *JAMA Internal Medicine* 173, no. 13 (July 8, 2013): 1230–1238, https://doi.org/10.1001/jamainternmed.2013.6473.

26. Howard Wainer, "The Most Dangerous Equation," *American Scientist* 95, no. 3 (May–June 2007): 249, https://www.americanscientist.org/article/the-most-dangerous-equation.

27. John Poppelaars, "The Most Dangerous Equation in the World," *LinkedIn* (blog), April 3, 2016, https://www.linkedin.com/pulse/most-dangerous-equation-world-john-poppelaars/.

28. Wainer, "The Most Dangerous Equation."

29. Ronald A. Fisher, *The Design of Experiments*, 6th ed. (Edinburgh: Oliver & Boyd, 1951), 13.

30. Edward H. Madden, "Aristotle's Treatment of Probability and Signs," *Philosophy of Science* 24, no. 2 (April 1957): 167, https://doi.org/10.1086/287530.

31. David L. Goodstein, "Richard P. Feynman, Teacher," *Physics Today* 42, no. 2 (February 1989): 73.

32. Jordan Ellenberg, *How Not to Be Wrong: The Power of Mathematical Thinking* (New York: The Penguin Press, 2014), chap. 6, Kindle.

CHAPTER 3

1. Elroy Dimson, Paul Marsh, and Mike Staunton, "The Growth Puzzle," *Credit Suisse Global Investment Returns Yearbook 2014.* https://plus.credit-suisse.com/rpc4/ravDocView?docid=dBC0Bv.

2. John Keynes, *The General Theory of Employment, Interest and Money* (New York: Macmillan & Co., 1936), 162.

3. John Miller and Scott Page, *Complex Adaptive Systems: An Introduction to Computational Models of Social Life* (Princeton and Oxford: Princeton University Press, 2007), chap. 2, Kindle.

4. Tulip mania facts are from Charles MacKay's classic tome, *Extraordinary Popular Delusions and the Madness of Crowds*, first published in 1841. See: Charles MacKay, *Extraordinary Popular Delusions and the Madness of Crowds* (Hampshire UK: Harriman House, 2018).

5. Richard Bookstaber, *A Demon of Our Own Design: Markets, Hedge Funds, and the Perils of Financial Innovation* (New York: John Wiley & Sons, Inc., 2007), chap. 2, Kindle.

6. Michael J. Mauboussin, *More Than You Know: Finding Financial Wisdom in Unconventional Places* (New York: Columbia University Press, 2007), chap. 34, Kindle.

7. William Bernstein, *Skating Where the Puck Was: The Correlation Game in a Flat World* (self-published, 2012), chap. 2, Kindle.

8. J. Willoughby, "Anyone Here Seen Alpha?" *Barron's*, March 27, 2006, https://www.barrons.com/articles/SB114324401090107976.

9. R.D. McLean and J. Pontiff, "Does Academic Research Destroy Stock Return Predictability?" *Journal of Finance* 71, no. 1 (February 2016): 5–31, http://www.jstor.org/stable/43869094.

10. "Forecasting stock returns: What signals matter, and what do they say now?" *Vanguard Research Whitepaper*. 2012, https://fairwaywealth.com/wp-content/uploads/Vanguard-Research-11-30-2014.pdf.

11. Amit Goval and Ivo Welch, "A Comprehensive Look at the Empirical Performance of Equity Premium Prediction," *National Bureau of Economic Research*, May 2004, http://www.nber.org/papers/w10483.

12. "Forecasting stock returns," *Vanguard Research Whitepaper*.

CHAPTER 4

1. Cixin Liu, *The Dark Forest*. Translated by Joel Martinsen (New York: Macmillan, 2008), Kindle edition.

2. For more on Hyman Minsky's financial instability hypothesis, see John Cassidy, "The Minsky Moment," *New Yorker*, January 27, 2008, https://www.newyorker.com/magazine/2008/02/04/the-minsky-moment.

3. William Green, *Richer, Wiser, Happier: How the World's Greatest Investors Win in Markets and Life* (New York: Scribner, 2021), chap. 3, Kindle.

4. J.P. Morgan, *Eye on the Markets* (Newsletter), September 12, 2012.

5. Tom Teodorczuk, "Global Macro Hedge Funds Struggle to Regain Top Form," *Barron's*, July 16, 2019, https://www.barrons.com/articles/global-macro-hedge-funds-struggle-to-regain-top-form-51563288900.

CHAPTER 5

1. However, Tom could have been right—see Chapter 9's discussion of "invisible histories."

2. Philip E. Tetlock, *Expert Political Judgment* (Princeton NJ: Princeton University Press, 2005), Kindle edition.

3. Jeff Sommer, "Clueless about 2020, Wall Street Forecasters Are at It Again for 2021," *New York Times*, December 18, 2020, https://www.nytimes.com/2020/12/18/business/stock-market-forecasts-wall-street.html.

4. Shawn Snyder, "Outlook 2020: Back to the Future," Citi Personal Wealth Management, January 2020, https://marketinsights.citi.com/Market-Commentary/Market-Outlook/Outlook-2020-Back-to-the-Future.html.

5. Andrew D. Goldberg, "Outlook 2020: Prepared for Challenges, Focused on Opportunity," J.P. Morgan Private Bank, 2019, https://privatebank.jpmorgan.com/content/dam/jpm-wm-aem/documents/PB-Outlook-2020.pdf.

6. Emily McCormick, "Stock Market 2020: Most Experts Predict Gains, Some Expect Losses," Yahoo Finance, December 19, 2019, https://www.yahoo.com/video/wall-street-strategist-forecast-for-sp-500-in-2020-211002824.html.

7. McCormick, "Stock Market 2020."

8. Tom Nichols, *The Death of Expertise: The Campaign against Established Knowledge and Why it Matters* (New York: Oxford University Press, 2018), chap. 6, Kindle.

9. Paul Krugman, "How Did Economists Get It So Wrong?," *New York Times*, Sept. 2, 2009, https://www.nytimes.com/2009/09/06/magazine/06Economic-t.html.

10. Andrew W. Lo, *Adaptive Markets: Financial Evolution at the Speed of Thought*, (Princeton, NJ: Princeton University Press, 2019), chap. 6, Kindle.

11. Lo, *Adaptive Markets: Financial Evolution at the Speed of Thought*, introduction, Kindle.

12. David Dunning, "We Are All Confident Idiots," *Pacific Standard*, October 27, 2014, https://psmag.com/social-justice/confident-idiots-92793.

13. Philip E. Tetlock, *Expert Political Judgment: How Good Is It? How Can We Know?* (Princeton NJ: Princeton University Press, 2017), chap. 2, Kindle.

14. G.A. Miller, "The Magical Number Seven, Plus or Minus Two: Some Limits on Our Capacity for Processing Information," *Psychological Review* 63, no. 2 (1956): 81–97, https://doi.org/10.1037/h0043158.

15. Graeme S. Halford, Rosemary Baker, Julie E. McCredden, and John D. Bain, "How Many Variables Can Humans Process?," *Psychological Science* 16, no. 1 (January 2005): 70–6, https://doi.org/10.1111/j.0956-7976.2005.00782.x.

16. Claire Tsai, Joshua Klayman, and Reid Hastie, "Effects of Amount of Information on Judgment Accuracy and Confidence," *Organizational Behavior and Human Decision Processes* 107, no. 2 (2008): 97–105, https://doi.org/10.1016/j.obhdp.2008.01.005.

17. Thomas Astebro and Samir Elhedhli, "The Effectiveness of Simple Decision Heuristics: Forecasting Commercial Success for Early-Stage Ventures," *Management Science* 52, no. 3 (2006): 407.

18. Tadeusz Tyszka and Piotr Zielonka, "Expert Judgments: Financial Analysts Versus Weather Forecasters," *Journal of Behavioral Finance* 3 (2002): 152–160.

19. Tyszka and Zielonka, "Expert Judgments," 152–160.

20. Nassim Taleb, *Antifragile: Things That Gain from Disorder* (New York: Random House, 2012), chap. 8, Kindle.

CHAPTER 6

1. Michael J. Mauboussin, *The Success Equation: Untangling Skill and Luck in Business, Sports, and Investing* (Brighton: Harvard Review Press, 2012), chap. 3, Kindle.

2. Figure created by author but adapted from a similar one in *The Success Equation*.

3. Berlinda Liu and Gaurav Sinha, "SPIVA® U.S. Scorecard," *S&P Dow Jones Indices Research Report*, Year-End 2021, https://www.spglobal.com/spdji/en/documents/spiva/spiva-us-year-end-2021.pdf.

4. Eugene F. Fama and Kenneth R. French, "Luck versus Skill in the Cross-Section of Mutual Fund Returns," *Journal of Finance* 65, No. 5 (2010): 1915–1947, https://doi.org/10.1111/j.1540-6261.2010.01598.x.

5. Mike Sebastian, and Sudhakar Attaluri, "Conviction in Equity Investing," *Journal of Portfolio Management* 40, no. 4 (2014): 77–88, https://doi.org/10.3905/jpm.2014.40.4.077.

6. Mauboussin, *The Success Equation*.

7. Data sourced from the CFA Institute.

8. Chart provided to author by Craig Lazzara, Managing Director, S&P Dow Jones Indices.

9. Hendrik Bessembinder, "Do stocks outperform Treasury bills?" *Journal of Financial Economics* 129, no. 3 (2018): 440–457.

10. Andrew Clare, Stephen Thomas, and Nick Motson, "Monkeys vs Fund Managers—An Evaluation of Alternative Equity Indices," Bayes (formerly Cass) Business School, University of London, April 3, 2013, https://www.bayes.city.ac.uk/faculties-and-research/research/bayes-knowledge/2013/april/monkeys-vs-fund-managers-an-evaluation-of-alternative-equity-indices.

11. But maybe we're starting the see the wheels come off as the FAANG stocks of Facebook, Apple, Amazon, Netflix, and Google have seen declines greater than the overall market in the first half of 2022.

12. See, for example: Noël Amenc, Lionel Martellini, Felix Goltz, Shuyang Ye, "Improved Beta? A Comparison of Index-Weighting Schemes," EDHEC Risk Institute, September 2011, https://risk.edhec.edu/sites/risk/files/improved-beta-comparison-index-weighting-schemes.pdf.

13. Clare, Thomas, and Motson, "Monkeys vs Fund Managers." Chart used with permission.

14. Brian R. Wimmer, CFA®, Sandeep S. Chhabra, and Daniel W. Wallick, "The Bumpy Road to Outperformance," *Vanguard Research Whitepaper*, July 2013, https://static.vgcontent.info/crp/intl/auw/docs/literature/research/bumpy-road-to-outperformance-TLRV.pdf?20140124%7C1455.

15. Data sourced from Cambridge Associates.

16. Bureau of Labor Statistics, "Survival of Private Sector Establishments by Opening Year," https://www.bls.gov/bdm/us_age_naics_00_table7.txt.

CHAPTER 7

1. Felix Richter, "Digital Camera Sales Dropped 87 Percent Since 2010," *statista*, February 7, 2020, https://www.statista.com/chart/5782/digital-camera-shipments.

2. Richard Watson, "Timeline of Failed Predictions (Part 1)," *FastCompany*, December 1, 2010, https://www.fastcompany.com/1706712/timeline-failed-predictions-part-1.

3. Ray Kurzweil, "The Law of Accelerating Returns," *Kurzweil: Tracking the Acceleration of Intelligence*, March 7, 2001. https://www.kurzweilai.net/the-law-of-accelerating-returns.

4. A regular piece of copy paper can only be folded seven times. This example ignores that issue.

5. Wikimedia Commons, "Price History of Silicon PV Cells since 1977," https://commons.wikimedia.org/wiki/File:Price_history_of_silicon_PV_cells_since_1977.svg.

6. Ajay Gambhir, Richard Green, Michael Grubb, Philip Heptonstall, Charlie Wilson, and Robert Gross. "How Are Future Energy Technology Costs Estimated? Can We Do Better?," *International Review of Environmental and Resource Economics* 15, no. 4 (2021): 271–318, http://dx.doi.org/10.1561/101.00000128.

7. Uber Technologies, Inc. S-1 Filing, April 11, 2019, https://www.sec.gov/Archives/edgar/data/1543151/000119312519103850/d647752ds1.htm.

8. Data source for chart: Alliance for Automotive Innovation, "Electric Vehicle Sales Dashboard," March 24, 2022, https://www.autosinnovate.org/resources/electric-vehicle-sales-dashboard.

9. Thomas Robert Malthus, "An Essay on the Principle of Population as It Affects the Future Improvement of Society, with Remarks on the Speculations of Mr. Godwin, M. Condorcet, and Other Writers," (London: Printed for J. Johnson, in St. Paul's Church-Yard, 1798), electronic edition by Electronic Scholarly Publishing Project, 1998, http://www.esp.org/books/malthus/population/malthus.pdf.

10. Data sourced from Our World in Data, https://ourworldindata.org/grapher/gdp-per-capita-in-the-uk-since-1270.

11. James Bates, "Japan's U.S. Real Estate Buying Plunges," *Los Angeles Times*, February 21, 1992, https://www.latimes.com/archives/la-xpm-1992-02-21-mn-2588-story.html.

12. "Nikkei 225 Index—67 Year Historical Chart," Macrotrends, https://www.macrotrends.net/2593/nikkei-225-index-historical-chart-data.

13. Daniel Yergin, *The Quest: Energy, Security, and the Remaking of the Modern World*, (New York: Penguin Books, 2012), chap. 16, Kindle.

14. "New York Urbanized Area: Population & Density from 1800 (Provisional)," Demographia, http://demographia.com/db-nyuza1800.htm.

15. "Greater London, Inner London & Outer London Population & Density History," Demographia, http://www.demographia.com/dm-lon31.htm.

16. Águeda García de Durango, "New York, Manure and Stairs: When Horses Were the Cities' Nightmares," *Smart Water Magazine*, June 9, 2019, https://smartwatermagazine.com/blogs/agueda-garcia-de-durango/new-york-manure-and-stairs-when-horses-were-cities-nightmares.

17. Kurt Kohlstedt, "The Big Crapple: NYC Transit Pollution from Horse Manure to Horseless Carriages," *99 Percent Invisible*, June 11, 2017, https://99percentinvisible.org/article/cities-paved-dung-urban-design-great-horse-manure-crisis-1894/.

18. Stephen Carlisle, "We Traded Carriages for Cars—Let's Embrace the Next Disruption," *Globe and Mail*, April 28, 2016, https://www.theglobeandmail.com/report-on-business/rob-commentary/we-traded-carriages-for-cars-lets-embrace-the-next-disruption/article29782316/.

19. Elizabeth Kolbert, "Hosed: Is There a Quick Fix for the Climate?" *New Yorker*, November 8, 2009, https://www.newyorker.com/magazine/2009/11/16/hosed.

20. The physical aspect—the number of transistors that can be fit on a chip—is reaching its limit, but the overarching principle may continue with further advancements in artificial intelligence and quantum computing.

21. Reda Cherif, Fuad Hasanov, and Aditya Pande, "Riding the Energy Transition: Oil Beyond 2040," *International Monetary Fund Working Papers*, May 22, 2017, https://www.imf.org/en/Publications/WP/Issues/2017/05/22/Riding-the-Energy-Transition-Oil-Beyond-2040-44932.

22. Carlisle, "We Traded Carriages."

23. Sam Korus, "The Automotive Industry Is on the Threshold of Massive Consolidation," *ARK Invest*, August 26, 2016, https://ark-invest.com/articles/analyst-research/automotive-consolidation/. Chart used with permission.

24. "Automobile History," *History.com*, August 21, 2018, https://www.history.com/topics/inventions/automobiles.

25. Federica Laricchia, "Global Market Shipment Share Held by LCD TV Manufacturers from 2008–2019," *statista*, February 21, 2022, https://www.statista.com/statistics/267095/global-market-share-of-lcd-tv-manufacturers/.

26. S. O'Dea, "Manufacturers' Market Share of Smartphone Subscribers in the United States from 2013 and [sic] 2022, by Month," *statista*, April 5, 2022, https://www.statista.com/statistics/273697/market-share-held-by-the-leading-smartphone-manufacturers-oem-in-the-us/.

27. Kleiner Perkins Caufield & Byers, "Internet Trends 2015," May 25, 2015, https://www.kleinerperkins.com/perspectives/2015-internet-trends/.

28. Nick Routley, "Internet Browser Market Share (1996–2019)," *Visual Capitalist*, January 20, 2020, https://www.visualcapitalist.com/internet-browser-market-share/.

29. Gerard Tellis and Peter Golder, "Pioneer Advantage: Marketing Logic or Marketing Legend?" *Journal of Marketing Research* 30, issue 2 (1993), https://doi.org/10.1177/002224379303000203.

30. Ricardo J. Caballero and Mohamad L. Hammour, "Creative Destruction and Development: Institutions, Crises, and Restructuring," *National Bureau of Economic Research Working Papers Series*, No. 7849, August 2000, http://www.nber.org/papers/w7849.pdf.

CHAPTER 8

1. Benoit Mandelbrot and Nassim Nicholas Taleb, "Mild vs. Wild Randomness: Focusing on Those Risks that Matter," in *The Known, the Unknown and the Unknowable in Financial Institutions*, eds. Frank Diebold, Neil Doherty, and Richard Herring, (Princeton: Princeton University Press, 2010), chap. 3, Kindle.

2. Javier Estrada, "Black Swans and Market Timing: How Not to Generate Alpha," *Journal of Investing* 17, no. 3 (Fall 2008): 20–34, https://doi.org/10.3905/joi.2008.710917.

3. Roger Lowenstein, *When Genius Failed: The Rise and Fall of Long-Term Capital Management*, (New York: Random House, 2000), 72.

4. Mandelbrot and Taleb, "Mild vs. Wild Randomness."

5. Robert Blakemore, "Non-Flat Earth Recalibrated for Terrain and Topsoil," *Soil Systems* 2, no. 64. (2018), https://doi.org/10.3390/soilsystems2040064.

6. Benoit Mandelbrot, "How long is the coast of Britain? Statistical self-similarity and fractional dimension," *Science* 156, issue 3775 (May 5, 1967): 636–8, https://doi.org/10.1126/science.156.3775.636. PMID: 17837158.

7. Benoit Mandelbrot, *The (Mis)behavior of Markets* (New York: Basic Books, 2001), 123–124.

8. Mandelbrot, *The (Mis)behavior of Markets*, 146.

9. Nassim Nicholas Taleb, *The Black Swan: The Impact of the Highly Improbable*, 2nd ed., (New York: Random House Trade Paperbacks, 2010), chap. 15, Kindle.

10. Estrada, "Black Swans and Market Timing," 22.

11. Data sourced from Pitchbook.

12. Mandelbrot and Taleb, "Mild vs. Wild Randomness."

13. Mandelbrot, *The (Mis)behavior of Markets*, prelude, Kindle.

CHAPTER 9

1. Daniel Kahneman, Jack L. Knetsch, Richard H. Thaler, "Anomalies: The Endowment Effect, Loss Aversion, and Status Quo Bias," *Journal of Economic Perspectives* 5, no. 1 (Winter 1991):193–206.

2. Amos Tversky and Daniel Kahneman, "Judgment under Uncertainty: Heuristics and Biases," *Science* 185, issue 4157 (September 27, 1974): 1124–1131, https://doi.org/10.1126/science.185.4157.1124

3. Tversky and Kahneman, "Judgment under Uncertainty."

4. Yuval Noah Harari, *Sapiens: A Brief History of Humankind* (New York: Harper, 2015), chap. 2, Kindle.

5. Angela K. Freymuth and George F. Ronan, "Modeling Patient Decision-Making: The Role of Base-Rate and Anecdotal Information: Study of Medical Treatments and Stories" *Journal of Clinical Psychology in Medical Settings* 11, no. 3 (September 2004).

6. Actually, they were told one of three stories: a positive, negative, or neutral story. I've excluded the results of the neutral story in this discussion for simplicity and clarity.

7. John Carreyrou, *Bad Blood: Secrets and Lies in a Silicon Valley Startup* (New York: Knopf Doubleday Publishing Group, 2018). Kindle edition.

8. Justin Wolfers, "Game Theory Says Pete Carroll's Call at Goal Line is Defensible," *New York Times*, February 2, 2015, https://www.nytimes.com/2015/02/03/upshot/game-theory-says-pete-carrolls-call-at-goal-line-is-defensible.html.

9. Stuart Firestein, "The Resulting Fallacy Is Ruining Your Decisions," *Nautilus*, December 7, 2017, https://nautil.us/issue/55/trust/the-resulting-fallacy-is-ruining-your-decisions.

10. Rolf Dobelli, *The Art of Thinking Clearly* (New York: Harper, 2014), chap. 32, Kindle.

11. Daniel Kahneman and Amos Tversky, "Prospect Theory: An Analysis of Decision under Risk," *Econometrica* 47, no. 2 (1979): 263–91, https://doi.org/10.2307/1914185.

12. Daniel Kahneman, *Thinking, Fast and Slow* (New York: Farrar, Straus and Giroux, 2011), 279–280.

13. Kahneman, *Thinking, Fast and Slow*, 285.

14. Ola Svenson, "Are We All Less Risky and More Skillful Than Our Fellow Drivers?," *Acta Psychologica* 47, issue 2 (1981): 143–148.

15. C. E. Preston and S. Harris, "Psychology of Drivers in Traffic Accidents," *Journal of Applied Psychology* 49, no. 4 (1965): 284–288, https://doi.org/10.1037/h0022453.

16. David Shariatmadari, "Daniel Kahneman: What Would I Eliminate If I Had a Magic Wand? Overconfidence," *Guardian*, July 18, 2015, https://www.theguardian.com/books/2015/jul/18/daniel-kahneman-books-interview#:~:text=The percent20most percent20damaging percent20of percent20these,he percent20had percent20a percent20magic percent20wand.

17. Max H. Bazerman and Don A. Moore, *Judgment in Managerial Decision Making* (New Jersey: Wiley, 2012), 23.

18. L. Rozenblit and F. Keil, "The Misunderstood Limits of Folk Science: An Illusion of Explanatory Depth," *Cognitive Science* 26, no. 5 (February 1, 2010): 521–562, https://doi.org/10.1207/s15516709cog2605_1.

19. Neil Irwin, "Nobody Really Knows How the Economy Works. A Fed Paper Is the Latest Sign," *New York Times*, October 1, 2021, https://www.nytimes.com/2021/10/01/upshot/inflation-economy-analysis.html

20. Jeremy B. Rudd, "Why Do We Think That Inflation Expectations Matter for Inflation? (And Should We?)," Finance and Economics Discussion Series 2021–062 (Washington: Board of Governors of the Federal Reserve System, 2021): 1.

21. Cameron Anderson, Sebastien Brion, Don Moore, and Jessica Kennedy, "A Status-Enhancement Account of Overconfidence," *Journal of Personality and Social Psychology* 103, no. 4 (October 2012): 718–35.

22. Cameron Anderson and Sebastien Brion, "Overconfidence and the Attainment of Status in Groups," *IRLE Working Paper* No. 215–10, April 2010, https://www.irle.berkeley.edu/files/2010/Overconfidence-and-the-Attainment-of-Status-in-Groups.pdf.

23. Paul C. Price and Eric R. Stone, "Intuitive Evaluation of Likelihood Judgment Producers: Evidence for a Confidence Heuristic," *Journal of Behavioral Decision Making* 17, no. 1 (December 16, 2003): 39–57, https://doi.org/10.1002/bdm.460.

24. Dominic Johnson and James Fowler, "The Evolution of Overconfidence," *Nature* 477 (September 14, 2011): 317–20, 10.1038/nature10384.

CHAPTER 10

1. While males are generally more overconfident than females, relative levels of overconfidence vary by area. Males tend to display more overconfidence than females in traditional masculine tasks.

2. Brad M. Barber and Terrance Odean, "Boys Will Be Boys: Gender, Overconfidence, And Common Stock Investment," *Quarterly Journal of Economics* 116, no. 1, (February 2001): 261–292, https://www.researchgate.net/publication/24091730_Boys_Will_Be_Boys_Gender_Overconfidence_And_Common_Stock_Investment.

3. Fidelity Investments, "Fidelity Investments: Women and Investing Study 2021," https://www.fidelity.com/bin-public/060_www_fidelity_com/documents/about-fidelity/FidelityInvestmentsWomen&InvestingStudy2021.pdf. The study didn't mention what percentage of men felt confident about selecting investments, but the implication was that men have more confidence.

4. "Fidelity's Best Investors Are Dead," *The Conservative Income Investor*, April 8, 2020, https://theconservativeincomeinvestor.com/fidelitys-best-investors-are-dead.

5. Amit Goyal and Sunil Wahal, "The Selection and Termination of Investment Management Firms by Plan Sponsors," *Journal of Finance* 63, no. 4 (2008): 1805–1847, https://EconPapers.repec.org/RePEc:bla:jfinan:v:63:y:2008:i:4:p:1805-1847.

6. Data source for chart: Goyal and Wahal, "The Selection and Termination."

7. "It Happened Here: The Apgar Score," *Health Matters: Stories of Science, Care and Wellness*, New York-Presbyterian Online Newsletter, https://healthmatters.nyp.org/apgar-score/.

8. Lee A. Green and J. Frank Yates, "Influence of Pseudodiagnostic Information on the Evaluation of Ischemic Heart Disease," *Annals of Emergency Medicine* 25, issue 4 (April 1, 1995), https://www.annemergmed.com/article/S0196-0644(95)70257-1/pdf.

9. Claire Kreiter, Marie O'Shea, Catherine Bruen, Paul Murphy, and Teresa Pawlikowska, "A Meta-Analytic Perspective on the Valid Use of Subjective Human Judgement to Make Medical School Admission Decisions," *Taylor & Francis Online Medical Education Online* 23, no. 1 (October 5, 2018), https://doi.org/10.1080/10872981.2018.1522225.

10. John W. Howard & Robyn M. Dawes, "Linear Prediction of Marital Happiness," *Personality and Social Psychology Bulletin* 2, no. 4 (1976): 478–480, https://doi.org/10.1177/014616727600200424.

11. John Bogle, *Enough: True Measures of Money, Business, and Life*, rev. ed. (Hoboken, NJ: John Wiley & Sons, Inc., June 1, 2010), chap. 3, Kindle.

12. Specifically, the 70/30 portfolio consists of: 5 percent three-month T-Bill, 25 percent Barclays 1-10 Municipal Bond Index, 37 percent Russell 1000, 12 percent Russell 2000, 15 percent MSCI EAFE, 2 percent MSCI EAFE Small Cap, and 4 percent MSCI Emerging markets. The portfolio is rebalanced annually.

13. Patrick Geddes, Lisa R. Goldberg, and Stephen Bianchi, "What Would Yale Do If It Were Taxable?" *Financial Analysts Journal* 71, no. 4 (June 9, 2014), http://dx.doi.org/10.2139/ssrn.2447403.

14. David Swenson, *Unconventional Success: A Fundamental Approach to Personal Investment* (New York: Free Press, 2005).

15. David Swenson, *Pioneering Portfolio Management: An Unconventional Approach to Institutional Investment, Fully Revised and Updated*, (New York: Free Press, 2009), 2.

16. Francis M. Kinniry Jr., Colleen M. Jaconetti, Michael A. DiJoseph, Yan Zilbering, and Donald G. Bennyhoff, "Putting a Value on your Value: Quantifying Vanguard Advisor's Alpha." *Vanguard*, August 16, 2019, https://advisors.vanguard.com/insights/article/IWE_ResPuttingAValueOnValue

CONCLUSION

1. Charles Darwin, *The Origin of Species by Means of Natural Selection, or the Preservation of Favoured Races in the Struggle for Life* (New York: Signet Classics, 2009), chap. XV, Kindle.

ABOUT
THE AUTHOR

John Jennings is president and chief strategist of St. Louis Trust & Family Office, a $15 billion national multifamily office. He is an adjunct professor at Washington University's Olin School of Business in its Wealth and Asset Management graduate program, writes on wealth management topics for *Forbes*, and is author of *The Interesting Fact of the Day* blog. He has finance and law degrees from the University of Missouri and a professional certificate in Investment Decisions and Behavioral Finance from Harvard.

Personally, he's of median height, a big fan of coffee, a lover of indie music, and a ravenous St. Louis Blues fan. He lives in University City, Missouri, with his wife and dog and has two grown daughters. You can connect with him through his firm's website (www.stlouistrust.com), his blog (www.theifod.com), or his author website (www.johnmjennings.com).